IMMORTALS
of
BRITISH SPORT

Published in 2013 by Vision Sports Publishing Ltd

Vision Sports Publishing Ltd
19-23 High Street
Kingston upon Thames
Surrey
KT1 1LL
www.visionsp.co.uk

ISBN: 978-1909534-18-6

© Ian Hewitt and Sampson Lloyd

Conceived and written by Ian Hewitt
Photography by Sampson Lloyd

Editor: Jim Drewett
Production editor: John Murray
Designer: Doug Cheeseman

WEBSITE
The website **www.sportingimmortals.com** contains a selection of images from this book and is intended to capture, through photographs, the continuing story of the immortals of British sport.

COVER PHOTOGRAPHY
Front cover: Stanley Matthews (sculpted by Julian Jeffery, Carl Payne and Andrew Edwards) photographed by Sampson Lloyd. Located at the Britannia Stadium, Stoke-on-Trent.
Back cover: W G Grace (sculpted by Louis Laumen) photographed by Sampson Lloyd. Located at Lord's Cricket Ground, London.

CONTENTS PHOTOGRAPHY
Old Tom Morris (sculpted by Paul Ferriter) photographed by Sampson Lloyd. Located at Rosapenna Golf Resort, County Donegal, Ireland.

IMMORTALS

of

BRITISH SPORT

A celebration of Britain's sporting history through sculpture

IAN HEWITT and SAMPSON LLOYD

CONTENTS

INTRODUCTION

I was travelling with my wife, Jenifer, around the Ring of Kerry on the glorious west coast of Ireland when the idea for this book originated. We arrived at the small, picturesque coastal village of Sneem and started to walk around a central square with its well-kept garden. Colourfully-painted shops and cottages provided a charming background. Sport, just for once, was far from my mind. And then I saw it.

Set in a neatly-hedged cutting in the square, a life-size statue came into view – unexpectedly prominent and almost incongruous in this picture-perfect setting. The figure seemed from another age – sturdy, ready to fight, at first glance an old-fashioned bare-knuckled pugilist, but on closer view a wrestler, eyes full of firm intent and arms poised for the contest. Who was he? Why was he there? I was about to discover the story of one of Ireland's greatest sportsmen, a member of an extraordinary family from Sneem: Steve 'Crusher' Casey. A champion rower, wrestler and boxer – a man even Joe Louis was afraid to fight.

How many other sporting statues of this kind were there around our islands? How many more stories of our sporting history could be celebrated through sculptures and memorials? Tracking down Britain's sporting statues and memorials became a journey of discovery into fascinating corners of our heritage.

The range is considerable and sometimes unexpected: figures whose achievements have brought pride and passion to a particular community or club; heroes who have so graced the national stage that statues honour them at the centres of their sport; sportsmen whose early deaths shocked or brought a premature end to a flowering sports career; stadium or team disasters that have left an indelible memory of tragedy; and a rich collection of four-footed heroes who have captured the public's love and affection. Sporting heroes represented in sculpture span centuries – from an 18th century Welsh mountain runner of legend, Guto, to modern Olympic heroes as recent as Tom Daley and Amy Williams.

I was struck how, collectively and by placing each subject in the era in which his or her sporting contribution was most prominent, this kaleidoscope of heroes and memories could offer a different and vivid view of the history of British sport.

A statue is, of course, just one tangible way of commemorating an individual or event. It expresses, though, an importance and emotion which we reserve for the truly exceptional. A well-designed sculpture or memorial, capturing an individual characteristic, can also add a distinctive and lasting dimension to our memory of the individual or occasion.

Reasons for commemorating a particular individual in bronze vary. Many statues will simply be a recognition of an outstanding sporting life. In other cases, a statue of a past hero provides a symbol of tradition and continuity for a club or stadium – many recent sporting statues have been associated with the construction

Alan Ryan Hall's sculpture of Steve 'Crusher' Casey captures the attention of visitors to the colourful Irish village of Sneem.

INTRODUCTION
continued

Philip Blacker's fine sculpture of Desert Orchid shines in the sunlight at Kempton Park.

of newly-built stadia. In each case, though, a statue or memorial reflects a judgment (by whatever body, club or council has commissioned it) that the individual or occasion is worthy of being remembered by future generations. Each provides its own insight into our sporting heritage.

Our first visit to photograph Britain's sporting sculptures was to Kempton Park. The racecourse was quiet and peaceful. Sun and showers created a dramatic light. The statue of Desert Orchid, steeplechase legend, shimmered in the sunlight. A venue and an equine star were both enhanced by the beautiful sculpture.

We discovered that very many of our public sporting sculptures have been created only within the last two decades or so. The trend continues with new statues already work-in-progress reflecting, it appears, a growing public interest in sporting sculpture as a medium for expressing civic identity or pride.

The works featured here are a personal selection. Other fine sporting sculptures or memorials no doubt exist around the country, including in private collections, but I hope we have not missed too many in public spaces.

This book, at its heart, is a celebration – a celebration of sporting heroes. Simon Barnes expresses it well for sports fans in *The Meaning of Sport*: "Heroes are the stuff of sport: without a hero there is no tale; without the truly exceptional performer, the narrative loses its fizz." It is our hope that, through the images in this book and the stories of these heroes, the reader can enjoy some of that "fizz" in our sporting heritage.

Let us journey through time and celebrate the memory of sportsmen and women (and animals) who have, through our statues and memorials, become immortals of British sport.

IAN HEWITT
July 1 2013

GUTO

"Run, boy, run." The instruction from his father sounded over the hillside as the young boy sped around the pastures rounding up the sheep. In the Welsh village of Mountain Ash, a delightful statue by Peter Nicholas continues the legend of Griffith Morgan (1700–1737), affectionately known as Guto of Nythbran Farm. He is our earliest sporting immortal.

The boy became the fastest runner in the region. His exploits were legendary. Aged 37, Guto was enticed out of retirement for a 12-mile race from Newport to Bedwas against a young challenger called Prince. Behind in the early stages, Guto surged past his opponent up the final hill to victory. Engulfed in congratulations by ecstatic followers, Guto sought out his sweetheart Sian. They smiled and kissed. She slapped him on the back in joy. Guto fatally collapsed and died in her arms.

He was buried in St Gwynno's Church in Llanwonno in one of the largest funerals the area had seen. A memorial gravestone, laid in 1866, recalls that final race "completed in seven minutes within the hour" (a pace which would outperform even the Olympic champion Mo Farah).

His grave, and now this fine statue of Guto running alongside a greyhound (left), are focal points of the famous Nos Galan (New Year's Eve) Road Races started in 1958 by Bernard Baldwin who reflected that "the sigh of the wind and the call of the wild will forever sing the sad requiem of the greatest runner that ever lived".

CHAPTER ONE

GAMBLING, SPORT &
THE EARLY VICTORIANS

We start with a sweeping view of the late 18th century and the first half or so of the 19th century.

Communications at the outset of this period were slow, the railway network had not developed and the major changes that urbanisation would bring in the late Victorian era were very much in the future. Sport in Britain was still very local. Running races and jumping competitions were many, as were forms of fighting or animal sports, but all differed from town to village. A few festive fairs or 'games', such as the Cotswold Olimpick Games originally promoted a century or so earlier by Robert Dover, were organised on a regular basis. Games and contests at this early time were enjoyed mainly for amusement and revelry.

Balls were certainly being kicked or thrown in towns and villages around the country, and increasingly in the leading public schools as team games grew in favour and popularity, but customs were all locally-based. Football and rugby would not develop separate identities or any uniform

rules until the 1860s and 1870s.

Of our modern sports, cricket was perhaps the earliest to take a recognisable form. The game had established early roots amongst the parishes and the villages. Matches were led with enthusiasm by members of the landed gentry keen to partake in local rivalry (and wagers). In Hambledon, in Hampshire, the village team – well-organised with many players paid in money or kind – became the acknowledged leaders of the sport for many decades until the formation of the Marylebone Cricket Club.

The principal spectator sports were those fuelled, essentially, by gambling. Aristocrats and the wealthy enjoyed opportunities to take part in, or promote, challenges and wagers. In addition to cricket, four sports in particular led to events at which substantial crowds would gather to enjoy the contests and to gamble on the outcome: horse-racing, prize-fighting, pedestrianism (foot-racing) and rowing. These were the sports which gave rise to our first sporting immortals.

ECLIPSE

Sire for the Ages

ECLIPSE
1764–1789

Bronze
James Osborne
Royal Veterinary
College, Hatfield
1989

It is an unlikely setting for our first sporting immortal: the entrance to the Royal Veterinary College in Hatfield, Hertfordshire. This is the story of a chestnut racehorse, with a white blaze on his head and a white 'sock' on his off-hind leg, who became one of the most important horses in the history of thoroughbred racing.

Horse-racing, by the mid-18th century, had moved from casual challenges (for wagers) between noblemen to a popular and relatively organised sport. Horses were being bred specifically for racing – 'thoroughbreds' descended from the three so-called foundation stallions of Arabian stock brought over to England in the late 17th century: the Byerley Turk, the Godolphin Arabian and the Darley Arabian (discovered by a merchant, Thomas Darley, and brought back from Syria).

Born during the period, and perhaps the day, of a solar eclipse and hence his name, Eclipse (1764–1789), was a descendant of the Darley Arabian. Bred by the Duke of Cumberland before being sold as a yearling, he grew strong and

Study of Eclipse (c. 1789) in the Royal Veterinary College (above).

fast in training. His prowess was spotted on the downs at Epsom by a flamboyant Irish gambler, Dennis O'Kelly. Eclipse's first race was in the Noblemen and Gentlemen's Plate at Epsom as a five-year-old in May 1769. Races were over long distances in those days, four miles or more, and held in heats. O'Kelly was confident that he knew something other punters did not. After the first heat, he bet that Eclipse would not only win the Plate but that, when he crossed the finishing line, none of his four rivals would be closer than the distance-post 240 yards away – 'nowhere' in racing terms. Eclipse won ... and the rest were nowhere. O'Kelly won his now legendary bet. And later he would buy the horse.

With a distinctive head-down style of galloping and ridden usually by jockey John Oakley, Eclipse was never stretched in any of his 18 races. He was the undisputed leading racehorse of his age. An even more successful career followed as a stallion. Eclipse himself sired over 300 winners. He also established a pedigree

A painting, from 1770, *Eclipse at Newmarket, with a Groom and Jockey,* by George Stubbs.

line without equal. It is estimated that over 90 per cent of all contemporary thoroughbreds have the male bloodline of Eclipse in their pedigree.

Eclipse died aged 24. A post-mortem was carried out by the renowned French veterinarian, Charles Vial de Sainbel, to discover 'the secret' of Eclipse. He reported on his powerful back legs and a huge-sized heart. His anatomical study was an important step in his campaign for a veterinary college in England, the

first of its kind, to study and further animal welfare. And so, the (now Royal) Veterinary College was founded.

A splendid two-thirds life-size statue of Eclipse, sculpted by James Osborne, is displayed in the entrance to the College. It was donated by the American breeder and philanthropist, Paul Mellon, to mark the bicentenary of Eclipse's death. Looking at its strong, simple lines, one can sense the power and the strength of this extraordinary horse.

"Eclipse first, the rest nowhere"
Dennis O'Kelly

DIOMED

First Derby Winner

DIOMED
1777–1808

Bronze
Judy Boyt
Derby Square,
Epsom
2001

Epsom is the home of the Derby, the blue riband event of the Flat racing season. It was in 1780 that the great race was first run and the winner was Diomed (1777–1808). In a shopping centre in Epsom, Derby Square, we can enjoy a striking sculpture by Judy Boyt which symbolically features that first Derby winner (near side) racing against the winner in 2001, Galileo (far side).

The leading figure in horse-racing during the latter half of the 18th century was Sir Charles Bunbury. Born in 1740, not far from Newmarket where his father was a vicar, Bunbury became a Member of Parliament for Suffolk – but he was more interested in the turf. He became Steward of the Jockey Club (formed in 1752 in Newmarket and the sport's accepted regulator). As the first 'Dictator of the Turf', Bunbury led many of the major changes that shaped the sport for modern times. Races became shorter in length and, as a result, more exciting. Shorter races were more suitable for fast, younger horses – leading to a quicker return on investment for their owners and more races during a day's meeting. The first Classics were established for three-year-olds: the St Leger in 1776, the Oaks in 1779 and the Derby a year later. The story goes that the name of the race was decided by a toss of a coin between Bunbury and Lord Derby. The latter won.

Consolation therefore for Bunbury that the first winner should be his fine horse named after the Greek hero, Diomedes. Of his 19 starts, Diomed won 11 times including 10 consecutive wins. After he ceased racing and moved to stud in America, Diomed became one of the most important stallions introduced into early American bloodstock – including siring Sir Archy, one of America's most successful racehorses. Diomed died aged 31 to much sadness in that country.

Derby day itself at Epsom became a mix of sport and festival, an occasion for a mass exodus from London to congregate on the downs for the spectacle. "The road to Epsom was crowded with all descriptions of people hurrying to the races, some to

The Finish of the 1862 Derby, oil painting by Henry Aitken Jnr (1862).

plunder and some to be plundered. Horses, gigs, curricles, coaches, chaises, carts and pedestrians covered with dust ..." reported *The Times* in 1793.

More than two centuries later, Galileo was an outstanding winner in 2001. Ridden by Mick Kinane, his devastating turn of speed led to a comfortable victory at Epsom. Grand-sired by the legendary Northern Dancer, Galileo has himself become one of the most valuable stallions at stud. He is the sire of the magnificent Frankel who retired unbeaten in 2012.

The glory of the sport, and of the thoroughbred, is resplendent in this vital sculpture – which also reflects the notable changes in riding styles of jockeys over the ages. Boyt's sculpture won the 2001 British Sporting Art Trust Award. It conveys majestically the sense of movement, power and pace of the racehorse.

"There was almost as much mourning over Diomed's demise as there was at the death of George Washington"
William Robertson, US racing historian

THOMAS LORD

Lord of the MCC

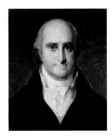

THOMAS LORD
1755–1832

Ceramic tile
Harold Stabler
(designer)
St John's Wood
Underground
Station, London

The history of cricket would have been very different without Thomas Lord (1755–1832). As with horse-racing, the sport was promoted in the 18th century by the nobility who organised teams to play for wagers. A lord or other aristocrat would act as patron for a village side which comprised both 'gentlemen' and talented locals.

The most famous village club was the Hambledon Club in Hampshire where Richard Nyren was a local landlord and, with noble patronage, the club's organiser. The club (motto: Wine, Cricket and Song) led the way in the second half of the 18th century in developing the rules of the game – including that the bat should be no wider than 4 ¼ inches. Large crowds watched (and wagered at) their matches. Erected in 1908, a memorial stone stands on Broadhalfpenny Down outside the village's Bat and Ball Inn. Hambledon's leadership continued until, as cricket became more fashionable in London, another club was formed which would influence the game both nationally and internationally.

Cricket as Played in the Mary-le-Bone Fields (c. 1744), by Francis Hayman.

A memorial stone from 1908 near Broadhalfpenny Down celebrates the great years of the Hambledon Club.

Born into a Yorkshire family whose fortune was lost in the Jacobite rebellion, Lord moved to London. Becoming a general attendant at a fashionable sporting club which played on the White Conduit fields in Islington, he earned extra money bowling in the practice nets against the 'gentlemen' batsmen. Members of the exclusive club sought a more private venue nearer to central London. Lord, ambitious and an entrepreneur, was invited to find and establish a new ground.

In 1787, Lord leased land on the Portman family estate. The White Conduit club reconstituted there as the Mary-le-Bone Cricket Club. A plaque on (now) Dorset Square recalls the historic birth of the MCC.

When the lease came up for renewal in 1811, Lord refused to pay the increased rent and moved to land on the Eyre family

"Cricket was the first team game in which the upper classes were expected to exert themselves without the aid of a horse"
Richard Holt, sports historian

estate in rural St John's Wood. It was not a popular site with the members. Fortunately in retrospect, Parliament decided that the proposed Regent's Canal should cross the land. He negotiated financial compensation and alternative grounds in St John's Wood. The MCC never looked back. A pavilion and tavern were erected. The ground was soon a major success attracting large crowds. Lord, then aged 70 and ever the businessman, sold the site in 1825 to a member, William Ward. The ground, though, continues to bear his legendary name.

The MCC became the strongest club in the land and its 'laws of cricket' were widely accepted. It became the governing body of 'first-class' cricket generally, organiser of England's touring teams and custodian of the spirit of the game.

Easily missed by hundreds of people passing daily, a tiled wall on a platform of the underground station at St John's Wood, originally designed by Harold Stabler, reveals a simple portrait of a man whose name has been at the forefront of cricket for more than 225 years.

A ceramic tile (above) reveals the profile of Thomas Lord in St John's Wood Underground Station and a plaque in Dorset Square (below left and below) recalls Lord and the birth of the MCC.

WILLIAM WEBB ELLIS

Rugby's Founder

WILLIAM WEBB ELLIS
1806–1872

Bronze
Graham Ibbeson
Rugby School,
Rugby
1997

Did one moment in 1823 change the course of a sport? Perhaps the stuff of legend, but a fine sculpture outside Rugby School embodies rugby's famous story.

Various kinds of 'folk football' had been played for years, if not centuries. They varied from town to village. On occasions, especially festival days, games could become unruly and violent. As the 19th century progressed, former pupils of the public schools sought ways of continuing in later university or business life the team games they had played at school. Each public school, though, had its own version of football. It was a quest for a common set of rules that would lead to the fledgling Football Association in 1863.

Several clubs, including Blackheath comprised largely of Old Rugbeians and brought up on a 'running and hacking' game, refused to join. Instead, representatives of 21 like-minded clubs met at the Pall Mall Restaurant in London in 1871 (a site now marked by a commemorative plaque) to establish the Rugby Football Union. Whilst many of the rules were very different from the game today, running with the ball in hand was allowed (although passing was frowned upon).

Keen to demonstrate that their game had a long tradition and was not 'primitive', a number of Old Rugbeians later started an historical investigation.

WILLIAM
WEBB ELLIS

continued

It appears that Rugby School in Warwickshire did indeed develop a unique form of football. H-shaped goals, for instance, are recorded in the 1830s and an early version of the oval ball seems to have been in use around that time. The most celebrated discovery was an article written in 1880 (by a former student, Matthew Bloxham, the one and only source of the famous story) which recorded an incident, more than 50 years earlier, involving a 17-year-old boy, William Webb Ellis (1806–1872), playing football at Rugby School. Apparently, Webb Ellis had caught the ball in his arms. He should then have stepped back and kicked ahead. Instead: "Ellis, for the first time, disregarded this rule ... and rushed forwards with the ball in his hands towards the opposite goal ..."

We do not know the outcome of that game ... but legend has it that this was the beginning of rugby football.

Webb Ellis himself was born near Manchester. William's mother, having lost her husband while serving in the Army, moved the family to Rugby to be within 10 miles of the Rugby Clock Tower and so qualify her children as local foundationers at Rugby School. William was at Rugby from 1816 to 1825. His later career had little more to do with sport, although he did play cricket at Oxford. He never, so far as we know, mentioned the 'rugby' incident. He went into the church, becoming rector at St Clement Dane's church in the Strand in London and later at Laver Magdalen in Essex (where a stained-glass window still commemorates

him). He died in the south of France in 1872 and is buried in Menton.

It is that alleged moment of enthusiasm, or cunning, in 1823 that is memorialised by a plaque at Rugby School and, worldwide, in the name of the trophy awarded to the winners of the Rugby World Cup.

Outside the school and framed by its rich architecture, a splendid statue of William Webb Ellis by sculptor Graham Ibbeson

was unveiled in 1997 by England's Jeremy Guscott. The statue, modelled on the sculptor's own son, shows a youth, in long sleeves and trousers, running with an oval rugby ball under his arm. It conveys a real sense of running movement. The statue bears the inscription: "The local boy who inspired the game of rugby football on the close at Rugby School in 1823." Perhaps mythical ... but a good and lasting story.

"Ellis rushed forwards with the ball in his hands"
Matthew Bloxham

ROBERT BARCLAY ALLARDICE

Champion Pedestrian

Running, jumping and throwing were pastimes commonly enjoyed, through the Middle Ages, as part of the 'fun and games' of the country fair or other festivals. As the 18th century progressed, a new kind of athlete emerged: the pedestrian – foot-racers who travelled the country taking on challenges, rather like the prize-fighters. Substantial crowds would attend to watch and to wager.

The landed gentry were never far from the piece. Indeed, many of the very earliest challenges were between members of the nobility on the prowess of their respective footmen. The public imagination became particularly enthused by feats of long-distance endurance against the clock. The most celebrated pedestrian of them all was Robert Barclay Allardice (1779–1854).

Born of a Scottish laird into a family noted for its strength, he realised early that his talent could be profitable. Known publicly as Captain Barclay after joining the Army, he became the most prominent walker and runner of his day, winning races and challenges over distances from 440 yards to 100 miles or more.

His most legendary feat came in 1809. The challenge: to walk 1,000 miles at one mile every hour of every day and night – 1,000 hours, nearly 42 days. No one had previously lasted beyond 30 days. It would clearly establish him as the country's champion pedestrian. At midnight on May 31 he set out on a roped-off half-mile course on Newmarket Heath, lit by lamps at night, over grass so flat it was said "you could have rolled a sixpence 100 yards on it" – observing a strict daily routine (including food, and ale, but rarely more than half an hour's sleep), forwards and backwards across the heath. By the final day, a crowd of more than 10,000 had gathered.

Reports of his achievement appeared in *The Times* alongside accounts of the Peninsular War against Napoleon. Barclay became a very wealthy man. His initial wager of 1,000 guineas had been multiplied many times over by side-bets.

His exploits made pedestrianism very popular in the 19th century, with crowds reaching 25,000. Not modest of his fame and prowess, he commissioned a marble statue of himself, modelled classically on Hercules "without a stitch of clothing", from Rome-based sculptor Lawrence MacDonald. It stood in the entrance hall to his ancestral Scottish home but its whereabouts are now unknown.

A contemporary record from 1809 of his feat exists, though, in the form of a hand-coloured engraving in the British Museum. Made by Charles Williams, the famous pedestrian is on Newmarket Heath in a splendid white flannel jacket – Captain Barclay, the most celebrated sportsman of the early 19th century.

ROBERT
BARCLAY
ALLARDICE
1779–1854

Hand-coloured
engraving
Charles Williams
British Museum,
London
c. 1809

"A task equally difficult was never before performed"
The London Chronicle, 1809

HARRY CLASPER

Hero of the North

HARRY CLASPER
1812–1870

Sandstone
George Burn
St Mary's Church,
Whickham
c. 1870

In the early part of the 19th century, the great rivers of the Thames and the Tyne were bustling with constant activity. Rowing flourished, as did the associated gambling and the drinking promoted by local publicans. It was a lively sport with challenges, lengthy races and unsophisticated rules. The rowers of the Thames and the Tyne were legendary sportsmen of the day, with crowds on race days often numbering tens of thousands and more for major events. Up on the Tyne, Harry Clasper (1812–1870) became the great hero. When he died, more than 100,000 people lined the seven-mile funeral route.

After starting as a miner, Clasper became an apprentice to a ship's carpenter. There, he gained valuable learning in boat design and construction which he put into effect. A Clasper-led crew, in a Clasper-built boat, became champions of the Tyne. They challenged the renowned London watermen, led by Robert Coombes (now

buried in Brompton Cemetery). The race took place in 1842 on the Tyne ... but the London watermen won.

Convinced that a more streamlined and lighter vessel was the answer, Clasper set off on a radical re-design. He was amongst the first to develop a keel-less boat for greater speed and to row with outriggers (the V-shaped struts that go out from the side of the boat to hold the oars) and curved blades. In effect, he designed the prototype for modern racing boats.

Triumph came in June 1845 when his newly-built boat, the *Lord Ravensworth*, with an all-Clasper crew, won the Champion Fours at the Thames Regatta by beating the London watermen. A huge civic reception confirmed his celebrity status on his return to Tyneside. A local song proclaimed: "*Oh! Harry's the lad, Harry Clasper for me! Haud away Harry! Canny Harry! Harry's the King of the Tyems an' the Tyne.*"

The Clasper boat and crew would stay supreme for a decade or more and Clasper, by today's standards, would enjoy millionaire status.

The great Harry Clasper died in 1870. He was buried in St Mary's Church in Whickham. On his tomb stands an elaborate sandstone statue by George Burn. A stately and somewhat severe-looking figure, dressed in normal day clothes and standing on a high pedestal under a gothic-style canopy, Clasper holds a piece of paper – perhaps he is proposing yet another design tweak to make his boat even faster?

Lithograph (c. 1844) of Harry Clasper rowing in a skiff on the Tyne.

"He took his strong arm and honest heart and hewed himself a pathway to fame and a sepulchre kings might envy"
Newcastle Daily Chronicle

ROBERT CHAMBERS

Although Harry Clasper himself never became, as a sole rower, a national sculling champion, he was the inspiration for two great Tyneside rowers who did. The first was Robert Chambers (1831–1868). He worked in local ironworks near Newcastle where he developed the strength which later brought him to the fore in rowing. He was coached and guided by Clasper.

'Honest Bob' achieved national fame when he won the sculling championship on the Thames in 1859 (the first non-Londoner to do so). He sadly died early at age 37 from tuberculosis. His was actually the first of the three memorable funerals of the Tyneside oarsmen (the third being James Renforth – see page overleaf) with over 50,000 people lining the route to Walker Cemetery.

A sandstone memorial (above), sculpted by George Burn, was erected over his grave. Dressed for rowing (with breeches and bare torso), Robert Chambers rests comfortably by a river bank with his oar by his side. His head, once removed by vandals, has now happily been restored.

JAMES RENFORTH

James Renforth (1842–1871) was the third of the great Tyneside rowers. Wonderfully strong, he became the world sculling champion in 1868 with victory over London's Henry Kelly. In 1870, he stroked a national four-man crew to win the world championship against a Canadian crew on the St Lawrence River near Montreal.

The following year, tragedy struck. Defending the championship, this time on the Kennebecasis River in New Brunswick, the same crew started well but the Canadian boat came back and, with something clearly wrong with Renforth's rowing, forged ahead. Renforth was swaying from side to side. He finally collapsed into the arms of the rower behind him, his great rival and friend, Kelly. Doctors could not save him. With huge bets at stake, rumours of poison persisted but a post-mortem confirmed natural causes, probably heart failure. His early death, so soon after Chambers and Clasper, brought gloom to the Tyne.

In 1872 a sandstone memorial, again sculpted by George Burn, was erected over Renforth's grave in Gateshead's East Cemetery. Restored after vandalism, the memorial was splendidly reinstated in 1992 beside the art gallery in the centre of the town. It has the feel of a dramatic classical tragedy. James Renforth is slumped against the bearded Henry Kelly with, as the *Illustrated London News* remarked, a "fading expression of consciousness". His death marked the end of an extraordinary era for professional rowing on Tyneside.

James Renforth dying in the arms of Henry Kelly, sculpted by George Burn.

TOM SAYERS

Champion Prize-Fighter

TOM SAYERS
1826–1865

Sandstone
Highgate
Cemetery,
London
c. 1865

One of the last great bare-knuckle fighters was Tom Sayers (1826–1865). Born in a slum district of Brighton, he developed his strength as a bricklayer before leaving for London and entering the world of prize-fighting. Although just 5ft 8ins and lighter than most, Sayers (the 'Napoleon of the prize ring') became widely recognised as the heavyweight champion of England.

On April 17 1860, one of the most extraordinary fights in history – and one of the last major prize-fights in England – took place in Farnborough in Hampshire. Sayers, now 34 years old, fought John Heenan. Taller, heavier and 10 years younger than Sayers, Heenan was America's champion. He had been enticed over to Farnborough by the £2,000 purse and the unofficial billing of the 'world championship'.

Pugilism had been one of the first sports to have introduced a written code. Rudimentary rules were published by champion fighter Jack Broughton (1704–1789) in 1743. They banned hitting a man when he was down and included the

John Heenan and Tom Sayers early in the great fight of 1860 (illustration).

"It's a man's game – it takes a game man to play it" *Tom Sayers*

introduction of 'rounds' with a rest period following a knock-down. Limited as they were, these rules essentially regulated the sport for a century or more. Broughton himself was buried in the west cloister of Westminster Abbey (where he was a Yeoman of the Guard). A memorial stone records this 'Champion Prizefighter of England'.

Prize-fighters were highly popular sportsmen of the day. Patronised by the landed gentry who would often provide safe venues away from magistrates seeking to outlaw disorderly assemblies, this brutal but popular sport attracted gamblers and supporters from all levels of society.

Bare-knuckle prize-fighting may have become clouded in illegality but the Sayers/Heenan fight attracted enormous publicity in the newspapers as excitement built. The secret date and venue were finally revealed. Special trains were laid on for the 7.30am start. A crowd of more than 12,000 gathered from all strata of society including, it is reported, famous figures of the day such as Charles Dickens and William Thackeray. Heavy betting, as always, took place.

The two fighters fought to a standstill for more than two hours and 35 rounds. Accounts differ as to which fighter was ahead. By the end, Heenan was virtually blinded. Sayers had a broken arm and was on the ropes, near strangulation. The makeshift ring-rope broke (or was it cut by one of the seconds?) as the crowd surged forward. The referee abandoned the scene. The police forced their way into the ring as

an unruly riot began. The fight was later declared a draw. A song from the 1860s records the tale: "*So! Hurrah my boys for Heenan and Tom Sayers we will sing, For they are the best and bravest ever fought in a British ring!*"

Sayers was encouraged by his supporters to retire and, indeed, an extraordinary public subscription of £3,000 was raised for him to do so. He would, in the following years, often be seen with his beloved bull mastiff, Lion, in the streets of Camden Town. Weakened by alcohol and pneumonia, he died barely five years after that great fight with Heenan.

In 2010, 150 years after the legendary fight, a commemorative plaque was unveiled in Brighton in his honour near the area where Sayers was brought up.

In a quiet corner of Highgate's West Cemetery in north London lies a distinctive sandstone memorial tombstone. On the day of his funeral, thousands thronged the streets and pubs closed in his honour. Story has it that Lion led the procession and later pined for him by his graveside. Fittingly, a life-size cast of Lion rests at the head of the distinctive grave – watching faithfully over one of England's great prize-fighters, Tom Sayers.

A bronze plaque by Carl Payne (above) recalls Brighton-born Tom Sayers.

DANIEL MENDOZA
BENDIGO THOMPSON
and WILLIAM PERRY

Many prize-fighters from the period leading up to Tom Sayers are commemorated around the country.

One of the most famous was Daniel Mendoza (1764–1836). Born in east London, his fights attracted the patronage of the Prince of Wales. Generally lighter than his opponents, he developed a more 'scientific' style of fighting with skilful side-stepping rather than simply exchanging punches in turn. The most celebrated Jewish athlete of his time, his popularity helped to change attitudes towards Jewish people in society.

He is recalled by a relief plaque commissioned from Louise Soloway by the Jewish East End Celebration Society and unveiled by Henry Cooper in 2008 in Mile End at Queen Mary, University of London.

Other fighters of the period now permanently commemorated include William 'Bendigo' Thompson (1811–1880). He was Champion of England in 1839 and a fighter beloved of the notorious supporters known as 'the Nottingham Lambs'. A distinctive burial monument stands in Nottingham and a concrete statue above a pub in Stainton near his birthplace.

In Tipton, near Wolverhampton, yards from the Fountain Inn which was once his headquarters, an imposing statue by Bill Haynes, erected in 1993, reveals William Perry (1819–1880) in fighting stance, a British champion popularly known as 'the Tipton Slasher'. His statue is a prominent reminder of the age of the prize-fighter.

Three of England's 19th century champion prize-fighters: Daniel Mendoza in east London (above left), Bendigo Thompson in Nottingham (above right) and William Perry in Tipton (left).

JEM MACE

Father of Modern Boxing

JEM MACE
1831–1910

Stone
Beeston
Churchyard,
Beeston
c. 1910

In the quiet rural setting of Beeston Churchyard in north Norfolk a white-cross stone commemorates 'Jem Mace Champion of the World'. Behind this simple memorial lies the story of a boxing champion, a womaniser, a man who travelled the world, made a fortune and died in poverty ... and who changed the style of boxing.

Born in Beeston and the son of a blacksmith who mixed with circus and fairground travellers, James 'Jem' Mace (1831–1910) was later known as 'The Gypsy'. He became a useful fighter in the fairground boxing booths of the area taking on all-comers. He was also a violinist, a fiddler. The story goes that, one day, some thugs broke his violin. As Jem showed his anger on them, someone said: "You should become a prize-fighter." Jem did so.

These were the last days of bare-knuckle fighting. In 1861 Mace won the title of Champion of England. The song rang out: *"Fill, fill your glasses to the brim and merrily let us sing, Jem Mace the Norfolk Hero now the Champion of the Ring."*

As pursuit of prize-fighting by the law increased, Mace set off for America where prize-fighting still flourished. In 1870, he fought Tom Allen in a famous bout at Kennerville near New Orleans and won – a fight widely recognising Mace to be the first Champion of the World. A local statue commemorates the fight.

The times were changing. New rules, largely drawn up by John Graham Chambers and promulgated in 1867 by the Marquess of Queensberry, were designed to soften the brutality of fights and to introduce glove-boxing. Mace was equally adept at this new form. Importantly, Mace (to quote his later obituary in *The Times*) had a style "of incomparable grace and effectiveness". He introduced skills of defence, feinting and footwork. He had "a profound contempt for the circular swings and crouching attitude adopted by American (or Americanised) boxers; in his opinion the straight left ruled the world". The modern style of boxing was born.

His private life was, by any standards, scandalous. He married three times – twice bigamously. He was said to have had two teenage mistresses, an affair with a famous American actress and 14 children by five different women. He travelled the world including working as a boxing instructor and promoter in Australia. A fortune was gained and gambled away. He ended his days as a penniless busker in poverty. His death in Liverpool in 1910 led to an unmarked grave in Anfield Cemetery – remedied only in 2002 with a black granite gravestone paid for by the Merseyside Ex-Boxers Association.

In Norfolk, though, Jem Mace was remembered as one of their own. A white-cross memorial to the champion was ceremonially unveiled in Norwich Cemetery soon after his death. In 1976, it was donated to Beeston Churchyard and placed beside the grave of his father. It is here that we recall the colourful story of the man who is regarded as the 'Father of Modern Boxing'.

"To Jem ... we owe the changes that have elevated the sport"
Jim Corbett, world heavyweight champion (1892–1897)

BOB FITZSIMMONS

If Norfolk claims Jem Mace, Cornwall is proud to have been the birthplace of Bob Fitzsimmons (1863–1917). Born in Helston to the son of a local policeman, Fitzsimmons migrated with his family as an 11-year-old to Timaru in the south of New Zealand. His father became a blacksmith and, working with him, Bob developed his strength. It was in a boxing competition in Australia, promoted by Mace, that Fitzsimmons was discovered and encouraged to become a fully-fledged professional fighter boxing, principally, under the Queensberry Rules.

Fitzsimmons travelled to America, now the centre of boxing, and earned a rich dividend. Fitzsimmons, bald-headed and thin-legged but carrying the penetrating power of a blacksmith, won the world middleweight championship in New Orleans in 1891. Then, in a famous fight in March 1897, he defeated the holder, Jim Corbett, in Kansas City to win the world heavyweight title. Wyatt Earp was among the well-known personalities who witnessed the duel.

By gaining the light-heavyweight title in 1903, Fitzsimmons became the first man ever to win three word championship titles at different weight divisions

Bob Fitzsimmons' birthplace in Helston is remembered by a plaque while a statue is planned to celebrate the legendary fighter. We can also enjoy in The Champion pub in Wells Street in central London a delightful stained-glass window (right), crafted by Ann Sotheran, featuring the great fighter.

Charles Alcock is
commemorated
by a monument at
his grave in West
Norwood Cemetery.
The FA Cup trophy
is prominent in
his legacy.

CHARLES ALCOCK

Pioneer of the Cup

It was in the 1860s that association football became a distinct sport. Team games had grown in popularity at public schools as the 19th century advanced and the quest began to establish a common set of rules for 'football' so that former pupils could carry on playing team matches in later life. Each school, though, had its own rules and traditions. In some, emphasis was placed on kicking and 'dribbling' with the ball on the ground; 'hacking' with the feet was usual, catching and holding the ball was generally allowed but most prohibited running with the ball in hand.

A major step came 150 years ago, in October 1863, with a meeting of 'clubs' formed in the London area by former pupils of different public schools (reputedly held at the Freemasons' Tavern in Great Queen Street). The group called themselves 'the Football Association'. Rules by which they would play 'association football', drafted by Ebenezer Cobb Morley, were agreed after much debate. Running with the ball and hacking were eventually prohibited. Morley became the first FA Secretary.

It was Charles W. Alcock (1842–1907) who was destined to play an extraordinary role in the game's development. Son of a shipping businessman from Sunderland, his family moved near London and Alcock was educated at Harrow. Aged just 24, he was elected to the committee of the FA and in 1870 became its Honorary Secretary. His ideas and drive would transform the game.

Alcock's landmark proposal came in 1871: "A Challenge Cup should be established in connection with the Association, for which all clubs belonging to the Association should be invited to compete." Prior to that, matches had been arranged on a haphazard basis.

The FA Cup, played on a knock-out basis, was the world's first-ever national competition between football clubs. (Alcock also happened to be the captain of the first winning side, the Wanderers!) The FA Cup soon became the nation's leading sporting competition. Geoffrey Green described it as "the spark that set the whole bonfire of football alight".

Alcock was also behind the introduction of international football. In 1870 he proposed that teams of Scottish and English players should compete against each other. Early matches, mostly comprising London-based players, were held at the Kennington Oval where the ubiquitous Alcock was Secretary of Surrey CC for many years. His influence would continue to extend over many aspects of the developing game, from the style of play to the growth of professionalism. Alcock would also become a major force in the organisation of county cricket.

In the undergrowth of West Norwood Cemetery, in south-east London, a monument at his grave (re-dedicated in 1999) commemorates this inspirational administrator. Prominently carved on the stone cross, and at the forefront of Charles Alcock's legacy, is the FA Cup trophy.

CHARLES
ALCOCK
1842–1907

Stone
West Norwood
Cemetery, London
c. 1907

"A founder of modern sport"
Sir John Major

WILLIAM PENNY BROOKES

Shropshire's Olympian

WILLIAM PENNY
BROOKES
1809–1895

Stainless steel
Adrian Reynolds
Linden Field,
Much Wenlock
2012

Were the seeds of the modern Olympic Games sown in Shropshire in the mid-19th century? In the small market town of Much Wenlock, the memory of William Penny Brookes (1809–1895) is proudly recalled. It was to his grave that Juan Samaranch, then President of the International Olympic Committee, came in honour in 1994.

Brookes was an extraordinary man. Local doctor, magistrate and philanthropist, he strongly believed that sport was good for all. In 1850 he started a 'class' for the local community which he termed the Olympian Class designed to "promote the moral, physical and intellectual improvement" of the neighbourhood "by the encouragement of out-door recreation".

The first meeting of the Wenlock Olympian Games was held later that year. It became a popular annual event with a variety of races and events (including contemporary pursuits such as tilting). Importantly, the events were open to "all grades of men" in the community regardless of their class. A colourful opening procession took place through the local streets. The custom began of rewarding the victors with a laurel wreath crown.

In 1858 Brookes learned about the proposed revival of the Olympic Games in Athens led by Greek financier, Evangelis Zappas. Brookes became an enthusiastic supporter and sent many suggestions. The initial Games in Greece, hampered by governmental interference, were not a success. But Brookes did not give up. He continued over the years to send letters to the King of Greece, the Greek ambassador in London and the Prime Minister advocating a revival.

If the cause was not taken up again in Greece, Brookes learned in 1885 of the activities of a young French aristocrat called Baron Pierre de Coubertin, who was an admirer of English sports as well as the virtues of physical vigour and group co-operation. He believed their introduction into France would help restore backbone to the nation.

Baron de Coubertin (aged 27), while visiting England, came at Brookes' invitation to Much Wenlock in 1890 where a special meeting of the Wenlock Olympian Games was held. Brookes then pressed the idea to him of a revival of the Olympic Games to start in Athens itself. Brookes had passed the torch to the younger man.

Two years later, Coubertin went public with his own proposal for the Games. He initiated a meeting of the International Athletic Congress in 1894. Invited as an honorary member, Brookes was too ill to attend. He died just four months before the first modern Games opened in Athens in 1896.

The memory of the contribution of William Penny Brookes to the Olympic Games movement may, internationally, have diminished – but not here in this corner of Shropshire. When the organising committee of the London 2012 Olympic and Paralympic Games revealed the name of the Olympic mascot for the summer Games, it was to Shropshire's delight. His name was 'Wenlock'.

"I come to pay homage to
Dr Brookes, who really was
the founder of the modern
Olympic Games"
Juan Samaranch

A memorial laid in
2012 in Linden Field
(left), the site of the
Wenlock Olympian
Games founded
by William Penny
Brookes. A memorial
(c. 1895) in Holy
Trinity Church, Much
Wenlock, and an
accompanying marble
plaque (above),
dedicated in 2012
prior to the London
Olympics.

CHAPTER TWO

AN ERA OF TRANSFORMATION

The last quarter or so of the 19th century and the beginning of the 20th century were years of momentous change.

Urbanisation was the major social development. Towns and cities grew rapidly as workers moved nearer the factories and other centres of employment in the new industrial economy. Time and money for enjoyment of sport by the working class were limited but increasing. The working week in most factories started to end at midday on Saturdays. Sports suited to the confines of urban life grew in popularity. Football, in particular, began to attract large Saturday afternoon crowds. Sport was not just for participants; it was becoming a major urban spectator attraction.

Communications were developing dramatically through the growth of the national railway network and the popularity of newspapers. Reports, results and the fortunes of a team could be followed. Matches could be played between teams across the country. The Victorian talent for organisation led to the growth of national governing bodies,

regulation of many of our great games and the start of national competitions – none more significant than the creation of the Football League in 1888. The first signs of international sport emerged (particularly in cricket, the sport of the British Empire).

For many Victorians (including leaders in the great public schools), sport encouraged virtues of exercise, competition, fair play and self-control. Clubs were formed to assist development of youth. Sport was viewed as 'a good thing'; amateur sport, that is. The seeds of tension between the sport of the 'gentleman amateur' and the dangers (or, for many, the opportunities) of sportsmen being paid as 'professionals' would start to grow in most sports. Each would grapple with this issue in its own way.

Many sporting heroes of this important era have been immortalised by statues and memorials around the country, a number quite recent. It is fascinating how, collectively, they now vividly reflect the heroes and events of this era of transformation in sport.

W G GRACE

The Champion

WILLIAM
GILBERT GRACE
1848–1915

Bronze
Louis Laumen
Lord's Cricket
Ground, London
1999

At Lord's, the home of English cricket, in the Coronation Garden in front of Thomas Lord's old roller, William Gilbert Grace (1848–1915) still bats with total authority. His standing in the game is undoubted and revered. W G Grace was 'the grand old man of cricket', a towering figure who dominated the game for decades.

By the 1860s, the game was still developing its structure. There were travelling professional 'elevens'. The county clubs were also growing in stature. Importantly, although not a representative side, the first international touring team to Australia visited in 1861–1862. (Two years later, a touring team would include E M Grace, an amateur from Bristol, who received £500 in expenses. His famous brother was inspired by this example.) The first official representative Test match took place in Melbourne between Australia and England in 1877.

W G Grace, son of a family doctor near Bristol, was in the meantime initiated into the county and touring teams of the day through his father's contacts with the Duke of Beaufort. Grace shot to prominence as a 15-year-old boy in 1864 when he scored 170 runs against the 'Gentlemen of Sussex'.

Statistics of his career are awesome: more than 54,000 first-class runs spread over an astonishing 44 seasons. In one spell, in just eight days in 1876, he scored 839 for Gloucestershire, his lifelong county, including two triple centuries (and when only one other player reached 1,000 runs during the entire season). He topped the first-class batting averages 12 times in the years between 1866 and 1880. Still opening for England at the age of 50, he was said to be the best-known Englishman of his day other than, perhaps, William Gladstone. His popularity transformed cricket into the nation's summer game and a leading spectator sport. By 1900, first-class matches were played before crowds that frequently rose to 20,000 or more.

Qualifying eventually as a medical doctor, he remained an 'amateur' throughout his career although his financial rewards from the game (particularly his compensation for touring Australia and a number of testimonials)

The great W G Grace (c. 1902), with bat in hand and the famous beard prominent (left).

"His bulk and stride carried cricket into the highways of our national life"
Sir Neville Cardus, writer and cricket correspondent

W G GRACE

continued

were beyond any level enjoyed or contemplated by others. This, and his love of gamesmanship, never qualified him as a 'gentleman' of the purist kind approved by the inner circles of the governing Marylebone Cricket Club (MCC). This, however, only served to increase his wider popular appeal.

The Guardian's obituary in 1915 summed up: "Dr. William Gilbert Grace was by common consent the greatest and most attractive figure that ever appeared on the cricket field. In his all-round mastery of the game, in the length of years during which he stood far above all his rivals, in the amazing sum total of his cricketing achievements, and by no means least of all in the popular interest he excited, no cricketer, living or dead, has ever approached him, and it is doubtful if any will."

At Lord's, this life-size bronze sculpture of WG reflects his imperial authority. It was not commissioned by the MCC but sculpted speculatively in Australia, with financial backing as part of a group of major sporting sculptures, by Louis Laumen. It was destined for the UK but by auction. Displayed at first, and fittingly, at Bristol in 1999 during a World Cup match between Pakistan and the West Indies, it was eventually bought by the MCC. It could surely have had no other home. Prepared after careful study from old film footage, the sculpture reveals Grace in imposing and easy batting action in his later years. His girth somewhat wider than in his early career, the cap (too small by

modern style) as always in place, his eyes full of concentration, the bat held above the ground due to his height, with hands apart, the legendary black beard adding age and authority – all captured in glorious sculpted detail. W G Grace seems to have been at the crease for years.

DICK BARLOW and ALBERT HORNBY

Two unexpected cricketers follow in our story: Dick Barlow (1851–1919) and Albert Nielson (A N) Hornby (1847–1925). Barlow was a resolute opening batsman for Lancashire, the original Stonewaller by nickname. A N Hornby was an Old Harrovian who captained England at cricket and also, twice, at rugby. Together, they were a formidable opening pair for Lancashire in the 1870s and 1880s. A fascinating insight into those days is that Hornby (a 'gentleman') would stride to the wicket at Old Trafford from the pavilion. Barlow (a paid 'professional') would join him from the professional's hut on a different side of the ground.

Hornby was captain, with Barlow and indeed W G Grace in the side, in the famous lost Test at The Oval in 1882 (the ninth Test between the two countries) when England were defeated by Australia on home soil for the first time. *The Sporting Times* issued an obituary notice that English cricket had died at The Oval on August 29 1882. "The body will be cremated and the ashes taken to Australia." England's captain, Ivo Bligh, promised that he would seek to regain "the ashes".

He did. Legend has it that the urn was handed over after a social match near Melbourne in December 1882 during the series won by England. The favoured version is that it contains the remains of a bail or a stump. It is displayed at the MCC Cricket Museum, perhaps the best-known memorial in sport.

When Barlow retired, he commissioned a glass-stained window of the famous

Lancashire opening pair with wicketkeeper Richard Pilling behind. Re-discovered a few years ago, the delightful window is now in the Long Room at Old Trafford.

A N Hornby and Dick Barlow's partnership is recalled with nostalgia in one of the best-known poems on English cricket, *At Lord's*, by Francis Thompson, recalling those days of the past: "*As the run-stealers flicker to and fro, to and fro: O my Hornby and my Barlow long ago!*"

A stained-glass window in the Long Room at Old Trafford (above) recalls Lancashire's stalwart opening pair, both of whom played in the losing Test match against Australia in 1882 that would lead to the Ashes urn (left).

MATTHEW WEBB

Swimming the Channel

Swimming was never the same after that day, August 24 1875, when Matthew Webb (1848–1883) set off from Admiralty Pier in Dover: the first man to swim the English Channel.

Born in Dawley in Shropshire, Webb became a merchant seaman and briefly commanded a ship (hence his oft-used title of 'captain'). A strong swimmer, he gained renown after a brave attempt to rescue a man overboard. Attracted by the publicity of failed attempts by others to swim the English Channel, and no doubt the potential rewards if successful, he decided to take on the challenge. He moved to London to train in Lambeth.

The 27-year-old Webb set off on that August day wearing a red silk bathing costume and smeared in porpoise grease. He swam (a journalist, Robert Watson, observed) with a "slow, methodical, but perfect, breaststroke" and with a "magnificent sweep of his ponderous legs". He kept going with the aid of "cod-liver oil, beef tea, brandy, coffee and strong old ale". Seven miles short of France, the tidal currents turned against him. Many hours later, in mid-morning on August 25 after a total of nearly 22 hours in the water and swimming around 40 miles, he made it to Calais. Webb gained £125 for his triumph, a generous publicly-funded testimonial and huge publicity.

Large crowds greeted his return. He became one of the best-known men in the country, and indeed internationally. Swimming became a widely popular sport. Dozens of new municipal baths were constructed around the country.

Webb himself became a professional swimmer participating in endurance races, exhibitions and various challenges. In 1883 he travelled to America and raced (and beat) the so-called US champion. Webb was then determined to tackle a challenge, for reward, swimming through a well-known whirlpool three miles below the Niagara Falls. It was one challenge too many. More than 10,000 people were reputed to have watched from the banks as he was rowed to the middle of the river. He dived in. Shortly afterwards, it was reported, "he abruptly threw up his arms and went under".

In 1909, just over 25 years after his death, a memorial to Webb was erected in the high street of his home town of Dawley in Shropshire (and was recently restored after unfortunate damage from an out-of-control lorry).

A year after that original memorial, in 1910, a head-and-shoulders statue followed on the seafront at Dover. It stands on a high stone plinth garlanded by seashells. A somewhat sombre but proud Captain Webb gazes out over the English Channel. Perhaps he is musing on his endeavours on that day in August 1875 when he set off into history. It would be nearly another 50 years before his feat would be emulated.

His fame endures, including in poetry. John Betjeman's *A Shropshire Lad* recalls the ghost of "*Captain Webb from Dawley ... Swimming along from Severn, And paying a call at Dawley Bank while swimming along to Heaven*".

MATTHEW WEBB
1848–1883

Bronze
Francis W Doyle-Jones
Marine Parade, Dover
1910

"Nothing great is easy"
Matthew Webb

WALTER WINGFIELD

Father of Lawn Tennis

WALTER
WINGFIELD
1833–1912

Bronze
Albert Toft
Wimbledon Lawn
Tennis Museum,
Wimbledon,
London
c. 1890

I n London SW19, the All England Lawn Tennis & Croquet Club is the home of one of the world's great sporting tournaments. In the Wimbledon Lawn Tennis Museum we pay tribute to Major Walter Wingfield (1833–1912).

As the railway network started to stretch out from the big cities, large houses with gardens developed in the rural suburbs and a middle-class culture embraced the use of 'lawns' for informal amusement. Croquet had been introduced in the mid-19th century, but could a more energetic summer garden sport be devised? Yes. In 1874 Wingfield obtained a provisional patent for a game played with rackets and the new vulcanised rubber balls that bounced on grass. He initially called it 'sphairistike' but later 'lawn tennis'.

The Field, read throughout the country shires, reproduced sections of Wingfield's booklet of rules which accompanied sets of equipment for his new game. The effect was extraordinary. The game swept through the English-speaking world. Others may have played similar games before him (and indeed Major Harry Gem had formed a lawn rackets club in 1872 at the Manor House Hotel in Leamington) but it was Major Wingfield who promoted the game towards its national, and international, status.

Wingfield's court had an hour-glass shape, the net narrower than the baseline. One side of the net was for serving and the other for receiving. Variants of the new game emerged. In stepped the Marylebone Cricket Club with an offer to establish a single set of rules, as they had for what was now called 'real tennis'. Some changes were made, pushing the server back to the baseline. But Wingfield's hour-glass-shaped court remained.

Lawn tennis fitted well into the middle-class social world of the late 19th century. It was a game that could be played by either sex and, indeed, at most ages. Tennis became, perhaps, the first truly national game. By 1914, there were over 1,000 clubs around the country.

Another development transformed the sport. At the prestigious All England Croquet Club in Wimbledon, then in Worple Road, a member proposed that a court be set aside for the new game of lawn tennis. The name of the club was changed to The All England Croquet and Lawn Tennis Club (note the order). New rules were adopted by the club, finally getting rid of Wingfield's hour-glass-shaped court. In 1877 the first lawn tennis championship was held, open to all amateurs. The Wimbledon Championships were born. The game became a major international competitive sport.

A first 'great' of the game at Wimbledon was William Renshaw (1861–1904). With his power and technical ability, he won a total of seven singles titles (an all-time men's record shared now with Pete Sampras and Roger Federer).

It is, fittingly, at the Wimbledon Lawn Tennis Museum that a bronze bust of a somewhat severe-looking Major Wingfield can be found. He is honoured as the father of the game.

"A new game has just been patented by Major Wingfield, late 1st Dragoon Guards, which, if we mistake not, will become a national pastime"
Army and Navy Gazette

FRED ARCHER

The Tin-Man

FRED ARCHER
1857–1886

Stained glass
Ann Sotheran
The Champion,
Wells Street,
London
1989

At the King's Arms, Cheltenham (right, top), a plaque on the door (right, bottom) recalls the childhood of Fred Archer.

The manner of his death still shocks. Fred Archer (1857–1886), the finest jockey of the Victorian era and aged just 29, reached for a revolver kept in a bedside cabinet and shot himself through the mouth.

In the late 19th century, horse-racing continued in popularity and the top jockeys were amongst the best-known of professional sportsmen. Earnings could be considerable – not only for the jockeys themselves but also their followers. Most famous of all was Fred Archer. Crowds would flock to see him. When he married in Cambridge in 1883, special trains were laid on to bring the cheering crowds to Newmarket. Upon his death, *The Times* reflected: "The news of his death has come with a sense of shock and almost personal loss to millions."

Archer was born in a small cottage in Cheltenham. His father was the landlord of the King's Arms; a memorial plaque proudly records the inn where Fred Archer "swallowed his earliest porridge". He was, from age 11, apprenticed to the trainer Matthew Dawson in Newmarket and later married Dawson's niece, Helen Rose. He became the retained jockey for Lord Falmouth and the powerful combination of owner, trainer and jockey enjoyed unparalleled success.

Archer rode his first public winner in his very first race at 13. By the end of his young life at 29, he had been champion jockey for 13 consecutive years – from 1874 to 1886 – and had ridden an astonishing

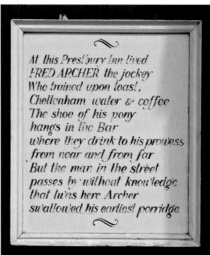

At this Prestbury Inn lived
FRED ARCHER the jockey
Who trained upon toast,
Cheltenham water & coffee
The shoe of his pony
hangs in the Bar
where they drink to his prowess
from near and from far
But the man in the street
passes by without knowledge
that 'twas here Archer
swallowed his earliest porridge

"Fred Archer was simply the best all-round jockey that the Turf has seen" *The National Horseracing Museum*

2,748 winners with 21 Classic victories (including five Derby winners). His success and careful attitude to money led to the nickname 'Tin-Man'. He was probably the most celebrated sportsman of his day, a legend in his own lifetime.

Why did he take his life? Was it fear of money troubles, the relentless strain of a tallish man (5ft 8ins or more) striving to make a difficult riding weight or, more likely, continued depression at the loss of his first child shortly after birth and then, a year later, the death of his wife giving birth to their second child – all compounded at the end by bed-ridden days with a fever? We shall never know. The sermon at his funeral described a career crammed with "a spending of physical force which left nothing remaining but the framework of a used-up life". The coroner's jury decided he suffered from "a state of temporary insanity". A simple tombstone stands over his grave in Newmarket, shared with his wife and infant child.

Now, a delightful glass-stained window of Fred Archer, colourfully crafted by Ann Sotheran, is included in the set of 'champions' that surround the interior of The Champion pub in central London.

The Archer legend continues. The story is told locally of a visitor who, returning home after a dinner in Newmarket, heard the clip-clop of a horse trotting down the road. He turned around but could see nothing and the sound ceased. The visitor later relayed his experience to a local jockey – who smiled: "Oh, that would be Fred. He goes for a ride occasionally."

YOUNG TOM MORRIS
W G GRACE
WILLIAM RENSHAW
and MATTHEW WEBB

Stained-glass windows in The Champion pub in Wells Street
in central London, all crafted by artist Ann Sotheran, provide
a delightful surround. Each colourfully displays a famous
'champion' of his time. In addition to boxer Bob Fitzsimmons
and jockey Fred Archer (featured earlier), sportsmen represented
include four names that resonated strongly in the late 19th
century: (from left) Young Tom Morris, W G Grace, William
Renshaw and Matthew Webb.

WALTER GEORGE

Original Miracle Miler

WALTER GEORGE
1858–1943

Bronze/stone
Recreation Ground,
Calne
1945

There was another 'WG' of the Victorian era, Walter Goodall George (1858–1943), now less well-known but an athlete who in 1886 established a world record that would last for nearly 30 years.

By the 1860s and 1870s a bitter divide existed between professional and amateur athletics. Professional 'pedestrians' continued to race in challenges around the country with large sums being waged on the outcome. Yet greed, corruption and race-fixing were rife. Victorian 'gentlemen' viewed professional racing with disdain.

Foot-racing as a 'pure' amateur sport had its origins in the cross-country runs popular at many public schools and universities. The amateur athletic national championships, first held in 1866, excluded not only professionals but (added the following year) also 'any mechanic, artisan or labourer'. After years of power struggles and political wrangling between rival clubs, the Amateur Athletic Association (AAA) was formed in 1880, with events open to all amateurs, in an attempt to unify and promote the sport. The inaugural AAA championships were held at Lillie Bridge in west London. The first mile winner was Walter George.

Born into a middle-class family in Calne in Wiltshire, he ran among the windswept hills for his health and later 'trained' by running alongside the Duke of Beaufort's hunt. (Many amateur athletic clubs had their roots alongside hunting; the names of Harriers, Beagles and Hare and Hounds still resonate.) On his family's

THIS PLAQUE WAS ERECTED
BY THE
CALNE TOWN COUNCIL
IN MEMORY OF
THE FAMOUS ATHLETE
WALTER GOODALL GEORGE
A NATIVE OF THIS TOWN.
IN 1886 HE SET UP A WORLD
RECORD BY RUNNING ONE MILE
IN 4 MINS 12¾ SECS.
THIS RECORD STOOD FOR 30 YEARS
AUGUST 1948.

"What a roar went up! Such a roar thrills me even now as I write this. It was stupendous" *A spectator*

move to Worcester, George worked in his father's chemist shop. His outdoor training was restricted and he developed his famous '100-up' exercise routine of exaggerated knee-lifts.

George won a total of 12 AAA championship titles and established records over distances ranging from 660 yards to 12 miles. With his distinctive black hair and moustache, he was very popular and the country's outstanding amateur athlete, racing before large crowds and, abroad, at venues such as New York's Polo Grounds and Madison Square Garden. He became a professional in 1885, principally to enjoy the fruits of a high-profile series of contests with professional Scottish runner William Cummings, then holder of the world mile record at 4 minutes 16.2 seconds.

The great mile race was on the red brick dust track of Lillie Bridge on August 23 1886. As they entered the fourth and final lap, Cummings edged ahead but George responded and burst clear with around 100 yards to go, Cummings collapsing to the track. The crowd, spellbound, waited for the timekeepers to pronounce. People stared at the blackboard with disbelief. The figures read: "4:12 ¾." The crowd erupted. George had beaten the record by an astonishing margin of nearly four seconds. His record stood for almost 30 years and no Briton matched it until Sydney Wooderson in 1937.

In Calne, two memorial plaques quietly but proudly record that extraordinary day in 1886. Walter George was the 'Original Miracle Miler'.

CHARLES BENNETT and HENRY TAYLOR

The Olympic movement produced its first British heroes at the start of the 20th century. The first British athlete to win an Olympic gold medal was Charles Bennett (1870–1948), a train driver from Dorset known as 'the Shapwick Express'. In 1900 in Paris Bennett led the field over a soft soil track to win the 1500 metres and won a second gold medal a week later with a combined British and Australian team in the 5000 metres. Two gold medals. He was hailed as a hero when he returned home to Dorset.

His story has now been rediscovered. At his grave in Kinson, near Bournemouth, a new headstone (left) was laid, before the London Olympics in 2012, commemorating the achievements of this unsung hero.

Another early Olympic star was Henry Taylor (1885–1951). Taylor learned to swim in local canals before training in new municipal baths in Oldham and Chadderton. In 1906 he gained the world record at 880 yards and then the gold medal in the 1500 metres freestyle at the interim Olympic Games in Athens. In 1908 the Olympic Games were held in London at the White City Stadium (with the swimming pool, the first purpose-built Olympic pool, in the middle area surrounded by the athletics track). Among swimmers from 14 nations, Taylor achieved glorious success by winning three gold medals – at 400 metres, 1500 metres and the 4 x 200 metres relay. He also represented Britain at the 1912 and 1920 Olympics, winning bronze medals in the relay.

It is at the old Chadderton Baths that a plaque (below) quietly reminds us of the achievements of Britain's most successful amateur swimmer of the 20th century.

BROTHER WALFRID

Celtic's Founder

BROTHER WALFRID
1840–1915

Bronze
Kate Robinson
Celtic Park,
Glasgow
2005

Industrialisation changed the landscape of Britain in the late Victorian era. For many, Saturday midday became the end of the working week. For the first time, working men found themselves with some leisure time and money to spend. Football, in particular, spread with great popularity.

Many philanthropic individuals and religious organisations saw sport as 'a good thing' and a way to develop 'moral character' in the 'lower' classes in the expanding towns and cities. It was the so-called doctrine of 'muscular Christianity'. Football clubs formed by church organisations included Aston Villa (promoted by the Villa Cross Wesleyan Chapel), Everton (as part of the St Domingo's Church Sunday School), Fulham (by St Andrew's Sunday School) and Southampton (by the young men of St Mary's Church). Others were founded by teachers' associations, factories or workplaces. Many clubs have distinctive stories but few have been so closely associated with their formative roots as Glasgow Celtic.

Andrew Kerins, later to be known as Brother Walfrid (1840–1915), made a journey as a 15-year-old, like so many others from Ireland, to escape from famine and political unrest but, sadly, only to squalor and poverty in Glasgow – probably then the most densely-populated city in Europe. Looked after by a religious group of Marist Brothers who brought care and education to the poverty-stricken of Glasgow's East End, Kerins decided that his own vocation would be with them and he became Brother Walfrid.

Sporting events were a way to help this charitable work. He sought to create a football team in Glasgow not only as a fundraising venture but as a social focus for the community. The Celtic Football and Athletic Club was formed in November 1887 in St Mary's parish hall. The name 'Celtic', proposed by Brother Walfrid himself, conveyed the link with the Irish. The Scottish League had not yet been formed. A circular was issued declaring that "the main object of the club was to supply ... funds for the maintenance of the dinner tables for the needy children in the missions of St Mary's, Sacred Heart and St Michael's".

Brother Walfrid later moved to teach and help in London's East End. He died aged 74. His link with Celtic was not forgotten. In 2005, funded largely by the club's supporters, a magnificent sculpture of Brother Walfrid, by Kate Robinson, was unveiled outside Celtic Park to commemorate the major part he played in the founding of the club.

The chair of the Memorial Committee, Eddie Toner, observed ruefully that modern football has been taken over by many of the values that Brother Walfrid would undoubtedly have opposed. The memorial would act "as a humble reminder of the club's origins".

A bronze relief on the statue's plinth recalls Brother Walfrid's support for children in east Glasgow.

"Walfrid gave our community a beacon in a dark, harsh and intolerant world"
Eddie Toner

WILLIAM McGREGOR

Father of the League

WILLIAM
McGREGOR
1846–1911

Bronze
Samantha Holland
Villa Park,
Birmingham
2009

As football grew from its amateur origins, clubs sought the best players to represent them. Footballers from working-class backgrounds were offered financial inducements by ambitious clubs (such as paid work, pub tenancies or other business opportunities). Many leaders, brought up in the 'amateur' ethic, opposed the introduction of professionalism, especially in the FA Cup. Tensions grew. The still highly influential Charles Alcock forcefully argued: "Professionals are a necessity to the growth of the game."

In July 1885, after many fractious meetings, the decision was taken. Professionalism was allowed, including for clubs playing in the FA Cup (but with strict rules of residency similar to those that applied in cricket). A schism in football was avoided.

Clubs, though, needed revenue to pay these professional players. The FA Challenge Cup attracted large crowds but it was the sport's only major competition. Friendly games were not always easy to arrange, frequently cancelled and often mismatches, and did not produce a regular income. Could football be structured to survive financially? In stepped William McGregor (1846–1911).

McGregor, a Scot who had moved to Birmingham to carry on business as a draper, was a director at Aston Villa, a club which paid many of its players. He realised that Villa needed regular competitive games for financial security. His solution? In March 1888 he wrote to Blackburn Rovers,

Bolton Wanderers, Preston North End and West Bromwich Albion. He proposed "that ten or twelve of the most prominent clubs in England combine to arrange home and away fixtures each season".

McGregor called a meeting in Manchester and, at the Royal Hotel, the Football League was formed – the world's first football league. It kicked off, with great publicity, on September 8 1888 with 12 founder clubs from the Midlands and the North. No southern clubs were interested. Preston North End were the first champions. Within a few years, leagues had been established in Scotland, Ireland and Wales – and a Second Division in England. Football developed at an astonishing speed.

McGregor has remained an unknown figure to most. Until 2009, when an impressive 7ft 6ins bronze statue was unveiled at the entrance to the main stand at Aston Villa by Lord Mawhinney, then chairman of the Football League, after six years of fundraising led by the Aston Villa Supporters Trust. Sculptor Samantha Holland explained: "He was a portly gentleman and, as the son of a draper, I imagine that he would have been well-dressed and had an eye for detail, so I put him in woollen trousers, a silk waistcoat, with a long morning coat, a cravat and an elegant cane."

The statue depicts a bearded William McGregor standing, elegant and somewhat Shakespearean in pose – and in his hand that letter proposing his ground-breaking vision for future league competition.

A plaque (above) on the site of the Royal Hotel in Manchester records the formation of the Football League in 1888.

"I beg to tender the following suggestion"
William McGregor

WILLIAM McCRUM

There are certain features of the game which we assume were there at the start. Not so. The penalty kick was the brain-child of William McCrum (1865–1932). Keener on sport than the family's local cotton mill, he was the goalkeeper for Milford Everton FC from County Armagh. McCrum deplored the deliberate fouling that was, to him, corrupting the game. Perhaps surprisingly for a goalkeeper, he persuaded the Irish Football Association to propose a new rule. A "penalty kick, to be taken from any point twelve yards from the goal line" may be awarded for an intentional trip or handball within that area. For purists 'the Irishman's motion' was contrary to the principles of a game played by 'gentlemen'. It was adopted by the International Football Board in 1891.

Housing was built in the 2000s on the site of the old football field in Milford. Permission was given provided the middle became a memorial park. The centrepiece, unveiled in 2010, is a bronze bust of William McCrum (above) by sculptor David Pettigrew.

ARTHUR WHARTON

Black Pioneer

ARTHUR
WHARTON
1865–1930

Bronze maquette
Vivien Mallock
2010

In a cemetery in Doncaster a grave remained unmarked for over 65 years. We now recall the story of Arthur Wharton (1865–1930), the world's first professional black footballer.

Born into an upper middle-class family in Accra (then in the Gold Coast, now Ghana), Wharton was the son of a missionary Methodist minister and a local mother in the British colony. Aged 19, Wharton went to college in Staffordshire to train as a preacher. He preferred sport. His talent was soon clear, particularly in athletics. Indeed, he won the 100 yards sprint title at the amateur athletics championships held at Stamford Bridge in 1886. He retained it in 1887 and thereafter became a 'pedestrian', taking part in various professional tournaments around the country until 1889.

His athletic prowess was, in the meantime, spotted by Darlington football club whom he joined as an amateur. One of the fastest men in England was selected to play as a goalkeeper. Not quite so odd as it sounds. In those early days, the goalkeeper could be challenged and shoulder-charged, whether he had the ball or not, and could race out anywhere in his own half. (It was not until 1912 that a goalkeeper was restricted to handling within a specific area.) Wharton used to "crouch by the post" and then speed out to the ball. He was also good at clearing the ball with "a prodigious punch".

His football career started before the founding of the Football League. The FA Cup was the game's main competition.

Wharton moved to Preston North End (shortly to be known as the 'Invincibles') and helped them reach the semi-final of the FA Cup in 1887. Despite acclaim, he was not chosen for England's annual fixture against Scotland and it would be a further 90 years before a black player, Viv Anderson, first represented England in an official international.

Wharton was an entertainer and, it seems, an eccentric. One paper described him as a "skylark". Although suffering some racist abuse, he was much liked. After a spell at Rotherham, he moved to Sheffield – as a paid professional, the first professional black footballer – and played briefly for Sheffield United in the First Division of the Football League after its formation in 1888.

After his football days, having been rejected as a civil servant in Ghana as a result of his "inappropriate" sporting background, Wharton became a haulage hand at a Yorkshire colliery but ended his days in alcoholism and poverty. His story was revived in 1997 by a Sheffield-led project entitled 'Football Unites, Racism Divides'.

His pioneering career is now being honoured more fully. A campaign for a statue in Darlington has active support. A maquette by Vivien Mallock of the proposed sculpture (a version of which stands in FIFA's headquarters in Zurich) dramatically reveals Wharton stretching high into the air.

The history of British sport is richer for the re-discovery of Arthur Wharton.

"One of the most capable goal-custodians in the country ... deserving of a place in any international team"
Northern Echo

OLD TOM MORRIS

Grand Old Man of Golf

OLD TOM
MORRIS
1821–1908

Bronze
Paul Ferriter
Rosapenna Golf
Resort, Downings,
County Donegal
2009

No individual had a greater influence on the growth of the game of golf in the 19th century than Old Tom Morris (1821–1908).

Born in St Andrews, Tom Morris was an apprentice to Allan Robertson, golf's first professional. He learned the skill of club-making and producing golf balls. Golf was a game for the affluent. Clubs were hand-crafted and balls were feather-stuffed. The new gutta-percha ball then came along. Robertson wanted to resist the new ball as damaging his trade; Morris saw its growing use as inevitable. They parted ways in 1851 and Morris went to Prestwick where he became Keeper of the Green. He would set golf on a new path – as a player, greenkeeper and course designer.

Prestwick, influenced by Morris, held a first championship in 1860 among

Old Tom Morris by
Brad Pearson in the
British Golf Museum
at St Andrews.

eight local professionals for a Challenge Belt. A year later, it was declared that the Belt "on all future occasions until it be otherwise resolved, shall be open to the world". The Open was born. Morris (to become known as Old Tom to distinguish him from his son, Young Tom, born that same year) came second in that inaugural tournament but he won the following year, and three further times over the following decade, with his slow, smooth swing. Old Tom, winning in 1867 at age 46, is still the oldest winner of the Open (only just, Tom Watson coming within an eight-foot putt of winning, aged 59, in 2009) and he continued to play in the event until 75.

Importantly, Old Tom was persuaded to return to St Andrews in 1865 to become the Keeper of the Green at the Royal and Ancient Golf Club – a position he held for nearly 40 years until his retirement in 1904. As greenkeeper he made a lasting contribution to golf history. He introduced the concept of top-dressing greens and many other innovations in course management. Bunkers were actively managed for the first time. Separate mown tee areas were established. Holes were metal-ringed. In course design, he helped to standardise the length of golf courses at 18 holes (even St Andrews once comprised 23 holes). He was widely consulted throughout the land as new courses emerged.

His hand is behind the design (or changes in design) of legendary courses such as Muirfield, Prestwick, Carnoustie, Royal Dornoch and Rosapenna. Old Tom died in St Andrews in 1908 aged 87.

A larger-than-life-size statue of the 'Grand Old Man of Golf', by American sculptor Brad Pearson, stands in the British Golf Museum at St Andrews and just down the road from the Royal and

Ancient. Interestingly, it was donated in 2004 by the Golf Course Superintendents Association of America (the American greenkeepers' association), on their 75th anniversary, to honour the contribution of Old Tom to the game.

It is over the links of Rosapenna on the north coast of Ireland that here, through a fine statue by Paul Ferriter, we see Old Tom Morris still keen to play the game to which he contributed so greatly.

"One of the most remarkable men – best of men and best of golfers – that ever missed a short putt"
Horace Hutchinson, The Book of Golf and Golfers

Three pioneers of golf in Scotland: John Rattray from Leith (left), Allan Robertson (below) and Young Tom Morris from St Andrews (far right).

JOHN RATTRAY and ALLAN ROBERTSON

It was among the professional and mercantile elite in the west of Scotland that the game of golf developed into its modern form. Playing over grassy land near the sea at Leith, a group in 1744 called themselves the Gentlemen Golfers (later to be known as the Honourable Company of Edinburgh Golfers). Rules of golf were, for the first known time, laid down for a competition. They were signed by local physician John Rattray (1707–1771), a founder member and first winner. A delightful statue by sculptor David Annand

(maquette shown above) is planned to honour Rattray and Leith's place in the sport's history.

It was a decade after Leith's first competition that the golfers of St Andrews started their own local competition for noblemen and gentlemen of Fife. The Society of St Andrews Golfers was formed and would later become the game's leading authority, the Royal and Ancient Golf Club.

As golf developed among the 'gentlemen' of Scotland, challenges on the links would take place for wagers backed

by noblemen and wealthy businessmen. Recognised by all during the mid-19th century as the outstanding golfer was Allan Robertson (1815–1859). Born in St Andrews, he was effectively the game's first professional.

His ball-making business in the town (producing the old 'feathery'), first founded by his father, was the best-known. On the course, he was rarely beaten. In the cathedral churchyard in the 'auld grey toon', a portrait carving on his tombstone is testament to his fame.

YOUNG TOM MORRIS

Growing up with his legendary father, Young Tom Morris (1851–1875) was a golfing prodigy. Bypassing the traditional caddying role, he started to compete as a professional from age 13. A year after Old Tom Morris had won his fourth and last Open, Young Tom won his first with a record low score (and is still, at 17, the youngest-ever winner of the championship).

Morris had won four consecutive Open Championships by the age of 21. With his third victory he won the original red leather Championship Belt outright. It was partly to find a way of avoiding such dominance that the championship was not held in 1871.

The decision was then taken to rotate the venue between three courses (Prestwick, St Andrews and Musselburgh) rather than always being held at Prestwick. A new trophy, the famous Claret Jug, was acquired and remains the trophy to this day. The first winner in 1872 was Young Tom Morris.

Young Tom brought a fresh approach to the game with his quick and wristy swing, the flourish of his driving and the flamboyance of his attire. Skilled with his rut iron and niblick, he developed pitch and chip shots over hazards with a height and accuracy which had not previously been achieved.

His story, though, ends in early tragedy. His young wife died in childbirth in 1875. Morris never recovered from the shock. He himself died on Christmas Day later that same year. A distinctive memorial by Young Tom Morris' grave (right) in St Andrews records "his many amiable qualities being no less acknowledged than his golfing achievements".

HARRY VARDON

Champion Golfer

HARRY VARDON
1870–1937

Bronze
Gerald Palmer
Royal Jersey Golf
Club, Grouville
2001

I f Old Tom Morris set the way, it was Harry Vardon (1870–1937) who took the game of golf to a new level. He won the first of his record six Open Championships in 1896 and was the leader of the famous 'triumvirate' of British golf along with J H Taylor and James Braid (a statue of whom stands prominently at Dalmahoy golf club).

With Braid and Taylor each winning five Open Championships, the trio dominated golf for two decades and did much to establish golf as an international sport. Vardon's own international status, as golfer and celebrity, was confirmed with victory in the US Open in 1900. He was, in modern-day idiom, golf's first superstar.

Vardon was born in Grouville in Jersey and grew up in a cottage on the edge of a common when, in 1877, permission was given for a golf course to be created going down to the water's edge. (The golf course is now the Royal Jersey.) Vardon would watch the gentlemen golfers and experiment with his own makeshift clubs and marble balls. His first job was as a gardener to a keen golfer.

Quickly developing a talent for the game, Vardon won competitions in England and became a 'professional', working at clubs such as Ripon, Bury and Ganton. He moved in 1902 to the South Hertfordshire Golf Club, in Totteridge in north London, and remained as their professional for 34 years. A discrete statue records the club's association with its most famous professional.

Struck by tuberculosis in 1903, Vardon's

game was never quite as sound afterwards – and his putting became shaky. It was a short missed putt on the final green that led to the play-off in the US Open won famously for the first time by an American, Francis Ouimet, in 1913. After Vardon's death, the PGA of America honoured his memory by awarding the Vardon Trophy annually to the player with the lowest scoring average on the US PGA Tour.

In Jersey a magnificent larger-than-life-size statue by Gerald Palmer was erected in 2001 close to the ground where Vardon first watched the golfers and started to play. The sculpture reflects his smooth, free-swinging action – despite the cumbersome jacket, shirt and tie which were still the order of the day. His power and accuracy were legendary, striking the ball with his hickory shaft clubs with a flight that was straight and true. The club is held with the overlapping grip (the little finger of the lower hand placed between the index and middle finger of the lead hand) which became known as the 'Vardon grip' and is used by the majority of golfers worldwide.

Harry Vardon's legacy is immense. He is a key figure in the history of golf.

> "Don't play too much golf.
> Two rounds a day are plenty"
> *Harry Vardon*

GWYN NICHOLLS

Prince of Threequarters

GWYN NICHOLLS
1874–1939

Wrought iron
Westgate Street,
Cardiff
1949

Rugby union's roots grew particularly deep in Wales. The 'amateur' game was not only supported by the middle class (as in England and Scotland) but became firmly entrenched amongst the miners and working class of the Welsh valleys. Soccer failed to gain a large popular following there and, importantly, professional rugby league made no headway. Some would say this was due in part to a blind eye turned by the Welsh rugby authorities to 'reasonable expenses' paid by many clubs to their players.

Arthur Gould (1864–1919) was the first superstar of Welsh rugby. His image was amongst the first of a sportsman to be used commercially. A fast threequarter back with a distinctive body-swerve and a good kicker, he played 27 times for Wales including 18 as captain. Under his captaincy, Wales won their first Home Nations Championship and Triple Crown in 1893. At Cardiff Arms Park against England, Gould was in rampant form. He scored two second-half tries in a 12–11 win and was carried shoulder-high from the pitch. Welsh supporters have always enjoyed a victory over England.

On his (first) retirement in 1896, a testimonial fund was raised to recognise his services to the game. Then, to Welsh glee, Gould was enticed out of retirement for one final season in 1897 but a mighty political storm arose. Gould was charged with 'professionalism' on the grounds that his testimonial made him no longer an amateur. Wales, in protest, sensationally

A postcard (c. 1897) featuring Arthur Gould running with the ball.

"He possessed that indefinable glamour which puts him on a pedestal, above all the rest"
Rhys Gabe, team-mate of Gwyn Nicholls

ARTHUR LINTON

Champion Cyclist of the World

ARTHUR LINTON
1872–1896

Plaster
David A Thomas
Cynon Valley
Museum, Aberdare
c. 1896

Cycling became a popular sport in the 1880s and 1890s after the invention of the chain-driven safety bicycle. No more so than in south Wales. The town of Aberaman in the Cynon Valley was, extraordinarily, home to four internationally renowned cyclists: the Linton brothers Arthur, Tom and Samuel and Jimmy Michael. It is Arthur Linton (1872–1896) whom we now recall.

Athletic, elegant and strong, Linton achieved fame and popularity which matched that of his contemporary, Welsh rugby's Arthur Gould. In 1893 Linton broke the world one-hour unpaced record, cycling over 22 miles at a track in Cardiff. He moved to Paris where professional cycling was raced before large crowds. Trained by the flamboyant but strict disciplinarian 'Choppy' Warburton, Linton beat the French champion cyclist, Debois, in a 100-mile race (distance races, in those pioneer days, were a huge attraction). He was called the 'Champion Cyclist of the World'. Linton set his mind on the biggest prize then available, the Bordeaux to Paris race over 360 miles.

Linton's triumph came in 1896. Supported by a team backed by Gladiator Cycles and carefully trained by Warburton, Linton outraced the leading Frenchman, Rivierre, in a sensational contest. The two rivals raced, hour after hour, on the open road until Linton surged forward to arrive ahead on the banks of the Seine. Controversy arose as Linton, finding the official bridge blocked, actually took a longer route (by around 300 yards) before racing, pain-wracked, to the finish line and to extraordinary scenes. He had finished first in the biggest race in the world. Yet the judges decided that two first prizes should be awarded, including to Rivierre, because Linton had crossed the wrong bridge. It was the race which may have inspired the watching Henri Desgrange later to establish the Tour de France.

For Arthur Linton, tragically, it was his last great victory. He returned to south Wales a conquering hero. Exhausted, he succumbed to typhoid fever and, aged 24, died just seven weeks after his triumph. Rumours circulated for many years that Linton's success, and his death, had been aided by drugs administered by the controversial Warburton. Subsequent investigation has produced no evidence to support this claim.

Linton's funeral brought national mourning. *The Aberdare Times* recorded: "Arthur Linton, the hero of many a battle and the initial 'Welsh World's Champion' has gone. There are few in the whole of the kingdom who have not at one time or another read of the marvellous performances of Arthur."

Funds were raised by local residents for a stained-glass window and a rolled gold-engraved lectern which still shines with Arthur's name in the town's St Margaret's Church. A bust of Arthur Linton stands prominently in the Cynon Valley Museum and a plaque at his former home recalls this hero of south Wales, the Bradley Wiggins of his day.

A gold-rolled lectern (above) in St Margaret's Church, Aberdare, recalls the national and international fame of Arthur Linton.

"He died in all his glory and at the zenith of his fame"
The Aberdare Times

DOUGLAS CLARK

Lion of the Northern Union

DOUGLAS CLARK
1891–1951

Bronze
Fliss Watts
Galpharm
Stadium,
Huddersfield
2007

Rugby developed rapidly after the formation of the Rugby Football Union (RFU) in 1871. Industrialisation and changes in Victorian society led to greater opportunity for working-class players to play sport and civic pride encouraged clubs to field the best players to represent them in competitions such as the Yorkshire Cup.

Tensions grew. How to deal with 'expenses' or other payments to good working-class players? Many traditionalists (both in the South and the North) were deeply disturbed by the incipient growth of 'professionalism' to which their brethren in football had, in their view, weakly

succumbed in 1885. Many clubs of the North, though, advocated not payment to players for gain but the ability to compensate them for lost work-time due to training and playing. Without such 'broken-time payments' the clubs could not recruit many of the best working-class players. A meeting in 1893 of the RFU, by a majority, rejected such payments as "contrary to the interests of the game and its true spirit". A group of the northern clubs saw no alternative but to break away.

Representatives of 21 Lancashire and Yorkshire clubs met on August 29 1895 in the George Hotel in Huddersfield. The Northern Rugby Football Union (to

A relief plaque (left) at the George Hotel, Huddersfield, recalls the formation of the Northern Rugby Football Union.

become the Rugby League) was formed. The game of rugby was split. Memorabilia at the hotel recall that momentous meeting. It would lead, in effect, to two different games after subsequent rule changes including, in 1906, the reduction in teams from 15 to 13 per side.

Douglas Clark (1891–1951), a successful wrestler from a young age, turned to rugby league and played most of his career at Huddersfield – 485 games including 11 Tests for Great Britain. A loose-forward, 'Dougie' was a mainstay during a period of great success for the Fartown club, the 'team of all talents' that won all four major cups in 1915 and many other honours.

International tours enjoyed high public profile. Clark played in the famous 'Rorke's Drift Test' in Sydney in 1914, the third and deciding test of the tour by the British Lions. In a bitterly-contested match, the touring side suffered heavy injuries. Clark himself returned to the field with a broken thumb in the first half before smashing his collarbone in the second half (and still trying to play on for a while). Reduced to 10 men with a full half an hour to go, the Lions held on – and indeed scored a dramatic late try – to win a famous 14–6 victory over the Australians. Clark later served in the First World War on the front line in France, earning the Military Medal for bravery. He also returned to wrestling with great success, becoming heavyweight champion.

In a ceremony at the George Hotel in Huddersfield in 2005, Clark was admitted to rugby league's Hall of Fame. Two years later, a sculpted torso and bust, by Fliss Watts, recalled his power, dignity and wrestling success. It now stands in Huddersfield's Galpharm Stadium. Dougie Clark is back in Huddersfield, where the Northern Union was born.

> "It was the most historic meeting in the history of rugby"
> *Tony Collins*

JACK HARRISON

War Hero

JACK HARRISON
1890–1917

Bronze/stainless
steel
Jenny Oliver
KC Stadium, Hull
2003

Sport is only a pastime. The horror of war brings that reality into stark perspective. No conflict has been more savage than the First World War during which so many lives were lost. And many were, of course, sportsmen. Careers were interrupted and, in many cases, ended. These were the young and fit, ripe for combat in defence of their country. They volunteered for action in large numbers. Sometimes virtually whole teams enlisted, such as football's Heart of Midlothian (who at the time were Scotland's leading team) and Clapton (now Leyton) Orient in England. Volunteers of leading sportsmen and teams had a major effect on recruitment.

The 17th and 23rd Battalions of the Middlesex regiment were even known as the Footballers' Battalions. The first was formed in 1914 amidst criticism that league football was continuing (as it did for a year) during wartime. Professional and amateur players, referees, administrators and supporters promptly enlisted and fought together in the trenches. Very many were lost on the killing fields of the Somme. A memorial to these Battalions, funded by the Football League, was dedicated in 2010 in the war cemetery at Delville Wood near Longueval in France. The Heart of Midlothian War Memorial has long been a distinctive feature in the Haymarket in Edinburgh.

Amongst the well-known sportsmen who made the ultimate sacrifice in the First World War were Ronnie Poulton-Palmer (England's rugby captain), Tony Wilding (New Zealand's Wimbledon singles champion), Gerard Anderson (world record 440 yards hurdler), Colin Blythe (England cricketer), Walter Tull (Northampton footballer and the first black officer in the Army), Sandy Turnbull (Manchester United's Scottish centre-forward) and many others.

Stories of valour and bravery are many. Those honoured forever with the award of the Victoria Cross, the highest decoration for valour in the face of the enemy that can be given to a member of the British forces, include two sportsmen from Yorkshire. One was Donald Bell (a member of the Yorkshire Regiment and, from Bradford Park Avenue, the first English footballer to enlist) who died in the Battle of the Somme and whose VC is displayed at the entrance to Harrogate Grammar School.

The other was Jack Harrison (1890–1917). A simple but exquisite memorial, designed by Jenny Oliver, was erected in 2003 outside the KC Stadium, the rugby league ground of Hull FC, for Harrison – more accurately, Temporary 2nd Lieutenant John Harrison VC MC of the East Yorkshire Regiment.

Jack Harrison was born in Hull. He became a good rugby league player, joining Hull in 1912 in a team that included the well-known Billy Batten. In the 1913/14 season, Harrison scored 52 tries – still a record for any one season at Hull – and a career total of 106 tries in 116 matches for the club. He was selected in 1914 for the international tour of Australia. But the First World War came first.

"His self-sacrifice and absolute disregard of danger was an inspiring example to all" *Citation for Victoria Cross*

A wartime poster from 1915 (above) encouraging recruitment to the Football Battalion.

CHAPTER THREE

HOPE, RECESSION &
THE INTER-WAR YEARS

As Britain emerged from the First World War, a mood of hope and liberation in the early 1920s was accompanied at first by a growing economy. Incomes increased significantly for those in employment. Some small weekly surplus could now be spent on enjoying sport and other pastimes. Football, in particular, enjoyed huge support in towns and cities throughout the country. Horse-racing produced memorable stars of the Turf.

The opportunity for a small bet, a flutter, was part of the enjoyment of sport for many. The football pools became a regular feature. Greyhound racing emerged as a significant sport and a comparatively cheap form of entertainment and betting, attracting large crowds as new purpose-built tracks were built around the country.

The development of the motor engine also attracted enormous interest. The new motor car itself was out of reach for most people but the motorcycle was less so – and motorcycle racing and speedway became popular sports.

If football was largely a sport for the working class and rugby for the middle classes, cricket continued to be a national sport – a sport for all (men). Cricket was also England's principal international sport with dramatic contests for the Ashes, at home and abroad, gripping the sporting nation. British tennis achieved a period of success not since seen among the men.

The Olympic Games gathered strength with the movement's ideals, appropriate for the time, of patriotism balanced with international fellowship through amateur sport. Scotland, Wales and Ireland continued to develop their own particular national passion and identity within the sporting framework of the British Isles.

The period between the two World Wars turned rapidly to years of economic recession but, despite the austerity, for the sporting public they continued to be years of passion, crowds and enjoyment.

Heroes from this period, many now immortalised in bronze, rank among the greatest names in the pantheon of British sport.

ERIC LIDDELL

The Flying Scotsman

ERIC LIDDELL
1902–1945

Bronze
Lesley Pover
Old College,
Edinburgh
University,
Edinburgh
1997

The London Olympic Games of 1908 had brought the movement to the forefront of the nation's attention. After the First World War, the Games increased in stature, coupling patriotism with aspirations of international harmony.

Baron Pierre de Coubertin's ideals of 'noble competition, sport, peace, culture and education' were exemplified no more strongly than in the life of Eric Liddell (1902–1945), winner of Olympic gold in Paris in 1924 – a life portrayed famously, if not with total accuracy, in the award-winning film, *Chariots of Fire*.

Born in north-east China, where his parents were missionaries of the Church of Scotland, Liddell went to boarding school at Eltham College in south-east London, a college for sons of missionaries. His headmaster later described him as 'entirely without vanity'. At Edinburgh University his talent for sport shone through. A fine rugby player, a fast and intelligent winger, he won seven caps for Scotland in 1922 and 1923.

His real strength as a sportsman was, though, as an athlete and his speed easily qualified him to represent Britain at the 100 metres and 200 metres in the 1924 Olympics. (Britain had been obliged to compete as a single nation from the outset of the modern Games.) The heats for the 100 metres, his best event, were due to be held on a Sunday. Liddell knew this ahead of the Games (contrary to the film) and he refused to run on the Sabbath. The 100 metres event was won by Harold

Abrahams (1899–1978). A blue plaque at the site of his former home in Bedford commemorates this other great British Olympic athlete from 1924.

Instead, Liddell was entered for the 400 metres and he qualified for the final. He first, though, won a bronze medal in the 200 metres. Then, with a sustained speed and stamina that surprised the favourites who expected him to flag over the longer distance in the final, Liddell burst home to win the gold medal in the 400 metres in a world-record time. "The secret of my success over 400 metres is that I run the first 200 metres as fast as I can. Then for the second 200 metres, with God's help, I run faster." No Scot had previously won an Olympic gold medal. He returned a national hero.

Liddell later went back as a missionary to Tientsin in China where he was ordained a minister. After the Japanese invaded Manchuria, he was interned in 1943 in a camp in Weifang where, amongst often brutal conditions, he remained for the duration of the war. He would not see freedom again. In 1945, he suffered a brain tumour and died.

In the Old College of Edinburgh University, against a photographic backdrop of the city skyline, a full-size statue of Scotland's hero by Lesley Plover continues to provide inspiration. A smaller version stands in the sports centre at Eltham College in south-east London. Eric Liddell's head-back, arms-outstretched, lung-bursting running style still has evocative power.

A plaque (above) in Bedford recalls Harold Abrahams, featured in *Chariots of Fire* with Scottish hero, Eric Liddell, whose 1924 Olympic gold medal (below) is in Edinburgh University.

"Eric Liddell has worthily attained to the company of the immortals who have brought honour and fame to our native land"
Lord Provost of Edinburgh

KITTY GODFREE

Wimbledon's Lady Champion

KITTY GODFREE
1896–1992

Bronze
Ian Rank-Broadley
All England Club,
Wimbledon,
London
2004

Kitty Godfree in action in the ladies' singles final at Wimbledon in 1923.

Sport, like a working career, was a preserve of male culture for most of the 19th century. Events at the Olympics for women were, until 1914, largely limited to figure-skating and swimming. By the turn of the century, though, the position had started to change in Britain even if sport for women at an elite level was largely for the privately-educated. In two sports, in particular, female participation was socially acceptable and prominent. Hockey became popular at many schools and The All-England Women's Hockey Association was formed in 1895. The other major sport was lawn tennis.

With the spread of suburbia and the role of the 'lawn' as a centre of middle-class amusement, lawn tennis became popular with both sexes. The sport produced many good female players. The most successful British player of the pre-war era was Dorothea Lambert Chambers (1878–1960). The daughter of a Middlesex vicar, she became a formidable champion with a relentless forehand and comparable determination, winning Wimbledon no fewer than seven times before the War. This great British champion has now been recognised by a plaque in Ealing placed by English Heritage.

Tennis was, for women, given a major boost after the First World War with the arrival of Suzanne Lenglen, the dashing Frenchwoman who dazzled the world of tennis with her play and fashion. Into this milieu stepped Kathleen 'Kitty' Godfree née McKane (1896–1992) and she became, twice, a Wimbledon singles winner.

A fine all-round sportswoman, excelling also as national champion at badminton, McKane's first and greatest triumph at Wimbledon came in 1924. She won a remarkable victory by beating the American Helen Wills in a pulsating final in three sets after trailing by one set and 1–4 (15–40). It would be the only loss suffered by Wills (later Wills-Moody) in singles at Wimbledon.

Two years later and now married, Godfree won again – this time taking her opportunity after the legendary Lenglen had walked out of Wimbledon following a row. Godfree also reached the singles finals at both the US and the French Championships in 1925. She was one of the first women to become a strong volleyer at the net and this helped her

"She showed Britain the way in the world of tennis"
Dan Maskell

A statuette of Kitty
Godfree by Hazel
Alexander in the
clubhouse of the All
England Club (below).

win several doubles championships with
different partners. (She and her husband,
Leslie, are the only husband-and-wife pair
to win the mixed doubles at Wimbledon.)

Tennis became for a short period an
Olympic sport and, at Antwerp (1920)
and Paris (1924), Kitty won five medals
(the most so far held by any tennis player)
including a gold medal in the doubles in
1920. She attended the 1988 Games in
Seoul, South Korea, when tennis was once
again played at the Olympics.

Since 2004, the ivy-clad facade of the
Centre Court at Wimbledon has provided
the backdrop for portrait sculptures
by Ian Rank-Broadley of five ladies –
yes, five British ladies – who became
singles champions after the move of the
Wimbledon Championships to the present
ground at Church Road in 1922. The first,
smiling and with her fashionable bandeau
in place, is the much-loved Kitty Godfree.

JACK HOBBS

The Master

JACK HOBBS
1882–1963

Wrought iron/steel
The Oval,
Kennington,
London
1934

Cricket retained its popularity in the 1920s among all classes as England's national summer sport. After the ravages of the First World War, cricket and England playing Test matches were symbols of 'Englishness', national prestige and stability. If W G Grace had been the star who led cricket out of the 19th century, it was Jack Hobbs (1882–1963) who was England's greatest batsman in the first decades of the 20th century, both before and after the First World War. He was 'the Master'.

John 'Jack' Berry Hobbs became cricket's most prolific batsman. Born near Fenner's in Cambridge (where his father was on the ground staff), practice perfected a technique which was coupled with steely determination. A plaque at Parker's Piece in Cambridge (far right) recalls those formative days of the Master.

Recommended to Surrey, it was clear to cricket judges that a player of the highest quality had arrived. He provided the batting backbone of Surrey and England for well over two decades. He scored more runs (61,237) and more centuries (197) in first-class cricket than any other player in the history of the game – nearly all scored from the top of the batting order.

The career of Hobbs was another interrupted by the First World War. His most spectacular period as a cricketer probably came before the War and, indeed, Hobbs himself claimed: "I wasn't half the player after the War as I was before." Yet, the majority of his career total of centuries were scored after he had turned 40 years

old and he remains, at 46 in 1929, the oldest man to score a Test century.

Poised in 1925 to equal the record 125 centuries of W G Grace in first-class cricket, the moment was eventually nigh at Taunton. Play was delayed for 25 minutes to allow all the spectators in the half-mile queue to enter and see the milestone. The century was achieved. Celebrations were all around the ground. Surrey's captain brought out a glass for Hobbs to toast the crowd. Most people thought it was champagne ... but, Hobbs being a teetotaller, it was just ginger ale.

Hobbs retired in 1934 and, at The Oval, Surrey honoured its greatest batsman by dedicating and naming the Jack Hobbs Gates at the main entrance to the ground he so graced. In 1953 Hobbs became the first cricketer, and the first professional sportsman, to be knighted.

Jack Hobbs in action in 1936 (below left). He is commemorated at the main entrance to The Oval (right, top) and recalled by a plaque at Parker's Piece in Cambridge (right, bottom).

"He was in every way the model of cricket's art and spirit"
Christopher Martin-Jenkins

The opening partnership for England between Hobbs and Yorkshire's Herbert Sutcliffe (1894–1978) became part of cricket's folklore. Their average score together was a remarkable 87.81, with very many of their 15 century partnerships coming in Tests against Australia. The Sutcliffe Gates, now no longer in use, were opened in 1965 in honour of the Yorkshireman at Headingley Cricket Ground.

Sir Jack Hobbs was, in 2000, named third (and the only Englishman) amongst five Wisden Cricketers of the 20th century. His name is admitted to the pantheon of cricket's all-time greats.

Sir Jack Hobbs
'The Master'
1882 – 1963
Born Barnwell, Cambridge
Learned cricket on Parker's Piece

Played for Cambs, Surrey & England
First professional to be knighted

61,237 runs, 197 centuries in first class cricket
Played in 61 test matches

HAROLD LARWOOD

The Nottinghamshire Express

Many claim with vigour that Harold Larwood (1904–1995), the most feared and celebrated fast bowler of his generation, was 'the quickest of them all'.

Cricket was England's leading international sport. Test matches with Australia and South Africa had been a major part of the sporting fabric since well before the end of the 19th century. Tests with the West Indies started in 1928, followed by New Zealand and India in the early 1930s. It was, though, the battles for the Ashes with Australia that were special. In the late 1920s, Don Bradman came along. Bradman and his 1930 Australian touring team were indomitable. How could England counter the force of the world's greatest batsman?

Harold 'Lol' Larwood was a slim, medium-height but broad-shouldered figure, brought up in and around the coalfields of Nottinghamshire and Derbyshire. "Down the mine I dreamed of cricket; I bowled imaginary balls in the dark; I sent stumps spinning and heard them rattling in the tunnels."

Playing for Nottinghamshire (for the same money he had earned down the pit), Larwood topped the season's bowling averages five times during a seven-year period from 1930 to 1936. He took 1,427 wickets over his career (at an average of 17.51) including 78 in 21 Tests but none had greater significance than the 33 wickets, at an average of 19 runs apiece, in the 'Bodyline' series in 1932/33 when England regained the Ashes in Australia.

Captain Douglas Jardine may have been the tactical brain but Larwood, supported by Nottinghamshire colleague Bill Voce, was the principal executioner of his plan – balls pitched short on the leg-side and aimed at or around the body of the batsman with five or six close short-leg fielders ready for any catch as the batsman took evasive action. Several did not succeed and were struck. By the third Test the Australian Committee formally cabled the MCC in England: "Bodyline bowling has assumed such proportions as to menace the best interests of the game ... In our opinion, it is unsportsmanlike." The charge was reluctantly dropped but, on the team's return to England with the Ashes regained, the MCC formally apologised.

Larwood never played for England again, partly due to strong remarks in a newspaper article when omitted from a subsequent Test series. He became the scapegoat. It is one of sport's ironies that, disillusioned with life in Britain, Larwood and his wife emigrated in 1950 to Australia. They sailed to Sydney on the same boat that had taken Jardine's MCC side to Australia.

In June 2002, his memory was vividly revived with the unveiling of a splendid nine-foot-high statue by Neale Andrew, full of suggested movement, in a pedestrian square in Kirkby-in-Ashfield in Nottinghamshire, Larwood's birth town. He is about to unleash another fearsome delivery with that famous rhythmic bowling action. Harold Larwood is back at the top of his form.

HAROLD
LARWOOD
1904–1995

Bronze
Neale Andrew
Kirkby-in-Ashfield
2002

"One of the rare fast bowlers in the game's long history to spread terror in opposition ranks by the mere mention of his name"
Wisden

MICK THE MILLER

The Wonder Dog

MICK THE
MILLER
1926–1939

Bronze
Elizabeth O'Kane
Killeigh,
County Offaly
2011

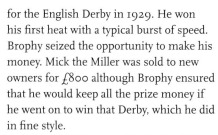

A major new spectator sport arrived in the late 1920s, offering a comparatively cheap opportunity for an evening out and a small gamble. That was greyhound racing. One dog captured the public's affection like no other: Mick the Miller (1926–1939).

The story starts with an Irish parish priest, Father Martin Brophy, in the village of Killeigh in County Offaly. Brophy liked the greyhounds and a gamble despite the Church's disapproval. Track circuits, rather than straight coursing, had just been introduced from America. Brophy hoped to produce a real winner. A pup, a brindle with a light white patch on his chest, particularly attracted his attention. He called him Mick the Miller.

Brought up by the priest's trainer, Mick the Miller won 15 out of his 20 races in Ireland. Brophy entered Mick the Miller

for the English Derby in 1929. He won his first heat with a typical burst of speed. Brophy seized the opportunity to make his money. Mick the Miller was sold to new owners for £800 although Brophy ensured that he would keep all the prize money if he went on to win that Derby, which he did in fine style.

Mick the Miller stayed in England for the rest of his life. Here, his record was supreme; a total of 46 victories in 61 races. He won five Classic races including becoming the first, and for a long time the only, dog to win the English Greyhound Derby twice (1929 and 1930). He even 'won' the English Derby race in 1931 for the third year in succession but the race was re-run (owing to a dubious decision after bumping by some dogs during the race) and Mick's age told against him in the re-run.

Long in the back, not particularly big but with strong shoulders and haunches, Mick the Miller was the canine superstar who captured the imagination of millions in those stringent days. He broke numerous track and world records in an unparalleled three-year career, including being the first to break 30 seconds over the Derby distance of 525 yards.

His final race was, as a five-year-old, in the St Leger at Wembley in 1931 over the longer distance of 700 yards. He held on (against dogs two years younger, including the dog that had defeated him in the re-run of the Derby earlier in the year) to win by a head amidst extraordinary scenes of jubilation among the 40,000 crowd.

"Never was there a dog more human" *Daily Mail*

He retired to stud but remained a celebrity, even starring in a cinema film. After his death, the great greyhound was restored through the skills of the taxidermist. For the people of Killeigh in Ireland, pride is still strong. In 2011, more than 70 years after his death, a graceful sculpture of Mick the Miller by Antrim artist Elizabeth O'Kane was unveiled and stands, with his eyes and ears alert, prominently on the village green.

Meanwhile, in Tring in Hertfordshire, behind the glass in the Natural History Museum, there he is: Mick the Miller, the most famous greyhound in racing history.

HERBERT CHAPMAN

Boss of the Arsenal

HERBERT
CHAPMAN
1878–1934

Bronze
Jacob Epstein
Highbury Square,
Highbury, London
1934

Crowds flocked to football grounds on Saturday afternoons in the 1920s and 1930s, enjoying some benefits from increased factory wages and sharing a collective identity with others through support of the local club. One man was at the forefront in shaping the game for the modern age: Herbert Chapman (1878–1934).

In north London, at Highbury, the former home of Arsenal FC – actually, in the entrance foyer to new apartments that now stand on the ground of the famous stadium – still prominent is a shining bronze head-and-shoulders bust of Herbert Chapman. He was the first great football manager.

Ironically, he was in the bath at Tottenham (one of the clubs where Chapman was a relatively undistinguished player) when a colleague suggested that Chapman should apply for a post available as player/manager at Northampton. He later managed Huddersfield whom he guided successfully to the First Division title on two occasions. He left in 1925 for Arsenal – then, if full of potential, a relatively unsuccessful club.

At Arsenal, his tactics transformed the team. He developed the strategy of a 'stopper' centre-half as a way of adapting to the new offside law (after 1925 only two, rather than three, opposition defenders were needed between the attacker and the goal-line), pushing the full-backs wider to cover the wings and bringing a forward back into midfield. Wingers were encouraged to cut inside and go for goal. Football became a game of fluidity. Chapman bought well and, with players like Charlie Buchan and David Jack, expensively. Arsenal won the FA Cup in 1930 (making up for a shock defeat in 1927 at the hands of Cardiff where a statue of Fred Keenor, the latter's captain on that memorable day, now graces the Welsh side's ground).

League title triumphs for Arsenal followed in 1931 and 1933 – the first London side to win the First Division title and, for Chapman, the first manager to win with two different clubs. Arsenal became the most feared side in the land. Chapman's vision also inspired or supported other important changes to the game: numbered shirts, matches under floodlights, white footballs and new stands.

Shock was felt around the country when, in January 1934, Chapman died aged 55 of pneumonia, just three days after watching, while suffering from a chill, an Arsenal third team match. The club, in tribute to their great manager, commissioned a portrait bust from one of the country's leading sculptors, Jacob Epstein, assisted by (the later reverend) Allan Wyon. It became a central point for decades as visitors entered the famous marble halls at Highbury. Now, outside the club's new Emirates Stadium, a full-size statue was unveiled in 2010 as part of the club's 125th anniversary celebrations.

A mighty figure in football's history, Herbert Chapman still conveys a formidable sense of authority.

Herbert Chapman still shows authority at the Emirates Stadium (above) and in the marble hall of Highbury Square (right).

"He had the one-eyed will to win of Don Revie, the passion for the game of a Bobby Robson and the footballing intellect of Arsène Wenger"
Alex Murphy, The Times

DOROTHY ROUND

Amidst Fred Perry's success, we should not forget the two Wimbledon triumphs of Dorothy Round (1908–1982). Yes, in 1934 there were British winners in both the men's and ladies' singles!

The girl from the Midlands, a Methodist Sunday school teacher, was a resolute competitor and one of the world's best over many years. Her two title victories in SW19 were won during an era which included the great Americans, Helen Wills-Moody (to whom Round lost in a dramatic three-set final in 1933) and Helen Jacobs (whom Round beat 6–3 in the final set in 1934 with an attacking display of driving and volleying which thrilled the crowd). The following year, she became the first overseas player to win the Australian ladies' singles title before winning again at Wimbledon in 1937. She also won the mixed title at Wimbledon three times in succession, twice with Perry. Britain was a proud tennis nation in the 1930s.

At Wimbledon, in front of the ivy-clad Centre Court, a head-and-shoulders bust of Dorothy Round (above) by Ian Rank-Broadley stands next to Britain's other two-time Wimbledon winner, Kitty Godfree. Meanwhile, for Priory Park in Dudley, near the tennis courts, a full-size action statue by John McKenna is planned of one of Britain's greatest tennis champions.

GOLDEN MILLER

The Miller

GOLDEN MILLER
1927–1957

Bronze
Judy Boyt
Cheltenham
Racecourse,
Cheltenham
1989

Steeplechasing has a long tradition separate from the Flat. No more important decision was made by the National Hunt Committee than to give permanently to Cheltenham, from 1911 onwards, the annual festival to promote the sport. The festival grew from strength to strength. In 1924 a new race was established: the Cheltenham Gold Cup. It became the 'blue riband' of the festival. And the horse that firmly established the event's reputation, and captured the public's imagination like no other, was Golden Miller (1927–1957).

Many regard Golden Miller as the greatest steeplechaser of them all. He dominated the Cheltenham Gold Cup with five successive wins from 1932 to 1936. In the magical year of 1934, adding to his Gold Cup win, he achieved an unprecedented double with victory in the

Grand National at Aintree.

Golden Miller (popularly known simply as 'the Miller') was bred in Ireland. Acquired by the somewhat eccentric Dorothy Paget, he was trained at Basil Briscoe's stables in Cambridgeshire. He won his first Gold Cup on his debut in 1932, ridden by Ted Leader. The following season, the Miller won his first five races including a second Gold Cup at Cheltenham. He was the leading racehorse of the day and (like his near namesake, Mick the Miller, in greyhound racing) had won the public's deep affection. Racing had never been more popular. Could the steeplechase double be achieved? Not in 1933. An attempt at the Grand National that same year failed.

In 1934 Golden Miller was ridden by Jerry Wilson. He triumphed for the third time in the Gold Cup at Cheltenham by six lengths. Again, he was entered for the Grand National and, this time, carrying top weight and with courage, he won in a new course record. It was the first time (and, so far, the only time) that a horse has won both of these great jump races in the same season. Golden Miller was a superstar.

A fourth Gold Cup victory came in 1935 in one of the great races of the century, a three-quarter-length victory in a thrilling finish and a record time. In 1936 a fifth successive Gold Cup victory confirmed his extraordinary dominance – and he would probably have won in 1937 but for snow causing the meeting to be cancelled. Aged 11, he was beaten for the first time in the Gold Cup in 1938. Many of the crowd were

Golden Miller relaxing after training in 1935 (left) and standing proudly in bronze at Cheltenham (above).

"A god on four legs" *Sydney Galtrey*

tearful. The great reign of Golden Miller had come to an end.

In his 52 starts, he had won a record 28 times. Part of the fabric of sport in the 1930s, he was as famous as any footballer or athlete. Crowds flocked to racecourses to see him. He lived to the ripe old age of 30. In 1989, more than 30 years after his death, a splendid half-life-size statue of Golden Miller, by sculptor Judy Boyt, was erected at Cheltenham Racecourse. High overlooking the parade ring, the Miller continues to be prominent at the course and festival that he helped to make so famous.

HYPERION

To the Flat. Outside the Jockey Club's offices in Newmarket stands a statue of one of the smallest horses ever to win Classic races. Hyperion (1930–1960), a chestnut, became one of the most important stallions of the 20th century.

Owned by Lord Derby but barely 15 hands high and measuring less than eight inches below the knee, Hyperion was an unlikely thoroughbred hero. Yet his fine racing style, speed and temperament led to nine wins out of his 13 races including, in 1933, victories in both the Derby and the St Leger. He retired to stud in Newmarket when five years old. It was as a stallion that he became a phenomenal success.

Hyperion himself sired the winners of over 750 races and was the year's leading sire in Britain no less than five times in the years 1940 to 1946 and again in 1954. Hyperion's daughters have also foaled the winners of over 1,000 races. His influence extended beyond Britain's shores to America (where Hyperion is the damsire of Nearctic who in turn sired the legendary Northern Dancer) and to Australia and New Zealand. Offered substantial sums to sell Hyperion to an American buyer, Lord Derby refused in Churchillian tones: "Even though England be reduced to ashes, Hyperion shall never leave these shores."

Hyperion's statue was commissioned by Lord Derby from leading equine sculptor John Skeaping. It now stands permanently and beautifully in the heart of Newmarket's High Street – a fitting tribute to the leading British-bred sire of the 20th century.

Hyperion, by John Skeaping, stands with authority by the Jockey Club Rooms in Newmarket.

HYPERION
1930 1960

JIMMIE GUTHRIE

Hawick's Flying Machine

JIMMIE GUTHRIE
1897–1937

Bronze
Thomas Clapperton
Wilton Lodge Park,
Hawick
1939

Motorcycle racing became a major sport in the late 1920s and the 1930s. The motor car was beyond the financial reach of most families but the motorcycle was more affordable and a popular attraction.

The first great British and international star of motorcycling was Jimmie Guthrie (1897–1937). Born near the Scottish Borders town of Hawick, Guthrie joined the 4th (The Border) Battalion in the First World War and, aged just 18, headed off on a tour of duty that saw action at Gallipoli in Turkey, followed by Palestine, Egypt and the western front in France. Ironically, it was the War that led to his sporting career. As a result of wounds first suffered at Gallipoli, he was transferred to duty as a signals' dispatch rider and developed his skill in handling motorcycles.

Quiet and determined, he joined the Hawick Motorcycle Club, racing on local

hill climbs and grass tracks. He entered the Scottish national championships, which he won – and he became, for a decade, one of the most successful motorcycle riders in Europe. Racing Norton bikes, he was a formidable competitor and set speed records at many tracks. In 1930 he won the first of six Isle of Man TT titles in a combination of 250, 350 and 500cc categories. Internationally, he was consistently a winner or runner-up. In 1935 alone, he won the Swiss, Dutch, German, Belgian and Spanish Grand Prix races and was European champion. Spectators everywhere loved his all-out streamlined style, chest as close to the bike's petrol tank as possible.

The German Grand Prix in 1937 turned out to be his last. An estimated 250,000 spectators had gathered at the Sachsenring circuit where Guthrie was immensely popular. Going into the last lap, flags were at the ready to greet another victory but it was not Guthrie who appeared for the final stretch. He had come off at a dangerous corner near the finish and had been thrown into the trees. The cause is still uncertain: was it due to another rider? Guthrie was taken to a local hospital and guarded by four German soldiers. He died from his injuries.

In Hawick, his funeral procession was lined by crowds for three miles. In 1939, a statue, sculpted by Thomas Clapperton, was erected in the town park. Jimmie Guthrie stands with elegance and old-fashioned dignity. Joggers and walkers daily pass by Hawick's great racing legend.

"In the mid-1930s, he was a household name all over Britain"
Hawick Archaeological Society

BERNARD LAURENCE HIEATT

An early well-known motorcycle racer was Bernard Laurence Hieatt (1909–1930). An air pilot from Reading, he created world records on the racetrack at Brooklands. He achieved a coveted 'star' in 1929 for lapping the famous track at over 100mph. The following year, leading a race during which he had already broken the 100 miles record and amidst rain and poor visibility, 21-year-old Hieatt attempted to overtake a straggler but struck a grass verge. Flung high into the air, he hit a concrete post and was killed instantly.

A memorial statue (erected in 1931) stands high on a plinth in Reading Old Cemetery (above).

STEVE CASEY

The Crusher

STEVE CASEY
1908–1987

Bronze
Alan Ryan Hall
Sneem,
County Kerry
2000

I n the picturesque village of Sneem, on the Kerry coast in Ireland, a life-size statue of a wrestler sets the scene for an extraordinary story. He is Steve 'Crusher' Casey (1908–1987).

Casey was one of a family of seven brothers born of a tough, sporting pedigree; their father was a well-known bare-knuckle boxer and their mother a champion oarswoman. Steve would grow to 6ft 4ins and 17 stone.

Across the country in Dublin, seismic events were taking place in Irish history. On 'Bloody Sunday', November 21 1920, 14 British agents and associates were murdered by Irish rebels. In the afternoon, pursuing suspects, British soldiers (the Black and Tans) together with auxiliaries and the local police went to Croke Park, home of Gaelic football, a symbol of Ireland's sporting national identity and a place where no 'British sports' should ever be played.

Thousands were gathered for a match between Dublin and Tipperary. Amidst chaos and confusion, an indiscriminate hail of shots was fired towards the crowd. The Tipperary captain, Michael Hogan, was killed at the side of the pitch along with 13 civilians. A plaque at the stadium commemorates the tragedy. The notorious incident caused deep anger. The Irish Free State (later the Republic) was established in 1922.

"Whether it came from my father, my mother or God himself, we were blessed by nature"
Steve Casey

STEVE CASEY
continued

Back to the Caseys. By the early 1930s, the brothers were excellent rowers, winning contests all around Ireland. The Olympics beckoned. Amidst continuing political wrangling, athletes born in what had since become the Republic were still eligible to compete for Britain. Steve and his brother Paddy were also members of the British amateur wrestling team in 1935, winning contests across Europe. Welcoming extra cash, they wrestled for money on some occasions. Later in the year, they returned to rowing and, with brothers Tom and Mick, the four won the All-England rowing championships.

The Caseys were ready to be selected for the Olympic team to represent Britain in the 1936 Olympics in Berlin ... but, at a late stage, were declared ineligible. They were deemed no longer pure 'amateurs' because they had fought 'professionally' in wrestling. Sporting history could have been very different. If they had gone to the Olympics in Berlin, they believed they would have won all six events in which they would have raced.

Instead, Steve Casey set off for America to pursue glory in wrestling. In 1938 he was crowned the undisputed wrestling heavyweight champion of the world. He would never be defeated before his retirement in 1947.

Casey was also a boxer of the highest strength and ability. In 1940 he defeated top US fighter, Tiger Warrenton. A reputed American journalist wrote: "All who saw the fight, including Jack Dempsey, were of the opinion that Steve would beat Joe Louis." Casey challenged Louis for the world heavyweight championship title. Louis declined to fight, the only refusal in his career. "Even the greatest run scared of the Sneem Machine," declared the *New York Post*.

In 1983, a family reunion was held publicly in Sneem. Only five of the brothers (now in their 70s) could make the trip. They climbed again into the same boat used in their glory days. They had not rowed together for 50 years but, wrote Jim Hudson in *The Legend of the Caseys*, the boat glided "as smoothly as a raindrop sliding down silk". Many in the crowd were tearful "watching the final performance of the greatest oarsmen and finest individual athletes Ireland had ever seen".

A powerful life-size statue, by sculptor Alan Ryan Hall, was erected in 2000 in the centre of Sneem. The Crusher is ready for any challenger.

In 2007, at Croke Park, a non-Gaelic sporting match was held and, in respectful silence before a home crowd of over 80,000, the strains of the British national anthem were heard there for the first time as the (all) Ireland rugby team played England. Sport continues to produce people and moments that inspire.

STEVE FAIRBAIRN
and JACK BERESFORD

Staying on or near water, exactly one mile from the Putney end of the Championship Course on the bank of the Thames, a stone obelisk (the Mile Post) bears prominently a portrait of Steve Fairbairn (1862–1938). Born in Australia, Fairbairn went to Cambridge and rowed four times in the Boat Race. He became an influential coach. His revolutionary rowing style encouraged his crews to slide in their seats to facilitate leg-drive and stressed the need for flowing movement. For many, he is the father of modern rowing.

Britain's great Olympic rower of the period was Jack Beresford (1899–1977), a 'gentleman' amateur with the Thames Rowing Club. Beresford won medals at five Olympic Games in succession from 1920 to 1936, a record since tied only by Steve Redgrave, including gold medals in 1924 (single sculls), 1932 (coxless fours) and 1936 (double sculls). A plaque at his family home in Chiswick, erected by English Heritage in 2005 and one of London's first sporting plaques, records this legend of the rowing world.

We also recall Tom Blower (1914–1955), from Nottingham and from a different social background. A marathon swimmer, he trained in the Trent and swam the English Channel in a record 13 hours 29 minutes in 1937. The 'Torpedo' also became the first to swim the Northern Channel between Ireland and Scotland and one of the few to swim the English Channel both ways. He is remembered (just) through a fading plaque at the John Carroll Leisure Centre in Radford.

Putney's Mile Post commemorates Steve Fairbairn (above) and a plaque recalls Jack Beresford (left).

ALEXANDER OBOLENSKY

The Flying Prince

ALEXANDER
OBOLENSKY
1916–1940

Bronze
Harry Gray
Cromwell Square,
Ipswich
2008

Two sensational tries by Alexander Obolensky (1916–1940) for England against the All Blacks at Twickenham in 1936, both founded on the searing pace of an athlete, have ensured lasting fame for the Russian prince. It was a romantic story that ended in tragedy. It is a story now recalled by an inspired sculpture in the centre of Ipswich.

Born in St Petersburg, the son of a prince who was an officer in the Czar's Imperial Horse Guards and a member of the doomed Russian aristocracy, Obolensky came to England in 1917 as a baby when his family fled Russia after the Revolution. A life of some style nevertheless continued here: boarding school in Derbyshire, Oxford University, a 'sportsman's fourth-class degree', a social life not without champagne and oysters, and success on the sporting field in athletics and rugby.

His pace (a hundred yards in less than 11 seconds) resulted in a surprise call-up aged 19 for England against the All Blacks – surprising partly because he was still officially a Russian! (His selection was dependent on his assurance that he would become a naturalised British citizen – completed a few weeks later.) There is a tale that he travelled by train to the match at Twickenham with the England captain. The pair got off three stops before Twickenham to warm up for the game by running the last two miles.

Then came those two tries before a packed 70,000 crowd at Twickenham;

tries shown widely through the Pathé newsreels at the cinema, black and grainy but still glittering. For the first, at full pace he side-stepped the New Zealand full-back to touch down. The second is regarded as one of the finest tries ever scored at Twickenham. Receiving the ball along the threequarter line, Obolensky turned infield – a highly unorthodox move at that time – and continued from right to left at an angle. The speed of the move surprised all as he flew diagonally for some 50 yards across the field wrong-footing defenders to score in the opposite corner. Known as 'Obolensky's match', it was England's first-ever win over the All Blacks.

Only three more international caps (and no more tries) were to follow. Club rugby became his focus including many games for Rosslyn Park. His sporting career was cut short by the Second World War. Obolensky took a commission in the RAF as the War approached. In March 1940 his Hurricane fighter crashed, in a freak accident, on landing at Martlesham Heath airfield near Ipswich during a training exercise. Obolensky was killed and he was buried in the town cemetery at Ipswich.

Many fine sportsmen lost their lives in the Second World War. Another well-known figure was Hedley Verity, the Yorkshire and England left-arm slow bowler who bowled the last ball in county cricket before it stopped for the War (and indeed topped the bowling averages that season). Wounded in action in Italy, he is reported to have said: "I think I have bowled my last over for Yorkshire."

"The blue-eyed Russian became the darling of the nation, a sort of Jonny Wilkinson with a title" *Financial Times*

ALEXANDER OBOLENSKY

continued

A plaque unveiled at Headingley in 2007 commemorates Verity and four other players who made the ultimate sacrifice.

For Obolensky, nearly 70 years after his death, a striking statue has been erected in the centre of Ipswich following a campaign led by a local businessman and supported by Roman Abramovich, the Rugby Football Union and many other donors, including former team-mates and widows of Second World War airmen. The statue, crafted by leading war memorial sculptor Harry Gray, was unveiled in 2008 by Princess Alexandra Obolensky.

The stone plinth of the strong, delightful sculpture is cut in the shape of the tailplane of the Hawker Hurricane in which Alexander Obolensky died. Atop the plinth, in bronze, are the muscular head and shoulders of the 'Flying Prince' with a rugby ball under his arm. Ready to run in full flight.

Harry Gray's iconic statue of Alexander Obolensky dominates Cromwell Square in Ipswich.

CHAPTER FOUR

POST-WAR BRITAIN &
SPORTING GREATS

The initial years of austerity after the Second World War were followed by a boom in the economy as the 1950s progressed. "You've never had it so good" became the political cry of the later years, but many will remember the whole decade as a glorious period for sport. Attendances at the major spectator sports have never been greater than in the late 1940s and early 1950s.

Leading sporting figures were hugely popular both nationally and, particularly, within their local urban communities. From football to cricket, from rugby union to rugby league, sporting heroes reflected passions that gave identity to the communities in which they played and helped to bind them together.

Yet none of these sporting 'greats' made personal fortunes from the game. The maximum wage remained in football, and at a modest level. The 'amateur' was still prominent in cricket. The influence of broadcasting was in its infancy and 'live' television was restricted to very few major events.

International sport continued to grow. The London Olympics in 1948 were a celebration and symbol of a rebirth of sport, and of a nation, after the Second World War. England's Test matches with Australia were often excitingly close and at the top of the sporting nation's attention. If the decade ended with the tragedy of the Munich disaster, football's fascination with European club competition grew with ever-greater enthusiasm from the mid-1950s.

Boxing, cycling and motor racing produced British world champions. Despite dramatic wake-up calls internationally on the football field, Britain's place in the sporting world remained strong and achievements were high in national esteem – never more so than when an English athlete broke the barrier of the four-minute mile.

The sporting passions of the late 1940s and the decade of the 1950s are well-reflected in a wonderful array of statues and memorials which now exist around the country recalling, with pride, many major figures in the history of British sport.

WILF MANNION

Golden Boy

WILF MANNION
1918–2000

Steel
Lewis Robinson
Normanby Road,
Middlesbrough
1998

The late 1940s were years hit by stringencies in the aftermath of the Second World War. Football was one of the key pastimes for a hard-working male population. Support for the local team provided a common passion. Players tended to stay with the same clubs. There was still little point, financially, in moving and few did.

Many players had promising careers interrupted by the War. Of all the figures that capture the romance, loyalty and yet sadness of these times, perhaps the most memorable is Wilf Mannion (1918–2000). With his distinctive blond hair and prodigious talent, Mannion was idolised by supporters of Middlesbrough. He was their 'Golden Boy'.

Mannion (like so many others) played his childhood football on the streets and the nearby waste grounds. His skills shone. Football offered an escape from the pits or the factory floor. He signed for Middlesbrough in 1936 and made his debut the following year. During a career halted by the War, he made 368 appearances for the club, scoring 110 goals and giving pleasure with his stylish play. Just 5ft 5ins tall, he won 26 caps for England and became part of that supreme forward line – Matthews, Mortensen, Lawton, Mannion and Finney. This combination attained a sublime level in 1947 with a 10–0 win away to Portugal. England ruled the football world, or so it seemed.

Yet there is sadness in the story of this gifted player. His full potential was restrained by the War (during which he served and suffered as a front-line soldier). He sought in 1948 to supplement his (maximum) football wage of £12 per week with a move to a lower club and an opportunity to take an outside job. Middlesbrough refused to let him go. He started a one-man strike but later relented. He subsequently did move in 1954 to Hull and wrote some bitter articles in the press after which he was actually banned for life by the Football Association. Although this was later rescinded, he never played league football again.

Wilf Mannion remains, for many, the special player of Middlesbrough's past. His memory lives on in the North-East and now permanently through a splendid eight-foot-high statue, sculpted by Tom Maley, erected in 2000 outside the Riverside Stadium. Elsewhere, beside a local park, decorative railings (designed by Lewis Robinson) bear fascinating steel representations of his football boots and number 10 shirt. They are known as the Golden Boy Railings.

"Wilf played football the way Fred Astaire danced"
Brian Clough

Wilf Mannion is still celebrated in Middlesbrough at the Riverside Stadium (left) and by the Golden Boy Railings (right).

GEORGE HARDWICK
JIMMY HAGAN
and JOE SHAW

Other sporting statues reflect the lasting affection in their community of footballing heroes of this period.

Also at Middlesbrough stands George Hardwick (1920–2004). 'Gentleman George'. A stylish centre-half (on the field and off), a firm tackler, an intelligent reader of the game and a born captain, he too became a local legend and is regarded as the club's best-ever defender. His debut for England (and, uniquely, as captain) was immediately after the War in 1946. A fine statue by Keith Maddison stands proudly at the club's Riverside Stadium. George Hardwick is again firmly in control, foot over the ball, watching his players.

Another player of the North-East revered for his loyalty and style of play was Jimmy Hagan (1918–1998). His name still resonates strongly with the supporters of Sheffield United. Renowned for his passing and shrewd tactical brain,

he was the team's conductor-in-chief. However, just one official England cap and a number of wartime internationals came his way. Hagan not only became an excellent manager but his managerial success was abroad – at Benfica, winning three successive Portuguese titles and the respect of players such as the great Eusebio who attended the unveiling in 2001 of Jimmy Hagan's statue by Kenneth Robertson. It stands in pride of place in the club's museum.

Another stalwart of Sheffield United recently recognised in bronze was Joe Shaw (1928–2007). As a left-half and later a centre-half, he played 714 games for the club including 632 appearances in the league (the club's longest-serving player) in a career spanning from 1949 to 1961. An imposing statue of Joe Shaw, by sculptor Paul Vanstone, stands at Bramall Lane.

Three stalwarts of the game: Middlesbrough's George Hardwick (above left), Sheffield United's Jimmy Hagan (above middle) and Joe Shaw (above right).

SAM BARTRAM
and BERT TRAUTMANN

Sam Bartram (1914–1981), born in County Durham, was literally the first name on the team sheet at Charlton Athletic for over 20 years and 623 games. His acrobatic saves, distinctive sandy-coloured hair and commanding presence endeared him to legions of fans. Just a handful of wartime internationals, though, came his way.

A centrepiece of Charlton's centenary celebrations in 2005 was the unveiling of a nine-foot-high bronze statue sculpted by Anthony Hawken (left) and paid for largely by fans' donations. Close to the club's main entrance, Sam Bartram stands as if to stride out on to the pitch. The delightful detail reveals the heavy, laced boots, the long shorts high on the waist, the gnarled, weathered hands, an old cap clutched and ready to be placed in the goalmouth – and a smile to greet the crowd.

Another much-admired goalkeeper was Bernhard 'Bert' Trautmann (1923–) who made over 500 appearances for Manchester City from 1949. German-born Trautmann was a paratrooper in the War. Captured and held as a prisoner of war in Lancashire, he declined repatriation at the end of the War, joining St Helens and then Manchester City to become one of the best goalkeepers in the land.

His skill and courage became legendary and no more so than in the 1956 FA Cup final. A brave save, diving at the feet of an onrushing forward, kept a winning 3–1 lead for City over Birmingham City. Trautmann played on – although a subsequent X-ray revealed a cracked vertebrae in his neck. A plaster statue (left), by Kari Furre, can be found within Manchester City's Etihad Stadium.

Two goalkeepers with more than 1,000 league games between them for single clubs: Charlton's Sam Bartram (above) and Manchester City's Bert Trautmann (right).

JACKIE MILBURN

Wor Jackie

Up in Newcastle, another hero forged a very special relationship with his community. Jackie Milburn (1924–1988) has been idolised by generations in the North-East. His goalscoring exploits in the number 9 shirt for Newcastle in the late 1940s and 1950s brought excitement to a region recovering, slowly, from the hardships of the Second World War. They have become the stuff of legend.

Folklore passes down that Jackie, born in the working-class coal-mining town of Ashington in Northumberland, wrote to Newcastle for a trial in 1943 after seeing an advertisement. He turned up with a pair of borrowed boots in a brown paper parcel. Including wartime matches, he scored 238 goals for Newcastle United during 14 years with the club – 200 in domestic league and cup competitions (still a club record, overtaken by Alan Shearer only with the benefit of goals in European club competitions).

Milburn was key to the club's FA Cup victories in 1951, 1952 and 1955 and won 13 caps for England. Newcastle was his only English league club. No player was more exciting to watch in the early 1950s than Milburn. It was not just his goals that excited the supporters; shirt billowing in the breeze, it was his speed and verve.

It was the 2–0 victory in the 1951 FA Cup final against Blackpool that is now most remembered. Milburn scored twice early in the second half. The second, taking a back-heel pass in an interchange with Ernie Taylor, was a thunderbolt 25-yard strike that flew into the roof of the bulging net – many still regard it as one of the finest goals scored at Wembley. A first-minute header in the 1955 FA Cup final against Manchester City simply added to his legendary record.

Milburn's iconic status grew even greater with time. A testimonial match was held 10 years after he had left the club. He worried that few spectators would turn up – but over 45,000 did. Newcastle's city centre came to a halt on the day of his funeral in 1988.

Two life-size statues, funded by public appeal, stand in his honour in the North-East (and a further may be planned). One in Newcastle, sculpted by Susanna Robinson, is high on a pedestal. Recently moved, again, it now stands yards from Milburn's favourite Gallowgate End at St James' Park. A right-foot shot is about to be unleashed for the top corner (assuming the ball is still there – it went missing several times in a previous location).

Another fine statue, by renowned sculptor John Mills, is situated in the main shopping street in Milburn's birthplace of Ashington. It shows him skilfully trapping the ball with his left foot and looking where next to pounce. The plaque remembers 'one of Newcastle United and England's greatest centre-forwards'.

For sports historian Richard Holt, Jackie Milburn "is arguably the most complete example of the professional footballer as a regional hero and symbol of community". 'Wor Jackie' to all Tynesiders.

JACKIE MILBURN
1924–1988

Bronze
Susanna Robinson
St James' Park,
Newcastle
1991

Tyneside hero, Jackie Milburn, is recalled by two statues: by John Mills in Ashington (left, far left) and by Susanna Robinson in Newcastle (top).

"He used to remind me of a wave breaking. He would just surge past defenders with his incredible pace. Everybody loved watching him" *Bobby Charlton*

STANLEY MATTHEWS

Wizard of the Dribble

STANLEY
MATTHEWS
1915–2000

Bronze
*Julian Jeffery, Carl
Payne and Andrew
Edwards*
Britannia Stadium,
Stoke-on-Trent
2001

England's football reputation internationally was still supreme in the late 1940s and early 1950s despite a shock defeat by the USA in the 1950 World Cup in Brazil, the first in which England had participated. One player, who did not play in that game, continued to enjoy a reputation as the game's greatest. Stanley Matthews (1915–2000) was, for well over two decades, the most revered footballer not just in Britain but throughout the world.

He played for England over a longer period than any other player before or since, the last of his 54 caps (together with 29 wartime internationals) being won in 1957 at the age of 42. His club career with Stoke and Blackpool spanned more than 30 years and nearly 700 appearances.

Born in Hanley, Stoke-on-Trent, he learnt early from his father, a well-known boxer, values of fitness and self-discipline. Joining Stoke City in 1932, Matthews made his international debut two years later before serving in the RAF during the Second World War.

His spell at Stoke ended in some turbulence when he wanted to leave for Blackpool where he owned a small shop. He was transferred in 1947. The Blackpool manager, Joe Smith, said: "You're 32. Do you think you can make it for another couple of years?" Matthews made it for another 18 years.

"In the days before television, his reputation was known in every country of the globe where football was played" *Bobby Charlton*

STANLEY MATTHEWS
continued

He was the 'Wizard of the Dribble' in the days when the winger (and Matthews invariably played out on the right) would take on the opposing full-back. Almost frail-looking and slightly bow-legged, his balance and ability to control the ball were combined with a sudden acceleration.

Football followers of the 1950s can still visualise the film of the 1953 FA Cup final, only the second to be televised. With the scores level at 3–3 in the final minutes, Matthews went past his defender and crossed back from the by-line for Bill Perry to strike home the winning goal. A nation cheered as Matthews, at the age of 38 and in his third final, won his first FA Cup winner's medal.

Matthews was the game's first global superstar. He was named the first Footballer of the Year in 1948, the first European Footballer of the Year in 1956 and, in 1965, he became the first professional footballer to be knighted. He was renowned throughout the world; on a coaching tour to Ghana shortly after its independence, Matthews was treated as if royalty and crowned 'King of Soccer'.

The second coming at Stoke came in 1961 when, aged 46, Matthews rejoined his former club. The following season, Stoke won the Second Division title and Matthews was voted Footballer of the Year for the second time.

The statue at Stoke shows Matthews at three different stages of his extraodinary career – as a teenager, at his peak in the 1950s, and aged 50.

STAN MORTENSEN

The 1953 'Matthews Final' is also remembered for the first (and, so far, only) hat-trick in an FA Cup final, scored by Stan Mortensen (1921–1991). With Blackpool losing 3–2 against Bolton Wanderers at Wembley with barely three minutes remaining, 'Morty' (with two goals already) took a free-kick from the edge of the penalty area. Stanley Matthews remarked of his Blackpool and England colleague: "I've never seen one taken as well. It flew, you couldn't see the ball on the way to the net."

Mortensen is another who learnt his basic skills in the backyards of the mining towns of north-east England. Declared unfit for further operational duties after a serious crash on a bombing mission while in the RAF and advised to give up his planned football career, he did not.

A career of 395 games at the top level for Blackpool brought 225 goals. He won 25 international caps and scored 23 goals including four on his debut, as England won 10–0 away against Portugal. A statue at Blackpool's Bloomfield Road by sculptor Peter Hodgkinson (above) simply, but movingly, says 'Morty'.

Matthews played his last match in February 1965, shortly after his 50th birthday. He later claimed he retired "too early". Always a fair player, he was never booked throughout his career. After his death, more than 100,000 people of all ages lined the streets of Stoke-on-Trent to pay tribute.

A first statue, by Colin Melbourne, was erected in Hanley's main shopping precinct. Pride of place now goes, though, to an imaginative larger-than-life-size three-figure statue at Stoke's Britannia Stadium (where Matthews' ashes are buried under the centre circle). The statue's plinth declares: "His name is symbolic of the beauty of the game, his fame timeless and international, his sportsmanship and modesty universally acclaimed. A magical player, of the people, for the people."

Crafted by three local sculptors working in collaboration (Julian Jeffery, Carl Payne and Andrew Edwards), it shows Matthews at three different stages of his career. The first is a teenage Stanley wearing the baggy shorts typical of football in the 1930s; the second reveals the number 7 at the peak of his career in the 1950s; and the third as a 50-year-old at the end of his playing days. The sculpture conveys the longevity of his career as well as a real sense of movement, with Stanley Matthews twisting and controlling the ball with magneticism, grace and balance.

Timeless. The Wizard of the Dribble.

TOM FINNEY

The Preston Plumber

TOM FINNEY
1922–

Bronze
Peter Hodgkinson
Sir Tom Finney
Way, Preston
2004

The 1950s were blessed with great footballers. Many were essentially one-club men and the pride of their communities. None was, or is, held in greater respect than Tom Finney (1922–). His entire league playing career was with relatively unfashionable Preston North End. He never won a league title or FA Cup winner's medal. Yet, for many, he is the most complete player English football has produced.

He was a local boy, living close to Preston's ground at Deepdale. He completed his apprenticeship in the family's plumbing business before signing as a professional in 1940. During the War, he played in various wartime matches but later saw action as a tank driver and mechanic with the Royal Armoured Corps in Montgomery's Eighth Army in Egypt. He was given a quick exit from the Army at the end of the War – not because he was a footballer but because he was a plumber!

Finney stayed with Preston throughout his league career. Making his debut in 1946, he was a fixture in the side until his retirement in 1960. His only winner's medal was as a member of the 1951 Second Division championship side. Preston were destined to be First Division runners-up twice and also runners-up in the FA Cup (in 1954, one of Finney's few poor performances on a big occasion). These were days of a maximum wage and strict club 'ownership' of a player's registration. He once was tempted by an offer from Italy after a successful England tour, but

Preston refused to sell. That was that.

His standing in the game was undoubted. Capped 76 times for England, he was often denied his favourite outside-right position by Stanley Matthews and he played 33 of those occasions on the left-wing. (The debate still continues: Matthews or Finney?) And he could play equally effectively at centre-forward. One match report in *The Times* vividly conveyed his skill: "There were three or four Arsenal defenders who dithered like old women on a zebra crossing every time Finney had the ball."

Added to his complete footballing skills, Finney possessed a quiet but firm dignity, respected still throughout the game as a 'gentleman of football'. Retiring as a player in 1960 after a persistent injury, he simply continued his successful plumbing business. He also became a magistrate and, for a period, chairman of the local health authority. He was knighted in 1998.

Tom Finney is the subject of one of the most imaginative sculptures in sport, sculpted by Peter Hodgkinson. Unveiled in front of the then National Football Museum at Deepdale in 2004 and entitled 'the Splash', it was inspired by a memorable photograph of Finney in a match in 1956 against Chelsea at Stamford Bridge. A large downpour before kick-off led to pools of water on the pitch. Having just beaten one defender and with the ball at his feet, Finney ended up in one of the pools of water.

As ever, the ball is perfectly under Tom Finney's control.

"Tom Finney would have been great in any team, in any match and in any age ... even if he had been wearing an overcoat"
Bill Shankly

BRIAN BEVAN

The Wizard from Oz

BRIAN BEVAN
1924–1991

Bronze
Philip Bews
Halliwell
Jones Stadium,
Warrington
1993

Rugby league has enjoyed a firm stronghold in the North ever since the 'split' from rugby union and the creation of the Northern Union in 1895. The founding clubs read like a roll-call of the industrial North: clubs like Oldham, Rochdale, Halifax, Leeds, Wakefield and Warrington. The game produced many great characters beloved in the North. Yet one of the all-time greats was an Australian.

High above spectators arriving at Warrington's ground is the figure of Brian Bevan (1924–1991). It is a remarkable story of an Australian's journey from Bondi Beach in south-east Australia to Warrington in north-west England; a winger who set records that may never be broken.

Born in Sydney in 1924, Bevan was at home on the local beaches, surfing, swimming and developing a frail body into a strong, athletic frame. He excelled at most sports but rugby league captured his enthusiasm as he went to local games, side-stepping telegraph poles en route. Then came the Second World War. Bevan joined the Royal Australian Navy. Shortly before the War ended, his ship went to England for a re-fit. The only contact he had here was an Australian friend of his father's who was working in the north of England. Bevan visited him and was taken to various professional rugby league clubs. A trial for Warrington followed and Bevan decided to sign for them in 1945. He played one match – and then had to go back to Australia to be demobbed.

Bevan returned to Warrington and was a fixture on the wing for 16 years. He was the league's top try scorer in his first season with a record 48 tries. He went on, over 620 games, to score an astonishing 740 tries for Warrington's first team and a career total of 796 tries including his last couple of years or so with Blackpool. He won two Challenge Cups and three rugby league championships with Warrington until his tearful farewell appearance, aged 37, on Easter Monday in 1962.

Knees often swathed in bandages, his outstanding speed and swerve – coupled with a side-step that left defenders grasping at thin air – made him a devastating match-winner. Tales of the tries he scored became legend in the pubs and clubs of Warrington. One, in a cup game at Wigan in 1948, came from a scrum under pressure five yards from the Warrington line. A passing movement reached Bevan. He was away, not down the touchline, but with a diagonal, swerving run through the centre, wrong-footing opponents in a 125-yard run.

In 1988 Bevan was one of nine original all-time greats to be inducted into rugby league's Hall of Fame. His only sadness was never having represented his home country, Australia, in an official Test.

A wonderfully imaginative sculpture by Philip Bews, unveiled in 1993 just two years after the death of the great Australian, shows Brian Bevan still running – in the sky, positioned between the tall steel rugby posts. High and untouchable in Warrington.

"Brian Bevan was the greatest I played against. He was a true gentleman. No one will near his record"
Billy Boston

WILLIE HORNE

Rugby league is at the heart of sporting life in the North-West. The game has a distinctive tradition of producing players whose commitment, style and 'grit' symbolise the aspirations and values of the game's supporters. A 'home-grown' star attracts particular affection. Barrow has many statues of industrial barons and other local worthies. Its most-loved hero, though, is rugby league legend Willie Horne (1922–2001).

Locals still recall that day in 1955 when Barrow, led by Horne – beat Workington Town 21–12 at Wembley Stadium to win the Challenge Cup final. Horne kicked five goals and a drop goal. (He was the first to perfect the 'round the corner' method of kicking, now, of course, standard in both codes.)

Horne played his whole career, 461 games, for Barrow. Relatively slight in build, his ability to create gaps with his speed or make the telling pass – often a heavy, rain-sodden ball thrown like a bullet to the wing – made him part of Barrow's

folklore. At one time, he was captain of Barrow, Lancashire, England and Great Britain. An international colleague summed up: "There are good players, there are great players and there's Willie Horne."

Renowned for his good sportsmanship, he is regarded as Barrow's greatest-ever player and became, in 1975, the first sportsman to be made a Freeman of the town. In his retirement, he ran a sports shop. His wife remarked that she would send him into a back-room because he would often prefer to give stuff away rather than sell it.

Horne now strides again through Barrow. He is in running flight, ball clutched to his chest, full of determination and honest endeavour. The statue, sculpted by Chris Kelly and two-and-a-half metres high, casts an imposing figure. The plinth displays bronze plaques depicting Willie Horne's career. The sculpture is a powerful and delightful reminder of one of rugby league's best.

Willie Horne, sculpted by Chris Kelly, strides through Barrow (above). Horne places the ball for a kick (above left), one of several bronze plaques on the statue's plinth.

GUS RISMAN
ERIC ASHTON
and BILLY BOSTON

Rugby league's knock-out Challenge Cup started in 1896. Despite the game's northern roots, Wembley has been the mecca of the competition for the sport's supporters since 1929, matching that of followers of the round-ball game. The final is one of the great days of the season. A sculpture celebrating rugby league is planned for erection in the near future at the new Wembley Stadium, already the site in bronze for football's Bobby Moore. The monumental work, sculpted by Stephen Winterburn, will represent the history of the sport, and its association with Wembley, through five of the game's greatest players. Three are recalled here.

Gus Risman (1911–1994), born in Cardiff, initially played rugby union before having 27 distinguished seasons as a rugby league player, mostly with Salford. A Challenge Cup victory for Salford in 1938 early in his career was followed,

astonishingly, by another triumph at Wembley Stadium for Workington in 1952 when aged 41 (he is the oldest Cup-winning player). Rugby league's Hall of Fame declares: "His monumental record, coupled with an exemplary demeanour on the field, made Risman one of the sport's most revered figures."

Alongside him in bronze, Eric Ashton (1935–2008) was one of the game's great players in the 1950s and 1960s. Signing for Wigan for £150 in 1955, he led the club six times in the Challenge Cup final, winning three of them, and became the first rugby league player to be honoured with an MBE. Regarded as a true professional, intelligent and a leader, he won 26 caps for Great Britain and captained his country 15 times over a period of great success.

At Wigan, Ashton formed a devastating partnership with Billy Boston (1934–), a winger whose turn of speed, side-step and strength led to an extraordinary 478 tries in 487 games for the club. Boston, born in Cardiff, was a pioneer among black players in rugby league and became one of the game's most prominent players. He was awarded the MBE in 1986.

Three rugby league greats being prepared by sculptor Stephen Winterburn for the new statue at Wembley Stadium: (from left to right) Gus Risman, Eric Ashton and Billy Boston.

ERIC EVANS

Pride of the Union

ERIC EVANS
1921–1991

Bronze
Peter Walker
Manchester Road,
Audenshaw
2009

Rugby union remained firmly 'amateur' throughout the 1950s. There were many, including in the North, for whom the 15-man game continued to be their sport.

There is a special pride in a community if a local sportsman achieves national and international glory. That pride, and the ability of sporting memories to live long within a community, is well-reflected in the unveiling of a fine statue of Eric Evans (1921–1991) in Audenshaw, on the outskirts of Manchester, more than 50 years after his time as the captain of England.

His background was classically 'union'. Evans attended the local grammar school where, like many, he enjoyed his first taste of sport. He played for Old Aldwinians and then began a career-long association with Sale at the outset of the Second World War before joining the Army where he became a member of the Border Regiment.

After the War, he qualified as a sports teacher at Loughborough College (to become fertile ground for so many fine sportsmen) before teaching at a technical college in Manchester. A fitness fanatic throughout his life, he trained at Old Trafford (often with the 'Busby Babes') and possessed a vigour and discipline that he would instil in colleagues.

Evans won his first cap, as a loose-head prop, in 1948 but did not become a regular member of the national team until 1951 (by which time he was England's first-choice hooker). He gained a total of 30 caps over a span of 11 years. In 1956, aged 37, Evans became the oldest man to captain England. Under his captaincy, in 1957, England won their first Grand Slam since 1928 – with a final victory over Scotland at Twickenham watched by a young Queen Elizabeth as Evans was carried high in celebration on the shoulders of his team-mates.

The Five Nations Championship (France had been re-admitted in 1947 after the War) was retained in 1958. Evans led England on 13 occasions – a record not surpassed until the days of Bill Beaumont – nine of which were victories.

After his retirement, he became a dedicated charity worker and was awarded the MBE both for his inspirational sporting achievements and his charity work for disabled children. He died in 1991 and his ashes were scattered on the pitch at Twickenham.

A splendid statue of Evans, sculpted by Peter Walker, was unveiled in 2009 as part of the borough council's programme to commemorate local figures through public sculpture. "We are always keen to celebrate the people and events that have helped to shape Tameside's history." On the road near the Aldwinians rugby ground, the sculpture, full of action, seeks to represent 'the strength, skill and vigour behind the sportsman'.

Eric Evans is shown, larger than life, ball in hand and shaking off a tackling defender at his ankles. He is a player in his thirties, leading his colleagues by example. The loose-fitting shirt, collar high around the neck, boots with knocked-in studs – all reflect a fine player of the 1950s.

"A local sportsman who achieved international glory"
Inscription on sculpture

KEN JONES

Wales' great all-rounder

In the valley town of Blaenavon, an amateur sportsman of the 1940s and 1950s is still at the centre of the community. This is the story of a Welshman who, uniquely, became an Olympic medal-winning athlete and a try-scoring winger ranking among the greats of Welsh rugby – Ken Jones (1921–2006).

A new recreation ground, incorporating the local rugby club, was opened in 1921 for the welfare of Blaenavon's growing mining community. It was also the year in which Jones was born. It was as a young boy on these local playing fields that his sporting talent was first spotted. An outstanding athlete at school in Pontypool and, later, training college in Cheltenham (he would become a teacher in this age of the sporting amateur), the Second World War came and Jones served, from 1945, in India. He won the All-India Olympiad sprint championships and an athletic career of high achievement beckoned.

His greatest thrill, and perhaps greatest achievement, came at the Olympic Games in 1948. Semi-finalist in the 100 metres, he won a silver medal as a member of Britain's 4 x 100 metres relay team. Captain of the British track and field team at the 1954 European championships, he again won a silver medal in the sprint relay team. He was also a bronze medallist at the 1954 Commonwealth Games.

Alongside, a rugby career as a winger blossomed. First capped for Wales in 1947, 'K J Jones (Newport)' was a fixture on the Welsh team sheet for the next 10 years – a remarkable 43 consecutive matches. On winning his 43rd cap, he became the most capped player in world rugby at that time. He played one more international. Cliff Morgan would remark: "Modest, unassuming, he had great charm and never wore his abundant talent and creative talents on his sleeve."

Jones' try-scoring was legendary, including a famous victory-clinching try against England in 1952 at Twickenham and another in 1953 against New Zealand at Cardiff Arms Park with five minutes to go and the scores level (the last Welsh victory over the All Blacks).

Perhaps his most sensational try came, though, in the fourth Test of the British Lions tour of 1950 against the All Blacks. The highly-respected New Zealand commentator, Terry Maclean, called it "the greatest try" at Eden Park. Jones, "the red panther of Wales", took a high pass on a break but with more than 50 yards to the try-line and with four All Blacks giving chase. Maclean wrote: "He ran at all times with the sinuous grace of a greyhound and now his long legs stretched forth over the green and driving onwards toward the goal." The whole crowd was on its feet, shouting and waving in "an expression of total joy".

Awarded the OBE in 1960 for services to Welsh rugby, Ken Jones is now recalled with pride by the community through a public-funded sculpture by Laury Dizengremel, unveiled in 2013. Clutching the ball to his chest, he is again sprinting to the try-line. The boy from Blaenavon who became one of Wales' finest.

KEN JONES
1921–2006

Bronze
Laury Dizengremel
Broad Street,
Blaenavon
2013

"When you watched him play, you felt a tingling of the spine ... the prickling of the scalp ... he was world-class"
Bleddyn Williams

LEN HUTTON

England's Batting Knight

LEN HUTTON
1916–1990

Stainless steel
Kate Maddison
Headingley Cricket
Ground, Leeds
2001

England's series of Ashes Test matches with Australia were at the centre of the country's sporting attention in post-war Britain. At the heart of England's team, and that of Yorkshire, was opening batsman Len Hutton (1916–1990).

Born into a cricketing family, he made his first-class debut for Yorkshire in 1934. A Test debut followed three years later. Then, in 1938, came one of cricket's legendary innings. Hutton scored 364 runs at The Oval against Australia in an innings built on sustained concentration and skill during more than 13 hours of play. It surpassed the record then held by Don Bradman for the highest individual score in Test history. It remains the highest Test innings by an Englishman.

Whilst serving in the Second World War as a physical training instructor, a broken arm in a gym accident led to a left arm two inches shorter than his right. Many believe that Hutton's post-war batting style showed greater caution as a result. Yet, highly-disciplined, he resumed a career of outstanding achievement in the 1950s.

In 1952 he was appointed captain of England – the first-ever 'professional' to be appointed. The firmly-established custom had been that a captain should come from the 'amateur' tradition. Hutton's career would prove an important stepping-stone towards the abolition of the game's distinction between 'gentlemen' and 'players'. The anachronism was finally abolished in 1962.

Under Hutton's leadership, England won the Ashes in 1953 and retained them in Australia in 1953/54. No side under his captaincy lost a Test series. The statistics of Hutton's career are formidable. He played 79 Test matches over nearly two decades, scoring 6,971 runs at an average of 56.67 – many against Australia with their top-class bowling attack of Lindwall and Miller. Hutton was knighted in 1956, joining Jack Hobbs as a cricketing Sir.

The chosen memorial for one of Yorkshire's finest was not a statue but, in the cricketing tradition, newly-designed gates – the Sir Leonard Hutton Gates – dedicated at the main entrance to Headingley. Hutton is placed at the centre playing a fierce and stylish drive over mid-wicket. Beside is a re-enactment of the scoreboard when he reached his historic score of 364 at The Oval against Australia in 1938.

On the other side is a scene from Headingley in the summer of 1990 when England played Pakistan and includes a number of Asian women in the stand wearing saris (controversially to some who declared the design inappropriate on the basis that Asian supporters did not feature in Hutton's time). Others supported the vision of the designer, Kate Maddison: "I felt it was important the design for the gates showed an unbroken link between the historic and the contemporary game."

The gates of Headingley are now open ... and Sir Leonard Hutton's place in the pantheon of the gods of English cricket is assured.

"Len Hutton was a batsman whose bat had no edges"
Fred Trueman

RANDOLPH TURPIN

The Leamington Licker

It was an unforgettable night: July 10 1951 at London's Earls Court. A British fighter out-boxed one of the sport's greatest legends, America's Sugar Ray Robinson, to win the world middleweight championship over 15 tough but glorious rounds. Randolph Turpin (1928–1966), or the 'Leamington Licker' as he was known, became an instant national hero.

Turpin, whose father had emigrated from British Guiana and later fought at the Somme in the First World War, was a boxer of rare calibre. As a nine-year-old, he attended a gym in Leamington run by a local policeman. A prodigious junior career followed. He became the Amateur Boxing Association's youngest ever champion – and the first black champion. It seems extraordinary now to relate but a ban, imposed by the British Boxing Board of Control on non-white boxers fighting for British titles, was only removed in 1948. As post-war immigration increased, black athletes would play a key role in British sport at the highest level – particularly in boxing, athletics, cricket and football.

While on national service in the Royal Navy, Turpin continued his boxing progress. He turned professional in 1946 and, aged 19, beat the existing British middleweight champion but, under the rules, he was too young to fight for the title itself! By 1950 he was officially the British middleweight title holder and ready for a world title fight against Sugar Ray Robinson and that triumphant night in 1951. After deafening applause, 18,000 fans in Earls Court joyously sang "For he's

a jolly good fellow". It was one of British boxing's greatest nights.

Turpin's hold on the world title lasted just 64 days. Robinson claimed a re-match in New York. It was a fight of great quality. A counter-barrage from Robinson, after a gash had opened above his eye, overcame Turpin and the fight was stopped with just seconds to go before the end of the 10th round. Turpin's career then started to slide, not helped by continuing personal problems including an alleged case of assault that was eventually settled out of court. Despite recovering the British light-heavyweight title for the third time, his career was fading and he retired in 1959.

His personal troubles continued. Business ventures failed and he was declared bankrupt in 1962. Attempts to return to the ring for a few fights were not successful. The glory days were well over. Struggling to cope, Turpin was found dead after a gunshot incident in 1966. He had apparently committed suicide aged 37.

In 2001, exactly 50 years after his famous world title victory, a striking statue of Randolph Turpin by sculptor Carl Payne, commissioned by the local council, was unveiled (by Henry Cooper) in Warwick town centre. A distinctive landmark, Turpin is in fighting stance, ready to strike. The first public sculpture in Britain for a black sportsman, it recalls the colourful and triumphant, and ultimately sad, career of one of Britain's most talented boxers.

Nothing, though, could take away the memory of that glorious night at Earls Court in July 1951.

RANDOLPH TURPIN 1928–1966

Bronze
Carl Payne
Market Square, Warwick
2001

"One cannot recall such a scene as that which followed the raising of his arm as the victor by the referee"
The Times

REG HARRIS

Bury's Cycling Maestro

REG HARRIS
1920–1992

Bronze
James Butler
The National
Cycling Centre,
Manchester
1994

British cycling has in recent years enjoyed a wonderful period of success at elite level. In the late 1940s and into the 1950s, Britain also had a world-class sprint cyclist.

Debonair, fluent French-speaker, colourful and stubborn, Reg Harris (1920–1992) was one of the country's most recognised and successful sportsmen in the years after the Second World War. He won both the amateur and professional world sprint cycling titles. He was voted Sportsman of the Year by the UK sports journalists in 1950. It would be another 50 years or more before men's British sprint cycling could, in Chris Hoy, boast a comparable successor.

Born near Bury in Lancashire of poor, working-class roots, Harris developed an early passion for cycling, financed by a job at the local paper mill. But the Second World War intervened. He joined the 10th Hussars and, as a tank driver in the western desert in north Africa, narrowly escaped death when his tank was destroyed by enemy fire. He was discharged, ironically, as medically unfit. Resuming his racing career, he joined the Manchester Wheelers and was among the first group of British riders to attempt to succeed on mainland Europe, the centre of world cycling.

These were still strict days of amateurism. Employed and equipped by a bike-maker, Harris just kept his amateur status. An ambition was achieved when he became the world amateur sprint cycling champion in 1947, winning his title on the Parc des Princes track in Paris. His heart was set on winning gold medals in the London Olympic Games of 1948 – partly, one suspects, because it would have greatly enhanced future sponsorship opportunities – but a car accident shortly before the Games ruined his preparation and his fitness. He had to be satisfied (which he was not) with two silver medals.

He did then turn professional. Harris became world professional sprint champion four times – in 1949, 1950, 1951 and 1954 – and broke five world records during this period. He retired in 1957 and was awarded the OBE. Disappointed that the national association did not seek to take greater advantage of his experience and critical of the standard of British cycling after his retirement, he was convinced that he could still race at the top – which, astonishingly, he did by returning in 1971 and then winning the British professional sprint title in 1974 ... at the age of 54.

At the velodrome in Manchester, the National Cycling Centre, a fine full-size bronze statue of Harris was unveiled in 1994. Delightfully sculpted by James Butler, Harris is shown in cycling action in the familiar hump-backed sprinter's pose. A real sense of movement is conveyed by the sloping plinth.

It is appropriate that the statue of Harris should now be prominent inside the National Cycling Centre, passed countless times in training by Britain's present-day world-class Olympic medal-winning squad. There is little doubt that Reg Harris would still like to be out there racing with them!

"I get tired of people telling me I wasn't as fast as him"
Chris Hoy

ROGER BANNISTER

Breaking the Barrier

ROGER
BANNISTER
1929–

Bronze
Eino
Royal Russell
School, Croydon
2004

Could the mile be run in less than four minutes? It offered a beautiful symmetry – four laps, four minutes – and held an intense fascination for the sporting world. On May 6 1954, Roger Bannister (1929–) reached a new peak in athletic achievement.

At the Iffley Road track in Oxford, there was a lull in the blustery wind just after 6pm. Bannister, a former Oxford man and now a medical student, was representing the Amateur Athletic Association against the University. He was Britain's finest miler. Bannister turned to his colleagues, Chris Brasher and Chris Chataway, and said: "Yes. Let's do it." Brasher set the pace for the first two laps. Bannister hung on in second place. Then Chataway took over at the third lap. When would Bannister make his break? With just 250 yards to go, he kicked hard for home with that glorious long-legged, wide-striding run. His face, white and drawn, blurred through the tape – totally exhausted. The chief timekeeper handed the result to Norris McWhirter, the announcer. The tension was raised further as he began:

"Ladies and gentlemen. Here is the result of the ... one mile. First, number 41, R G Bannister, Amateur Athletic Association and formerly of Exeter and Merton Colleges, Oxford, with a time which is a new meeting and track record,

"I found longer races boring.
I found the mile just perfect"
Roger Bannister

ROGER BANNISTER
continued

and which – subject to ratification – will be a new English native, British national, All-Comers, European, British Empire and world record. The time was 3 ..." ... and the rest was drowned in cheers and uproar. Yes, 3 minutes 59.4 seconds, the barrier had been broken.

Bannister's triumph provided another major boost to the country's morale. Britain had now emerged from the dark days of the War. The hope and celebration of the Coronation of a new Queen Elizabeth in 1953 had been followed by the dramatic news that a mountaineering expedition, British-led by John Hunt, had conquered Everest, the world's highest peak. Now came Bannister's triumph. Despite the professionalism in approach, this was also a triumph for the 'amateur' and, perhaps, even more admirable for that. Bannister would shortly resume a medical career and become a highly distinguished neurologist. He was knighted in 1975.

The record had its roots in Bannister's relative failure in the Helsinki Olympics of 1952. He had expected to challenge for the 1500 metres, and then retire. He came fourth. Determined, he applied himself, importantly with a greatly increased attention to training, to a new goal ... the four-minute mile. Shortly after his rival's landmark run in Oxford, Australian John Landy broke Bannister's new record. The two great milers met in the Empire Games in Vancouver. A sculpture in Vancouver, by Jack Harmon, recalls that stunning moment when Landy, leading in the final lap, glanced sideways over his left shoulder

Roger Bannister's supreme moment is celebrated (presently in Croydon) by Finnish sculptor Eino (left and right, top) and by a plaque at Oxford's Iffley Road (right, bottom).

... and Bannister passed him on the right side to victory in the 'Miracle Mile'.

Bannister's four-minute mile was broadcast live on BBC radio and recorded for television. Other athletic dramas featured prominently in the limited televised sport of the period. Later in 1954 at the White City, Chris Chataway set a world record in the 5000 metres with a thrilling victory over Russian Vladimir Kuts. He was voted BBC Sports Personality of the Year.

Bannister was followed in 1955 by another fine athlete, Gordon Pirie. His battles, also often televised, with long-distance legends Emil Zatopek and Vladimir Kuts remain vivid memories of the period. Pirie, although never an Olympic gold medal winner, broke five world records during his career – none more memorable than in 1956 when he took the 5000 metres record and then, later that year, shattered the 3000 metres record. Yorkshire-born, Pirie was brought up in Coulsdon, Surrey, where a plaque recalls his achievements.

Bannister's own extraordinary achievement is recalled by a simple plaque at Iffley Road. It also inspired the world-renowned Finnish sculptor, Eino. A keen runner (he often trained with such athletes as his great countryman, Lasse Viren), Eino created a striking sculpture in 2004 in his American studio – not at the behest of any commission but inspired by his own admiration for Bannister. It has, since May 2008, stood in the grounds of the Royal Russell School, Croydon, where Eino

spent some teaching time. A permanent home still awaits. Full of raw texture and expression, as if still made of its original clay, the bronze sculpture captures the moment as Roger Bannister is about to breast the tape in his legendary run.

Eino calls his work 'Paradigm'. It represents a supreme moment when a barrier was broken and the sporting world changed.

OXFORDSHIRE BLUE PLAQUES BOARD
Here at the
Iffley Road Track
the first sub-four minute mile
was run on
6th May 1954
by
ROGER
BANNISTER
UNIVERSITY OF OXFORD

STAN CULLIS and BILLY WRIGHT

Legends of Molineux

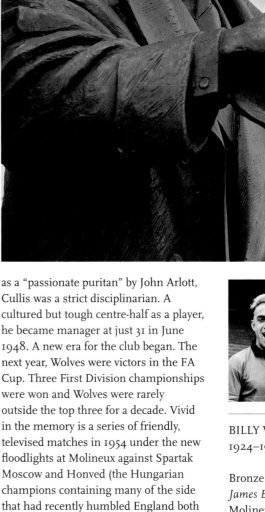

STAN CULLIS
1916–2001

Bronze
James Butler
Molineux Stadium,
Wolverhampton
2003

Football was at a fascinating stage in the early 1950s. Club loyalties remained strong and the league programme was lengthy. England had not taken international football very seriously, not joining FIFA when it was formed in 1904 and, indeed, not playing in the FIFA World Cup until 1950 in Brazil. The 1–0 loss there to the USA was simply seen as a freak result. Then, in 1953 at Wembley, England's fortress, along came the Hungarians with Hidegkuti, Puskas and the other 'Magical Magyars'.

England were mesmerised and destroyed. A first home loss for England to a team from outside the British Isles was a deep shock and the 6–3 lesson was compounded by the emphatic 7–1 defeat the following year in Budapest. English football started to wrestle with the challenges of the new order – but in a context where the domestic Football League and the FA Cup were still central. It was Wolverhampton Wanderers who took on these challenges most strongly in the mid-1950s.

The manager, and driving force, was Stan Cullis (1916–2001). Aptly described as a "passionate puritan" by John Arlott, Cullis was a strict disciplinarian. A cultured but tough centre-half as a player, he became manager at just 31 in June 1948. A new era for the club began. The next year, Wolves were victors in the FA Cup. Three First Division championships were won and Wolves were rarely outside the top three for a decade. Vivid in the memory is a series of friendly, televised matches in 1954 under the new floodlights at Molineux against Spartak Moscow and Honved (the Hungarian champions containing many of the side that had recently humbled England both at Wembley and in Budapest). These dramatic victories, played with a passion and flair still warmly remembered, contributed greatly to England's

BILLY WRIGHT
1924–1994

Bronze
James Butler
Molineux Stadium,
Wolverhampton
1996

"Our supporters get more entertainment from watching Wolves than any other two teams together" *Stan Cullis*

IVOR ALLCHURCH and BERTIE PEACOCK

The Welsh national football side enjoyed much success in the late 1950s. At the heart of the team was Ivor Allchurch (1929–1997). Allchurch, a ball-playing inside-forward, played most of his football career (including 445 league games) for Swansea. He became the first Welsh player to earn more than 50 caps and was at the centre of the Welsh success at the 1958 World Cup in Sweden where the team reached the quarter-finals, losing 1–0 to eventual winners Brazil. A statue, sculpted by Michael Field, for Swansea's all-time great player was erected at the club's new Liberty Stadium in 2005 (above left).

Northern Ireland also reached the quarter-finals of the World Cup in 1958. One of their fine players was midfielder Bertie Peacock (1928–2004). Born in Coleraine, Peacock started his career locally before making over 400 appearances for Celtic. Part-time manager of Northern Ireland for a three-year spell (giving a first international cap to an 18-year-old George Best), he also returned to Coleraine as manager for 13 years. Co-founder of the youth Milk Cup, Peacock was awarded the MBE in 1986. A life-size statue (above right), by Ross Wilson, was unveiled in 2007 in the heart of Coleraine.

enthusiasm to embrace the introduction of European club competitions.

On the pitch, the team was led by Billy Wright (1924–1994). He was the captain who led the team out and played, as England coach Walter Winterbottom put it, with "a heart of oak".

Joining Wolves as a schoolboy in 1938, he played 541 games for Wolves until he retired, aged 35, in 1959. A midfield wing-half for much of that time, he moved to centre-half for the later part of his career. A tenacious tackler, he exemplified the discipline and fitness demanded by his club manager, Cullis. "Win the ball and give the simplest pass" was his basic creed.

Wright was Footballer of the Year in 1952 and runner-up to Alfredo di Stefano as European Footballer of the Year in 1957. He was the first player, worldwide, to reach a century of international appearances (105 England caps, including 90 as captain); he was, remarkably, an ever-present in the national team for eight consecutive years.

Wolves' fortunes started to decline in the 1960s and Cullis was suddenly dismissed early in the 1965 season, the first high-profile sacking in England of a top-line manager. The shock was felt throughout Wolverhampton and beyond. For some, the club has never recovered.

Wright, awarded a CBE in 1960, died of cancer in 1994. The town of Wolverhampton came to a standstill on the day of his funeral. Sturdy, single-minded, a driving force for his team – a leader. These qualities are reflected in the larger-than-life-size statue sculpted by local artist James Butler and unveiled in 1996. Bedecked in the club's gold-and-black strip, Billy Wright is again leading his team out at Molineux.

Cullis died, aged 84, in February 2001, seven years after the death of his great captain. A characterful sculpture, again by James Butler, was unveiled in 2003. It stands at Molineux not far from Billy Wright, the club captain during that reign of Stan Cullis – a reign that is still recalled with awe and pride.

DUNCAN EDWARDS

Pride of Dudley

DUNCAN
EDWARDS
1936–1958

Bronze
James Butler
Market Place,
Dudley
1999

Movingly and permanently, the Munich memorial clock at Old Trafford recalls the date of the tragedy – February 6 1958. At 3.04pm on that fateful day, British European Airways flight 609 crashed on take-off after a refuelling stop. The dead included eight players of the Manchester United squad returning from a European Cup tie in Belgrade: Geoff Bent, Roger Byrne, Eddie Colman, Mark Jones, David Pegg, Tommy Taylor, Liam Whelan and Duncan Edwards.

Having nearly missed a league match after a European fixture due to a delay on a regular flight the previous year, Manchester United chartered a plane for the away tie against Red Star Belgrade. United drew 3–3 and clinched a place in the European Cup semi-finals for the second year running. The return flight left Belgrade in sunshine but Munich was shrouded in low cloud, freezing sleet and snow. The anti-icing equipment was used for the landing for the fuel stop. The players disembarked. Just over an hour later, the flight was cleared for take-off but aborted by the pilot due to an uneven tone in the engine. A second attempt likewise – described as a 'slight engine fault' to the passengers. Everybody disembarked again.

A third take-off was attempted. The plane failed to gain height and crashed into a perimeter fence and a nearby house. The port wing and part of the tail were ripped off. The fuselage hit a wooden hut, causing a truck filled with tyres to explode. Twenty-one people were found dead. Edwards and

A stained-glass window (right) is dedicated to Duncan Edwards in Dudley's St Francis Church.

"He could do anything, play anywhere, and the world awaited the full scale of his glory" *Bobby Charlton*

DUNCAN EDWARDS

continued

the co-pilot died later from their injuries.

In 2008, on the 50th anniversary of the tragedy, a new version of a memorial plaque was installed at Old Trafford and is sited on the ground's East Stand.

Duncan Edwards (1936–1958) was, and still is, the pride of Dudley in Worcestershire. Aged just 21 and already a fixture in the Manchester United team, he was at the heart of the 'Busby Babes'. Edwards fought for 15 days after the Munich crash. News of his death had to be kept from Matt Busby, fighting for his own life, for fear of the effect it would have on him.

As a youngster, Edwards was made captain of England Schoolboys. He was always destined for greatness. Signed as a professional by Manchester United in the early hours of his 16th birthday, he made his first-team debut a few months later. He became the youngest player to win a senior England cap when he played, aged 18 years and 183 days, against Scotland in 1955.

By the time of Edwards' young death, he had already played 177 times for Manchester United and won two league championship medals and 18 full international caps. Mostly a driving left-sided wing-half, Edwards could play anywhere – with many games at centre-half and centre-forward.

The disaster ripped the heart out of the Busby Babes side – league holders, European Cup semi-finalists and, many still believe, on the verge of being one of the game's greatest teams. The tragedy became a sad, but important, part of the heritage of the club. The strength of feeling and support helped it to rebuild and become one of the world's most popular and successful clubs.

In St Francis Church in Dudley, two stained-glass windows depicting Edwards were dedicated to his memory in a ceremony three years after his death. All the survivors of the Munich crash attended.

In October 1999, Dudley's pride in the memory of Edwards was further reinforced with a larger-than-life-size statue, sculpted by James Butler, standing high on a plinth in Dudley Market Place. Duncan Edwards is again in England action, full of power and strength. A towering figure.

Separately, the memorial Munich clock, a simple two-faced clock attached to the south-east corner of the stadium at Old Trafford, shows the date of the disaster – never forgotten.

The Munich clock at Old Trafford commemorates the tragedy (below); Duncan Edwards in training as a 17-year-old (below left).

STIRLING MOSS

Born to Race

Motor racing became a highly popular, if dangerous, sport in the 1950s. Cars were small and ill-protected. Grand prix drivers ran to their cars at the start. Overtaking and driving skills were paramount. Britain possessed, proudly, one of the very best. Stirling Moss (1929–) has been part of the basic fabric of motor racing for 50 years and more. He is universally respected as one of the best-ever racing drivers: the 'greatest driver never to win the world championship'.

At the entrance to the Mallory Park Circuit, south of Leicester, major figures of motor sport – all with strong connections with racing in the Midlands – are recalled in a series of life-size bronze statues lovingly commissioned by Chris Meek, owner of the circuit and himself a former racing driver, and all crafted by Scottish sculptor David Annand. Standing distinctively among them is the people's champion, Stirling Moss.

Moss was born into a motor racing family and destined to race from a young age. He competed, at the highest level, from 1948 to 1962. Out of the 527 competitive races he entered during his professional career, he won an astonishing 212 times – including 16 Formula One grand prix events. As with many other drivers of his era, he competed in many different types of car and races. Moss was as gifted at the wheel of a sports car as a grand prix car. His great victories in sports car racing include the 1955 Mille Miglia, the famous 'thousand mile' open-endurance road race held in Italy. His versatility and all-round driving skills were extraordinary.

His first Formula One victory came in 1955 in the British Grand Prix, then held at Aintree, where he finished ahead of the legendary Juan Fangio. It was a first Formula One victory for a British driver in a British-built car. Four times second, the world championship came agonisingly close in 1958 when he narrowly missed out on the title to rival Mike Hawthorn, even though the latter only won one race compared to the four of Moss. (Moss would have won the title today under the current points scoring system.)

His preference for driving British-manufactured cars may have cost Moss a number of races and titles. Yet, triumphs in glorious demonstration of his racing skill were many. In 1961, competing against the more powerful and state-of-the-art Ferrari, Moss won the Monaco Grand Prix in a Lotus 18, his third success there and regarded by many as one of the best Formula One races ever.

His career in grand prix racing ended in 1962 when he was badly injured in a crash at Goodwood that forced his retirement. He was knighted in 2000. His name is still synonymous with motor racing in Britain.

Yes, whilst driving, he was once stopped by the police and challenged with the famous question: "Who do you think you are? Stirling Moss?" Moss quietly explained. Few sportsmen have become part of the language – and few remain so respected.

STIRLING MOSS
1929–

Bronze
David Annand
Mallory Park
Circuit,
Kirkby Mallory
2006

"Stirling Moss is a national institution"
Murray Walker

MIKE HAWTHORN

The Farnham Flyer

MIKE
HAWTHORN
1929–1959

Bronze
David Annand
Goodwood Motor
Circuit, Chichester
2005

On the south coast near Chichester, at Goodwood's motor racing circuit, we find a moving tribute to Mike Hawthorn (1929–1959). He was the golden boy of motor racing. He drove fast, lived with style, had fun ... and died young at the age of 29.

Hawthorn was the first British Formula One motor racing champion. In 1958, although only winning one grand prix to the four victories that year of fellow countryman Stirling Moss, Hawthorn's greater consistency in his Ferrari won the title by just one point over his gallant and senior rival. He became the first in a now long and illustrious line of British drivers

to win the prestigious Formula One drivers' title.

Born in Yorkshire in Mexborough (where there is a memorial plaque), Hawthorn's family moved to Farnham to run a local garage – and to be near the Brooklands racetrack for young Michael. His racing career took off in 1952 when he was spotted, and later mentored, by Jaguar's racing manager, Lofty England.

Hawthorn came into international prominence when he beat the great Argentinian driver, Juan Fangio, in the 1953 French Grand Prix; for over 150 miles there was scarcely a length between them as Hawthorn held on for a famous victory. He was clearly destined for motoring greatness. His charm, broad grin and bow-tie lifted everyone's spirits. He was nicknamed 'Le Papillon' (the butterfly) by the French.

As lead driver for Jaguar in the 1955 Le Mans race, he was involved, if indirectly as he pulled into the pits, in the terrible crash behind that killed more than 80 spectators. Jaguar eventually won but the race had been overshadowed by motor racing's worst disaster. Hawthorn was deeply affected.

Even in his year of Formula One triumph, in 1958, there was sadness. His great racing friend, Peter Collins, was killed at Germany's notorious Nurburgring track. Hawthorn felt disillusioned. About to be engaged to a beautiful fashion model, Jean Howarth, he announced his retirement shortly after clinching his title.

Just months later, on January 22

Mike Hawthorn, sculpted by David Annand, faces the pits at Goodwood with mentor Lofty England, whose hand is on his shoulder, during their Jaguar days.

"If he had been born a decade earlier John Michael Hawthorn might have been a heroic Spitfire pilot in the Battle of Britain"
Motor Sport Hall of Fame

1959, Hawthorn died in a car accident on the A3 Guildford bypass in Surrey. It was front-page headline news. The exact circumstances remain unclear. Driving his highly-tuned British racing green Jaguar saloon, he had spotted a racing friend ahead. He overtook and then skidded off the road at a wet corner, fatally hitting a tree.

The headstone on his grave in Farnham's West Street Cemetery bears a distinctive stone carving of a wreath surrounding a racing car, coloured highlights to the carving being added in 2004. Flowers are still renewed regularly.

Since 2005, a charming life-size bronze sculpture of Mike Hawthorn with Lofty England, sculpted by David Annand, stands facing the pits at Goodwood racetrack more than 50 years after his death. It was funded entirely by donations. Hawthorn is walking, relaxedly, with England's hand on his shoulder in their days at Jaguar. It is a warm sculpture reflecting the friendship of the two men. Hawthorn's bow-tie shines in the sun.

CHAPTER FIVE

THE SIXTIES, WORLD CUP & ALL THAT

The beginnings of major developments in sport were born in the 1960s.

No social factor in this period affected sport more than the growth in television. At the beginning of the 1950s, fewer than 10 per cent of households possessed a television; by the end of the 1960s, only 10 per cent did not. Even if sport broadcast on television was (compared with today) limited and often only shown in highlight form, sport had spread from being primarily a 'live' experience to include a potentially vast television audience.

In football, the early 1960s saw the end of the maximum wage and the lowering of restraints on transfers between clubs. Star players began to acquire a bargaining strength beyond any previously held. The move to professionalism, however defined, was unstoppable in most sports. The days of 'shamateurism were coming to an end'. Tennis, among others, went 'open'. Cricket abolished the quaint distinction between 'gentlemen' and 'players'.

The growth of television, combined perhaps with increased worldwide travel by the public generally, led to greater interest in international competition. In football, the World Cup and the European Cup provided stories that are integral to memories of the decade.

Major domestic sporting events, including the Derby, the Grand National and Wimbledon, enhanced their nationwide popularity with the support of television. Britain continued to produce world champions in motor racing.

Other trends and influences became apparent. Women in elite sport started to feature more prominently in the public's attention, particularly in athletics and tennis. Ominously, at the end of the decade, the menacing spectre of a major problem of drugs in sport manifested itself darkly for the first time.

Many of the great sporting figures of the 1960s (including several still, happily, with us) have been honoured in fine statues and memorials. Indeed, there are around the country probably more public monuments of sporting heroes of the 1960s than of any other decade.

JOHN CHARLES

The Gentle Giant

JOHN CHARLES
1931–2004

Bronze
*David
Roper-Curzon*
Elland Road, Leeds
2006

S everal sporting stars straddle, of course, the decades of the 1950s and the 1960s. We start with one. If there is a top table in the pantheon of British football, a place would be held by John Charles (1931–2004).

Born in Swansea, he learnt his football (with his brother Mel) in the local park. He joined the groundstaff at Swansea but it was Leeds United who signed him as a 17-year-old. He played 327 games for the Yorkshire club.

The youngest player to be capped by Wales (aged just 18), his skill and power marked him out early as an exceptional player. He helped Leeds win promotion to the First Division in 1956 and, in his first season in the top flight, was the division's leading scorer. Powerful, agile, 6ft 2ins tall, perfectly balanced, quick and versatile, he was as good a centre-half as he was a centre-forward.

Captaining Wales in April 1957, Charles was watched by Umberto Agnelli, owner of Juventus. Two months later, Charles was transferred for a then world-record fee of £65,000. He is reported to have received a £10,000 signing-on fee at a time when British players merely received £10 for a domestic move.

Charles was an instant success in Italian football – succeeding where, later, the likes of Jimmy Greaves, Denis Law, Ian Rush and Paul Gascoigne would not (with Rush, allegedly, declaring: "It's like living in a foreign country"). Against the defensive play and tight tackling of the Italian *catenaccio*, Charles was supreme.

As Juventus won the 1957/58 Serie A league title for the first time for many years, in his first season, he was the Italian league's top scorer and voted player of the year. Early on, Charles acquired a reputation for never using his great strength unfairly. In Italy he was labelled, with great esteem, 'Il Gigante Buono' – the Gentle Giant.

He helped Wales through to the quarter-finals of the World Cup, in Sweden in 1958, for the first and only time. Two more Serie A league championships for Juventus followed in 1960 and 1961 and two Italian Cup wins. Over five sublime seasons and 155 games for Juventus, he scored 93 goals – a remarkable goal-rate given the defensive nature of Italian football. In many a game, Charles would score and then be instructed to revert to centre-half in order to protect his team's lead.

In 1962, he returned briefly to Leeds (principally for family reasons) with spells at other clubs as his game, troubled by a knee injury, lost its edge. Several times he would return as a visitor to Turin.

Affection for John Charles among the fans of Juventus, the *tifosi*, was lasting. His steel grey hair and broad grin would still be recognised with affection. In 1997, Charles was voted the club's best-ever foreign player.

In the entrance to the banqueting suite at Leeds' Elland Road ground, a memorial bust, sculpted by David Roper-Curzon, stands of this colossus of a player. John Charles CBE. The Gentle Giant.

"When we were at Juve, the two most important people for most Italians were the Pope and Il Gigante"
Omar Sivori, team-mate of John Charles

JOHNNY HAYNES

Fulham's Maestro

Few years have been more significant for British football than 1961. It saw the break-up of the maximum wage (then £20 per week), one of the most significant developments in the game's history. George Eastham was pursuing his court battle to overcome the tyranny of a retain-and-transfer system that enabled a club (in his case, Newcastle) to prevent a player moving to another by retaining his 'registration' even after his contract of employment had ended. Players' bargaining rights, certainly those of the top players, changed dramatically.

Fulham's Johnny Haynes (1934–2005) moved quickly after the end of the maximum wage. Remembering well that the club's extrovert chairman, Tommy Trinder, had earlier claimed proudly that Haynes was worth £100 per week, he knocked on his chairman's door. Haynes will go down in football history not only as 'the Brylcreem Boy' (one of the first product endorsements by a footballer) but as the game's first £100 per week player – although, it is said, he never received another increase.

Haynes was, by far, Fulham's leading player for most of the 1950s and 1960s. He was 'the Maestro', renowned for his passing skills: the 40-yard pass threading the defence; the reverse pass; the pass into space where instinctively he knew a team-mate was (or ought to be) running – a repertoire that gained him a worldwide reputation. He was also a perfectionist, as demanding of himself as he was renowned

for rebuking team-mates who did not play to his standards. Often, the rebuke was simply in his stance, hands on hips, an accusing look at a player who had failed to fulfil his plan.

Haynes captained England 22 times between the reigns of Billy Wright and Bobby Moore. Disappointing campaigns in the World Cups of 1958 and 1962, and a subsequent car crash, meant that his England career never matched his universal reputation. By 1966, his style did not meet the taste of Alf Ramsey and his more workmanlike team approach.

As a Fulham player, Haynes has no equal in the club's history. A one-club man, for 18 years, despite temptations to join a bigger club later in his career. He led Fulham, a Second Division side for much of that period, to promotion to the First Division in 1958. His huge contribution is reflected in the bare statistics: 657 appearances for Fulham (594 in the league), the club's all-time record; 157 goals; and, with 56 international appearances for England, still the club's most capped player.

Johnny Haynes' statue, designed by William Mitchell and sculpted by Douglas Jennings, was unveiled in 2008 and stands on a plinth outside Craven Cottage. He is in typical pose. Hands are on his hips, perhaps less menacing in look than in some tales of the past, but still with a slightly quizzical expression and furrowed brow. His foot is on the ball, in the words of the statue's designer, as though "he'd just killed a lion in the jungle".

JOHNNY HAYNES
1934–2005

Bronze
Douglas Jennings
Stevenage Road,
Fulham,
London
2008

"He's the best passer of the ball I've ever seen. It was as if he possessed his own internal guided missile system"
Pelé

JIMMY HILL

The campaign to break the maximum
wage was led vigorously by Jimmy Hill
(1928–), as chairman of the Professional
Footballers Association (PFA), and Cliff
Lloyd, its secretary. Hill was then still a
player (if relatively modest) with Fulham.
Fifty years later, a statue of him (above), by
sculptor Nicholas Dimbleby, was erected
outside the Ricoh Stadium at Coventry
City, the club where (then at Highfield
Road) he became manager for six eventful
years and later returned as managing
director and chairman. After the last game
at Highfield Road, the crowd acclaimed
him as his Sky Blue song rang out.

Hill enjoyed an extraordinary range
of roles in football: player, union leader,
coach, manager, match official (stepping
out, memorably, once to volunteer as a
substitute linesman in a First Division
match), director, chairman – and then
television executive and presenter.

Jimmy Hill was an innovator. No
change, though, had a greater impact
on the game than the abolition of the
maximum wage in 1961.

BILL NICHOLSON

The 1961 season was also a landmark
year on the pitch. Tottenham Hotspur
became the first team in the 20th century
to achieve the 'double' of the league
championship and the FA Cup. The
European Cup Winners' Cup was secured
in 1963 – the first British club side to win a
leading European competition. The driving
force of the club, and its most respected
figure, was manager Bill Nicholson
(1919–2004).

As a right-half, he was a key member
of the famous 'push-and-run' team, under
Arthur Rowe, that won the 1951 title.
Becoming manager in 1958, Nicholson
fashioned a team of fluency and skill with
players such as Danny Blanchflower, John
White and, later, Jimmy Greaves but with
a strong centre/midfield with Maurice
Norman and Dave Mackay.

A statue is planned for Tottenham's
new stadium. In the meantime, a portrait
bust (above) inside the portals of White
Hart Lane is a proud reminder of the
'glory, glory' days under their most
successful manager.

HENRY COOPER

Our 'Enry

HENRY COOPER
1934–2011

Plaque
Old Kent Road,
Southwark,
London
2008

Britain has produced many brave boxing heavyweights but none has gained more public affection than Henry Cooper (1934–2011). There is no statue yet for one of Britain's most popular boxers of all time (one is being promoted by the London Ex-Boxers Association) but simply a plaque – one that may go unnoticed by most – along the Old Kent Road in south-east London. It is on the wall of the building, just above the old Thomas a Becket pub, where Cooper trained for 14 years, from 1954, six days a week. This was where 'Enry's 'Ammer, his trademark left hook, was developed.

No list of sporting memories of the 1960s is complete without recalling that night, in June 1963, when 'Enry's 'Ammer sent a stunned Cassius Clay onto his back at a packed Wembley Stadium.

Sloped against the ropes at the end of the fourth round, Clay was 'saved by the bell'. His manager, Angelo Dundee, allegedly widened a tear in Clay's glove to give him more time to recover between the rounds. In the next round, Cooper's eye was badly cut open. His chance was gone. Three years later, they met again when Muhammad Ali (as Clay became known) was world heavyweight champion. The fight ended, with Cooper bloodied and exhausted, in the sixth round. Yet his courage and engaging honesty won the admiration and affection of countless millions of fans – not only in Britain but around the world.

Cooper's professional career lasted

17 years. He fought 55 fights, winning 40 of them. He won the British and Commonwealth heavyweight titles in 1959 in a gruelling fight with Brian London and added the European title in 1968. Cooper, carefully guided throughout by manager Jim Wicks ('the Bishop'), retained his British title for over 12 years until 1971, losing in a controversial points decision to Joe Bugner.

Born in Southwark, Henry Cooper (knighted in 2000, the first boxer to be so honoured) was the clear first choice of the people of Southwark when they voted in 2007 for a recipient of the council's blue plaque scheme. The Thomas a Becket pub, and the gym, may have gone, but Our 'Enry will be long remembered.

"Clay is down! And as the bell goes Clay has just been dropped ... What a beautiful punch from Cooper!"
BBC commentary

FRED TRUEMAN

Fiery Fred

FRED TRUEMAN
1931–2006

Bronze
Graham Ibbeson
Canal Basin,
Skipton
2010

Cricket attendances may have started to fall as the 1960s progressed but one player continued to capture the public's attention like no other, as he had for most of the 1950s as well: Fred Trueman (1931–2006).

Trueman was born in Stainton just 300 yards from the border with Nottinghamshire – 300 yards of consequence; nobody has been more associated with Yorkshire and Yorkshire cricket. His impact on the game, and people's love of the game, was enormous. When Trueman played, people watched.

His first-class career spanned three decades from his Yorkshire debut in 1949. We include him here as a hero of the 1960s since it was in 1964 at The Oval, with Australia's Neil Hawke being caught at slip after another fiery delivery, that Trueman became the first cricketer to reach 300 wickets in Test matches. This eventually became a career total of 307 wickets at an average of just 21.57 runs each. It would probably have been even more but for several disagreements with the authorities.

Trueman gained more than 2,000 first-class wickets at a miserly average of 18.29 runs each and helped Yorkshire to the championship on six occasions during a period of the county's dominance that he loved. He claimed 100 wickets a season no fewer than 12 times.

Colourful anecdotes about Trueman abound, from the time when the Rev. David Shepherd dropped a catch off his bowling ("You may close your eyes when you're praying but I wish you'd keep them open when I am bowling") to his suggested title for his biography: "The definitive volume on t'finest bloody bowler that ever lived."

Retiring as a player in 1968, he became a lively and knowledgeable media commentator (despite his frequent declarations of apparent astonishment: "I don't know what's going on out there"). He was awarded the OBE in 1989.

Trueman never lost his love of Yorkshire and his belief in its old-fashioned values. It was to Skipton that he retired and where he wished any memorial to stand. He now has his wish. One of the great fast bowlers in history, he is still bowling with menace and style by the canal in Skipton through a larger-than-life-size statue by Barnsley-born sculptor Graham Ibbeson.

The sculpture captures the vigour and excitement as 'Fiery Fred' releases another wicket-bound delivery. It accentuates his flopping hair and the physical power of a bowling action involving, as John Arlott put it, "a belligerent spring in his run ... like a storm-wave breaking on a beach ... followed through with so mighty a heave that the knuckles of his right hand swept the ground". It was "a performance of drama, skill and character which held the attention as few bowlers have ever contrived".

There is, one suspects, just a hint of a knowing smile on his face as the ball hurtles towards the batsman.

"No one seized the public imagination as this dark-haired, brown-eyed, pale-faced, heavy-shouldered Yorkshireman"
John Arlott

COLIN CHAPMAN and JIM CLARK

Lotus and the Quiet Champion

COLIN
CHAPMAN
1928–1982

Bronze
David Annand
Mallory Park
Circuit,
Kirkby Mallory
1998

JIM CLARK
1936–1968

Bronze
David Annand
Kilmany, Fife
1967

The 1960s were vintage years for Britain's standing in motor racing's Formula One. Two figures, bound together in sporting history but with very different personalities, were supreme: Colin Chapman (1928–1982) and Jim Clark (1936–1968). At the entrance to the Mallory Park Circuit in Leicestershire, both are recalled among a fine collection of sculptures, all by Scottish sculptor David Annand, celebrating great British figures from the world of motor racing.

Although not a champion racing driver, immediately recognisable to racing aficionados of the 1960s and 1970s, but perhaps less so to others, is a moustachioed figure in a short-sleeved shirt. Colin Chapman was probably the most influential innovator in the history of British motor racing.

With a degree in civil engineering and a background in the RAF, Chapman was convinced that aeronautical engineering techniques could be applied to the motor racing car. He formed his own company, Lotus Cars, built his own car and raced for a while before developing a team and entering the world of Formula One with extraordinary success.

Chapman, with his team at Lotus, revolutionised Formula One. Major innovations included the design of a full monocoque chassis (a one-shell unibody replacing the previously separate body and frame), using materials and design from aeroplane technology. Aerodynamics were improved through the use of front and rear wings; radiators were moved to the sides away from the front of the car; the driver's position was reclined to reduce drag; and numerous other significant technical improvements were pioneered. Chapman also exploited, dramatically, the opportunities for sponsorship and advertisements.

On the track, Chapman found his perfect partner in driver Jim Clark. Clark was the son of a Scottish farmer, from Kilmany in Fife.

A statue of Jim Clark (right) stands in Kilmany, the village of his birth. Clark chats to Colin Chapman in the pits at Brands Hatch in 1964 (below).

"He just enjoyed driving cars as fast as they could be made to go, and almost without effort he found he was better at it than anyone else"
Murray Walker, on Jim Clark

King George VI Chase in December 1966 (still finishing second). He was in plaster for four months, recovered but never raced again, retiring to his owner's farm at Bryanston in County Kildare. Arthritis set in and, sadly, he was put down at the early age of 13.

In 1971 a less-than-full-size statue of Arkle by Doris Lindner was erected near the paddock at Cheltenham where the great horse reigned supreme. He is still the emperor of all he surveys.

In 2014, on the 50th anniversary of his first Gold Cup success, another statue of Arkle will be unveiled. Sculpted by Emma McDermott, it is planned to grace the main street in Ashbourne, a stone's throw from where the great horse was reared, trained and retired.

To the Irish, Arkle was known simply as Himself. He was a national treasure, one of their own. So Irish that he was reputed to have enjoyed two bottles of Guinness in his feed each night.

ALF RAMSEY

The General

Perhaps the outstanding memory of British sport in the 1960s is England's victory in the football World Cup in 1966. The architect was manager Alf Ramsey (1920–1999). At the moment of the final whistle, fans around the ground cheered and England's bench rose in celebration – except for the still, inscrutable, seated manager.

First, we recall his days at Ipswich Town. A seven-foot-high statue of Ramsey stands close to the entrance to the ground on Portman Road. Born in Dagenham in south-east London, Ramsey had a successful playing career as a stylish right-back with Southampton and then league championship-winning Tottenham. He won 32 caps for England. Retiring as a player in 1955, a new era began as he took over as manager at Ipswich in the lowly Third Division South.

Ramsey guided his unfashionable team to promotion to the Second Division within two years, then four years later to the First Division and, the following year, to the astonishment of nearly all in the football world, straight to the 1961/62 league championship. All achieved without notable stars but based on a solidarity of purpose, team morale, strong work ethic and shrewd tactics.

Ramsey was appointed England manager in 1963 (succeeding the 16-year reign of coach Walter Winterbottom for whom a bronze bust was unveiled in 2013 at the National Football Centre). Ramsey took complete control and fashioned the team to the style that he demanded.

The World Cup was, of course, won by England in 1966 at Wembley in extra-time – Ramsey's exhortation to his players, after West Germany's late equaliser in normal time, receiving, as ever, the loyalty of his team: "You've won it once, now go out and do it again." He remains the only England manager to have won the World Cup.

Ramsey was knighted in 1967. His later years with England were less successful and he was sacked, unceremoniously, upon the failure to qualify for the 1974 World Cup. After a short spell at Birmingham, he retired and returned to live quietly in Ipswich.

Sometimes introverted, stubborn, unsmiling but with a firm and focused gaze, Ramsey was 'the General' (his nickname as a player). A portrait statue of Ramsey is away from public view at Wembley. It is the full-size statue at Portman Road by Sean Hedges-Quinn (himself a long-time Ipswich fan), unveiled in 2002 nearly 40 years after Ramsey's league championship triumph, that captures the focus and sense of authority of the man.

Alf Ramsey is relaxed, with his left hand gently in his pocket, formally suited, tie perfectly in place. Bobby Charlton, present at the unveiling, remarked: "If Alf was trying to explain something or there was a point he was trying to make that he didn't want you to forget, that was the look he had ... spot on."

The statue is a well-known landmark for supporters in Ipswich. "Meet me at Sir Alf."

ALF RAMSEY
1920–1999

Bronze
Sean Hedges-Quinn
Portman Road,
Ipswich
2002

"Alf made us proud to wear the England shirt"
Alan Ball

BOBBY MOORE

England's Captain

BOBBY MOORE
1941–1993

Bronze
Philip Jackson
Wembley Stadium,
Wembley,
London
2007

On the pitch, England's captain for Alf Ramsey was Bobby Moore (1941–1993). Moore holding the World Cup aloft at Wembley on July 30 1966 is one of the enduring images in football. When he climbed the steps to the Royal Box, millions on television saw him stop and wipe his hands on the velvet cloth before shaking hands with the Queen. He was football's English gentleman.

Born and brought up in London's East End, Moore's promise was recognised early by West Ham – a club with a growing reputation, under Ron Greenwood, for cultured football and a fine academy for developing young talent. Moore shone and was soon made club captain. He played 642 games for West Ham. Appointed also as England's captain in 1963, at just 22 – one of Ramsey's earliest decisions – he was the manager's general on the pitch. With a total of 108 England caps, he was captain an astonishing 91 times.

As a defender, Moore's defining characteristic was his ability to read the play and anticipate danger or the right move. Moore always looked for the creative option. With barely a minute to go in the 1966 World Cup final, England were clinging to a one-goal lead and spectators were on the pitch. ("They think it's all over.") Moore received the ball outside

"My captain, my leader, my right-hand man.
He was the spirit and the heartbeat of the team"
Alf Ramsey

BOBBY MOORE
continued

England's penalty area and team-mates, along with most in the crowd, screamed for him to boot it into the stands. No, Moore had seen a 40-yard pass into space for Geoff Hurst ... and history. ("It is now.")

Moore was not particularly quick nor a strong header of the ball. "I don't think he wanted to spoil his hair," joked Greenwood. Sometimes his club form lacked an extra drive brought out by the big occasions but, according to Greenwood, "when the bugle sounded he would always find another 20 per cent". He left West Ham for Fulham in 1974 and retired in 1978 after a short period in US soccer. He was sadly struck down by cancer and died in 1993, aged just 51. His reputation is undiminished and, indeed, his stature grew even more as England failed to repeat those glory days of 1966.

A stunning, twice-life-size sculpture by Philip Jackson was unveiled by Sir Bobby Charlton at the new Wembley Stadium when it was opened in 2007. Still evoking an image of grace and control, ball under his foot, arms folded and a steely gaze, Bobby Moore now looks down from the front of Wembley Stadium over Wembley Way with Caesar-like style. Around the plinth are outlines of all the members of the 1966 England team, with Moore still firmly at the helm.

Relief work on Bobby Moore's sculpture at Wembley reflects his leadership of England (above). The inscription on the sculpture of the cap (below) reads 'World Championship Jules Rimet Cup 1966'.

MARTIN PETERS, GEOFF HURST, RAY WILSON and JIMMY ARMFIELD

Across in east London, close to West Ham's Upton Park ground, another splendid eight-foot-high work (right) by Philip Jackson, unveiled in 2003, celebrates the contribution of West Ham's golden trio to that World Cup victory: Martin Peters (1943–), still cool and a little distant from the others, hat-trick hero Geoff Hurst (1941–) and Bobby Moore holding the Jules Rimet trophy on high.

The only non-West Ham player of the four, left-back Ray Wilson (1934–), has his fist clenched. At the time, his face was in a grimace (bearing the weight of Moore on his shoulder) but the sculptor allowed himself one change from reality: Wilson now bears a smile.

The sculpture stands on circular steps, easily accessible on a main street. Young children inspect with curiosity. Their fathers tell them of that day in 1966.

Still in the England squad for the 1966 World Cup finals was former captain Jimmy Armfield (1935–). One of Blackpool's greatest players, he is celebrated at their ground through a nine-foot-tall statue by sculptor Les Johnson, unveiled in 2011.

Jimmy Armfield and Geoff Hurst are also found together (with Italy's Simone Perrotta from a later era) in an imaginative sculpture by Andrew Edwards unveiled in 2010 in Ashton-under-Lyne, on the outskirts of Manchester. (Armfield is on the left, Hurst on the right.) The work is part of Tameside council's project to honour local figures through public sculpture. The reason? All three are players, born in the area, who have gone on to win World Cup winners' medals.

World Cup winners Jimmy Armfield, Geoff Hurst and Simone Perrotta – all born in the local area – are commemorated in a sculpture in Ashton-under-Lyne (left). Near Upton Park, Martin Peters, Hurst and Ray Wilson celebrate with captain Bobby Moore (right).

JIM BAXTER

Slim Jim

Football has enjoyed a long tradition of fervent support in Scotland. Since the earliest days of soccer in the 19th century, Scotland has prided itself on playing the 'dribbling game' with emphasis on skill and passing.

No matches have been greeted with more fervour than those against the 'auld enemy'. Successes have been occasions for national celebration. The 'Wembley Wizards' of Scotland's 5–1 win at Wembley in 1928 attained legendary status. It was, therefore, a triumphant day at Wembley in April 1967 when Scotland won 3–1 against an England team that, less than a year earlier, had been crowned world champions on the same pitch.

A symbol, and midfield architect, of that glorious Scottish victory in 1967 was Jim Baxter (1939–2001). Alex Ferguson said that his performance could have been "set to music".

Born in the small mining village of Hill O'Beath in Fife, Baxter joined Raith Rovers as a part-timer. After two years of national service, he was signed up by Glasgow Rangers in 1960. He was a clear talent, an attacking left-half with left-foot skills of which others could only dream, a tactical vision for the telling pass and a confidence that could lift a team.

He was 'Slim Jim'. His five years with Rangers were years of dominance for the club. Honours included winning three Scottish league championships. For Scotland, he won 34 caps and was only once on the losing side against England.

The Scotland team was blessed with players such as Dave Mackay, Paddy Crerand, John White, Denis Law ... and Baxter. Perhaps his best international performance was actually in 1963 when Scotland defeated England 2–1 at Wembley despite being reduced to 10 men. Baxter was superb and scored both of Scotland's goals. The following year, Scotland beat England 1–0 at Hampden Park. Baxter was man of the match.

He was a talent whose best years were spent (too early) by his mid-twenties. Drink and other temptations, particularly after a period out of the game with a broken leg, affected his fitness. He tried to make a fresh start at Sunderland, and then Nottingham Forest, before a return spell at Rangers. The spells of brilliance were fewer and the 'slim' look had gone.

Yet, on that day at Wembley in April 1967, the swivel of the hips, the caress of the ball with the left foot, the moments of ball-juggling and the midfield dominance in the Scottish blue – they were all there again. With Baxter playing 'keepy uppy' with the ball, taunting the English to the roars of the Scots, Geoffrey Green, in *The Times*, described him as "reducing the tempo to a walking pace while he teased the wounded bull like a matador".

Jim Baxter died of cancer in 2001 aged 61. Two years later, a life-size statue by Andy Scott was unveiled in Baxter's home town of Hill O'Beath. Baxter is still a Scottish icon. Here, in his home town, the ball is still being caressed by that magical left foot.

JIM BAXTER
1939–2001

Bronze
Andy Scott
Hill O'Beath, Fife
2003

"Treat the ball like a woman; give it a cuddle, caress it a wee bit, take your time, and you'll get the required response"
Jim Baxter

JOCK STEIN

The Big Man

JOCK STEIN
1922–1985

Bronze
John McKenna
Celtic Park,
Glasgow
2011

If 1966 had been England's year in football, 1967 certainly belonged to Scotland. The national team's victory over England at Wembley in April was followed six weeks later by a triumphant night for a Scottish club in Lisbon. No manager has attained more revered status in Scotland than Jock Stein (1922–1985).

"Right, lads. You've made history. Go out and enjoy yourselves." Stein, manager of Celtic, the first British side to play in the European Cup final, gave his last instructions to his team as they went out on that warm Lisbon evening on May 25 1967 to take on the Italian champions, Inter Milan.

Within six minutes, Celtic were 1–0 down to a penalty. The Scottish side responded with a relentless display of attacking football. Wave after wave of attack. The famous (or infamous) Inter Milan defensive wall – the *catenaccio* – held firm. Twice the crossbar was hit but the goal would not come. Then, deep into the second half, the ball swept into the path of attacking left-back Tommy Gemmell to strike, stunningly, an equaliser from outside the penalty area. More attacks and, just five minutes from the end of normal time, Celtic scored the winner through Steve Chalmers. The jubilation in Scotland was as great as for the victory at Wembley just weeks earlier.

It was a great moment for Stein. After a strong playing career with Celtic (including captaining the club as it won its first post-war Scottish league championship),

injuries in 1956 forced his retirement. A few years later, a managerial career began at Dunfermline. Celtic came calling in March 1965. It was a momentous decision – not least because Stein became the club's first protestant manager. His charisma and man-management skills revitalised the team after a barren period. Scottish titles were regained. In the glorious year of 1967, Celtic won the domestic treble for the first time in the club's history – and then became European Cup champions.

Stein, awarded the CBE in 1970, was badly injured in a car crash in 1975 and, if reluctantly, stood down as Celtic manager. After a 44-day spell in charge of Leeds United (extraordinarily, the same length as the reign of Brian Clough that had ended four years earlier), he was appointed full-time manager of Scotland in 1978 and led them to the 1982 World Cup. Scotland were on course again in 1985 for qualification for the next World Cup finals in Mexico. It was during a qualifying match at Ninian Park against Wales that 62-year-old Stein, forever urging his team, suffered a fatal heart attack near the end of the game.

To mark the 25th anniversary of his death in 2010, a statue of Celtic's great manager, by Scottish sculptor John McKenna, was proudly unveiled the following year outside the entrance to the stadium. Stein is holding the huge European trophy. He will forever be regarded as the 'Big Man' – big in heart and stature and big in the history of football for that glorious night in Lisbon.

"We did it by playing football. Pure, beautiful, inventive football"
Jock Stein

BOBBY CHARLTON DENIS LAW and GEORGE BEST

The United Trinity

BOBBY
CHARLTON
1937–
DENIS LAW
1940–
GEORGE BEST
1946–2005

Bronze
Philip Jackson
Sir Matt Busby
Way, Old Trafford,
Manchester
2008

Across from the main entrance to Old Trafford, Matt Busby now faces three of his finest players from the late 1960s. An imposing statue (also sculpted by Philip Jackson) stands to celebrate that team and, in particular, the magical trio of Bobby Charlton, Denis Law and George Best: 'the United Trinity'.

The unveiling ceremony, in May 2008, took place three years after the death of George Best and exactly 40 years (to the day) after Manchester United lifted the European Cup for the first time.

Charlton, Law and Best are revered in the history of the Red Devils. Each won the coveted European Player of the Year award during the period from 1964 to 1968. They represent, in Charlton's words, the "colour and excitement" that Busby sought from his team.

Bobby Charlton (1937–) was the oldest. Making his debut as an 18-year-old in 1956 and fitting into the championship-winning side of 1956/57, he was in the 'Busby Babes' team (he scored twice in Belgrade) that suffered the horror of the Munich disaster. Charlton, injured, survived and became integral to the team's rebuilding.

A glorious playing career with the club brought (in terms of honours) three league championship titles, an FA Cup winner's medal and 100 caps for England with a record 49 goals (two against Portugal in the World Cup semi-final of 1966 at Wembley are instantly recalled). At first an inside-forward and then moving to the left-wing, he became essentially a deep-lying centre-forward-cum-midfielder, a position that suited him and the team perfectly. The image of Bobby Charlton advancing to the penalty area and unleashing a fiercely-struck shot from distance is a compelling memory.

"Bobby Charlton embodies to me what being great really is"
Alex Ferguson

BOBBY CHARLTON
DENIS LAW and
GEORGE BEST

continued

It has been said that, for a decade or more, four words in the English language could be understood by more people, anywhere around the globe, than any others: "Bobby Charlton, Manchester United."

Denis Law (1940–) was a record signing in 1962 by Busby and critical to the rebuilding of United. Full of aggression and agility, with a keen sense of opportunity, the Scot was a born goalscorer. A frail-looking youth, his playing background is sometimes forgotten. Law played for Huddersfield and Manchester City before leaving, one of a band of British players (Jimmy Greaves was another) to be tempted by the riches of Italian football, for Turin. He found it "a prison for a footballer".

Law was snapped up by Busby and became a United legend. Injured at the time of the European Cup final, he was nevertheless the team's key striker. So often he would score a seemingly simple goal, a short sharp strike or header, followed by the trademark celebration – captured here in this statue – the arm in the air, hand clutching his sleeve, finger pointing to the sky. Denis Law was the pioneer of the distinctive goal celebration.

George Best (1946–2005), the mercurial Irishman, was the youngest and perhaps the most gifted of the trio. Combining speed, balance, vision, courage and strength with either foot, he was a winger with a striker's eye for goal. His exploits (on and off the field) were legendary. On the field, none more so than in 1966 in the quarter-final of the European Cup. The Reds were defending a slender 3–2 lead from the first leg in the return match against a Eusebio-led Benfica in Lisbon.

Busby recalled: "Our plan was to be cautious, but somebody must have stuffed cotton wool in George's ears." Within 10 minutes, Best had destroyed Benfica with two goals – one a mazy run from the halfway line.

Best became the first celebrity icon of British football in a television age – succumbing, sadly, to an extravagant and debilitating lifestyle for the tempted. It was a sign of things to come; the time when the life of a star footballer changed. Best could not cope and the influence of Busby could no longer restrain him. The great years were gone. He left United at 27. The demons of alcohol had taken over, and a liver transplant failed to stem years of abuse.

Best died in 2005 aged 59. Perhaps only now are we again able, with joy, to recall those times of utter brilliance from one of football's most talented players.

In Belfast, George Best remains an iconic figure for the Northern Irish. In Manchester, Philip Jackson's fine statue brilliantly represents not only a tribute to three of United's finest but a tribute to a team, a style and a magic that were the best of the 1960s.

Three of the all-time greats of the Red Devils: Bobby Charlton (above left), Denis Law (above middle) and George Best (above right), and (preceding page) all together in 2000 after receiving lifetime achievement awards.

"Maradona good. Pelé better. George Best"
Irish saying

ANGELA MORTIMER and ANN JONES

Wimbledon Winners

ANGELA
MORTIMER
1932–
and
ANN JONES
1938–

Bronze
Ian Rank-Broadley
All England Club,
Wimbledon,
London
2004

Tennis was a sport in which women were playing an increasingly prominent role – whether in participation, spectator support or competitive play. Kitty Godfree had set the way at Wimbledon's new Centre Court in the 1920s and Dorothy Round was a winner in 1934, the same year as Fred Perry's first victory, and 1937. It was not until the 1960s, though, that another British winner came along – and then there were two of them.

In 1961, there was even an all-British ladies' final at Wimbledon with Devon's determined Angela Mortimer (1932–) edging out Essex's Christine Truman in a tense three-set final. Mortimer's fine driving groundstrokes, astute play and determination had won two previous Grand Slam titles – the French Championships in 1955 and the Australian title in 1958. Losing finalist in 1958, her Wimbledon victory in 1961, at 29, was her finest moment.

Another British player who won the French Championships, a gruelling event on the slow clay courts of Paris, was Warwickshire's Ann Jones (1938–), or Ann Haydon as she then was. She won the French Grand Slam title in 1961 and again in 1966 to establish herself as one of the most consistent and leading players of her day.

Her formative sport, as for Perry in the 1930s, had been table tennis – a fast-growing sport in post-war Britain – and Haydon became national champion and a finalist in the world championships. It was on the world tennis stage, though, that she became most well-known.

A long career in the upper echelon of the game (she reached a world ranking of number 2) culminated in 1969 when, at the age of 30 and by then married, she achieved her Wimbledon singles triumph – defeating two of the world's greatest players in the process, Australia's Margaret Court in the semi-final and American Billie-Jean King, the holder, in the final. Determined and skilful, it was her 14th challenge for the title and her finest triumph.

For the curious-minded, Ann Jones became the first left-handed woman to win the Wimbledon title.

"Ann Jones gave British lawn tennis one of its finest moments"
Lance Tingay

Ann Jones seals victory in the 1969 Wimbledon final (left). Angela Mortimer (above) and Jones (above right) are commemorated in bronze in front of the Centre Court.

Tennis had gone 'open' in 1968. No longer was Wimbledon barred to professionals. 'Shamateurism' was over. The world's best men's player, Australia's Rod Laver, could again compete – and win. Jones was amongst the first women to take advantage of the new regime, joining King and others to form the first professional female touring group in tennis as well as playing in the Grand Slam championships.

Jones became the second female winner at Wimbledon in the 'open' era.

Bronze head-and-shoulders portraits of Britain's post-1922 ladies' champions, sculpted by Ian Rank-Broadley, now stand against the backdrop of the ivy-clad frontage of Wimbledon's Centre Court. They include, proudly, Britain's two Wimbledon winners of the 1960s – Angela Mortimer and Ann Jones.

CHAPTER SIX

HEROES OF THE SEVENTIES

As the 1960s moved into the 1970s, Liverpool and Leeds continued their sustained battle at the top of English football – punctuated by Arsenal's double-winning triumph of 1971. The World Cup victory of 1966 would not be repeated in 1970, although England's campaign in Mexico left many memories. The FA Cup was still highly popular throughout the country and the 1970s produced memorable upsets.

Strong British managers continued to inspire the leading football teams and the decade saw, at their best, many figures whose reigns will last in sporting memory. Off the pitch, the tragedy at Ibrox Stadium in 1971 would, devastatingly, be just one of a series of stadium disasters over the next two decades.

In rugby union, the Five Nations Championship enjoyed great popularity – aided by the attraction of colour television (first introduced into sport at Wimbledon in 1967). The late 1960s and the early 1970s were years of success for the Welsh rugby team with players worthy of the rugby gods. No greater smile was enjoyed throughout Northern Ireland, and Britain as a whole, than that of Mary Peters in 1972 winning Olympic gold in the pentathlon in Munich.

The 1970s were also golden years for horse-racing. Outstanding thoroughbreds created tales that would be celebrated in racing history. As ever, it was another decade of triumph for Britain's greatest post-war jockey, Lester Piggott. On the motor racing tracks (motorcycle and Formula One) there were both triumphs and sadness.

A number of the leading sporting figures of the era are no longer alive – some suffering the poignancy of an early death. Others recalled in bronze are still very much with us. If televised sport and sponsorship brought greater financial rewards and celebrity status (some would say, too easily) to leading sportsmen, it is notable – and warming – that sculptures and memorials recall figures from this decade whose substance, character and enthusiasm represent the best in sport.

GORDON BANKS

A Hero Who Could Fly

GORDON BANKS
1937–

Bronze maquette
Andrew Edwards
2011

A first memory of the 1970s is a moment of supreme sporting skill.

England, world champions, were playing against Brazil in Mexico in the 1970 World Cup. It was still 0–0. The flowing Brazilian attack surged forward. Jairzinho beat a defender on the right and crossed. Pelé, at the back post, rose imperiously and a goal seemed certain. Scuttling back from the near post, Gordon Banks (1937–) dived down and slightly backwards as the ball headed for the net. Astonishingly, his outstretched hand scooped the ball upwards from the line and over the bar. Banks himself said: "As soon as I got my hand to it, I thought it was going in the top corner. But after I'd landed, I looked up and saw the ball bounce behind the net and that's when I said: 'Banksy, you lucky prat'."

England would eventually lose 1–0, and later depart in the quarter-final after throwing away a 2–0 lead against West Germany, but a lasting memory remained of an extraordinary moment of skill.

Born in Sheffield and playing for Leicester City, Banks became England's first-choice goalkeeper under Alf Ramsey and a rock in the England team under Ramsey that won the 1966 World Cup. Seventy-three England caps in total – and only nine times on the losing side; just 57 goals conceded, a miserly average per game. Safe as Banks of England. He was awarded the OBE in 1970.

Later joining Stoke City (for whom he played 246 games out of his total 703 English club appearances), he became an 'adopted son' of Stoke. A statue, by local sculptor Andrew Edwards, now stands in a local school near Stoke – perhaps drawing some jealousy from fans at Leicester City. The sculpture shows Banks holding the Jules Rimet trophy high after England's 1966 triumph. A second statue by Edwards is planned. A maquette commemorates Banks in action with two of his memorable saves including that glorious moment in the 1970 World Cup.

These works have their own special story. Banks was the inspiration for an Irish fan, Don Mullan, who wrote a book, *A Hero Who Could Fly*, a personal life-story explaining how a scrapbook of Banks' career had helped Mullan overcome dyslexia and, even more significantly, led him away from a life of violence into which he was in danger of being drawn in those troubled times in Northern Ireland. An inscription on the plinth of the first sculpture is taken from Don

A maquette (above) by Andrew Edwards reflects two great saves by Gordon Banks, including 'that save' against Brazil in 1970 (left).

"I had already began to celebrate the goal ... I couldn't believe it hadn't gone in" *Pelé*

A statue of Gordon Banks holding aloft the Jules Rimet trophy stands in Madeley School in Stoke (right) to the pleasure of local children.

Mullan's book: "... across the water, on a neighbouring island with whom we Irish had been at war for centuries, I had a hero who could fly. His name is GORDON BANKS. From being a timid, fearful young boy he taught me that impossible doesn't exist. Unknown to him he helped save a young fan from making choices that had brought too much sorrow and sadness to Irish and British alike. Who knows? Perhaps it was his best save ever."

The sculpture was unveiled in 2008. It was a key symbol of a charity event, a 'Celebration of Peace through Sport', and the unveiling was attended not only by Gordon Banks and his family, but also by Pelé himself and South Africa's Archbishop Desmond Tutu. Sport can be a force for peace.

JOHN GREIG

The Ibrox Disaster

JOHN GREIG
1942–

Bronze
Andy Scott
Ibrox Stadium,
Glasgow
2001

Football experienced, horribly, a series of stadium disasters in the 1970s and 1980s.

Ibrox Stadium in Glasgow was the tragic scene in 1971. Now, a statue of John Greig (1942–), a figure bearing dignity but with a slightly furrowed brow, stands at Ibrox. He is wearing an armband. Voted in 1999 by the club's supporters as 'the greatest-ever Ranger', Greig made 755 appearances for the club, won 44 Scottish caps and was captain of Rangers when the team won the European Cup Winners' Cup in 1972.

Greig was also captain in January 1971 for the 'Old Firm' derby at Ibrox. The atmosphere was intense. It was 0–0 for 89 minutes and then Jimmy Johnstone scored to put Celtic in the lead. Many Rangers supporters turned for the exits. They missed Colin Stein's equaliser in the last moments of stoppage time. There was confusion, excitement and pressure amongst the crowd as the game ended. Had many turned back at the roar? Did someone stumble and fall, bringing others down behind? Was it the packed pressure of people leaving and giving rise to a crushing concertina of bodies and injury?

At the exit by stairway 13, a notorious bottle-neck, the pressure was too great. Heavy steel barriers twisted and were mangled out of shape under the weight and pressure of the exiting crowd. Bodies were crushed. Sixty-six people died and hundreds were injured.

The memories of football stadium disasters carry a heavy and shocking resonance. The loss of life, when people have come simply to enjoy themselves at a game, seems totally incongruous.

On the 30th anniversary of the tragedy, a memorial monument was unveiled to honour the victims. Blue plaques display the names of persons killed in 1971 and in two fatal incidents at Ibrox in previous years. Every year, at the home game closest to the date of the disaster, the club lays a special wreath at the memorial.

The statue of John Greig stands atop the monument. The work of sculptor Andy Scott, assisted by Alison Bell, it is a recognition of a fine and dignified player but also, and more, a symbol of permanent commemoration of a tragedy. Greig is facing to his left – towards the corner exit where the tragedy occurred.

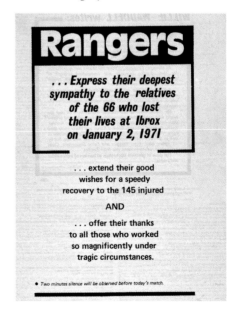

Rangers

. . . *Express their deepest sympathy to the relatives of the 66 who lost their lives at Ibrox on January 2, 1971*

. . . extend their good wishes for a speedy recovery to the 145 injured

AND

. . . offer their thanks to all those who worked so magnificently under tragic circumstances.

● *Two minutes silence will be observed before today's match.*

An announcement in the Rangers match programme after the 1971 disaster.

"It's something that will never leave me. It's etched on my mind"
John Greig

LESTER PIGGOTT

The Long Fellow

LESTER PIGGOTT
1935–

Bronze
William Newton
Haydock Park
Racecourse,
Newton-le-Willows
2005

The 1970s were magical years for racing on the Flat. One rider continued to dominate public attention and affection, as for two previous decades and years to follow, like no other. Four of his nine Derby victories came in this decade. Lester Piggott (1935–) is probably the greatest Flat jockey of all time.

Near the entrance to Haydock Park racecourse, a sculpture pays tribute to this icon of the sport. It originated from the wish of Piggott's wife, Susan, to mark his 70th birthday. She commissioned a small bronze from William Newton, a former jockey, to illustrate the span of Lester Piggott's extraordinary career – showing him riding both his first winner, The Chase, as a 12-year-old boy in 1948, and his last winner, Palace Gate Jack, in 1994 when aged 58. Both winners were at Haydock Park. The resulting work was shown to those in charge at Haydock Park

and a larger, one-third life-size sculpture of Piggott was promptly commissioned. It is appropriately entitled 'From Start to Finish'.

Lower in the saddle in his sensational teenage years, his early riding style contrasts dramatically with the distinctive high bottom-in-the-air style of his adulthood to counter his 5ft 8ins height – tall for a jockey (hence his nickname the 'Long Fellow'). His record is astonishing. He rode, in the words of Peter O'Sullevan, with "an obsessive, single-minded thirst for winners", achieving more than 4,000 winners domestically and, worldwide, more than 5,300 in over 30 countries. These included 30 Classic victories in England alone and he was champion jockey 11 times.

His Derby winners are a roll-call of great racehorses: Never Say Die (1954), Crepello (1957), St Paddy (1960), Sir Ivor (1968), Nijinsky (1970), Roberto (1972), Empery (1976), The Minstrel (1977) and Teenoso (1983). The Lester Piggott Gates at Epsom, dedicated in 1996, incorporate paintings (by artist Roy Miller) that commemorate the legendary jockey's triumphs in the blue riband of Flat racing.

The son of a successful National Hunt jockey and trainer, Piggott was born to racing. His first Derby winner came at the age of just 18. He had, and often chose, the best rides – but he was given them because he was the best. For the public, his very presence gave excitement to any race. For racing connoisseurs, he combined the best of racing skills.

"No jockey has exercised a greater hold on the imagination of the sporting public" *Peter O'Sullevan*

Off the track, Piggott failed to declare his full racing income to the Inland Revenue. Sentenced in 1987 to three years in jail, he served just more than a year in prison. He was, though, stripped of his OBE.

Piggott astonished most by returning to the track in 1990 as a jockey at the age of 54. Less than two weeks after picking up the reins again, he won a famous victory on Royal Academy in America's prestigious Breeders' Cup Mile. It was one of sport's greatest comebacks. Even Lester Piggott, once memorably described as having a face "like a well-kept grave", found a smile.

VINCENT O'BRIEN
and NIJINSKY

Michael Vincent O'Brien (1917–2009) was, for very many, the greatest racehorse trainer of the 20th century. The quiet Irishman, with an acute eye for the truly promising yearling and a relentless pursuit of perfection, built training stables at Ballydoyle in County Tipperary without equal in the British Isles.

His first great horse was steeplechaser Cottage Rake whom he trained to victory three times in the Cheltenham Gold Cup. Three Grand National winners in succession, three Champion Hurdles and many other successes in National Hunt followed before he turned to concentrate on Flat racing with unprecedented success. He trained the winners of the Epsom Derby on six occasions between 1962 and 1982, along with 10 other English Classics, 27 Irish Classics and three Prix de l'Arc de Triomphes. Asked to place O'Brien in racing's pantheon, Lester Piggott simply said: "Of course Vincent was the greatest – look at the figures."

In the 1970s, O'Brien and owner Robert Sangster, with son-in-law John Magnier, established the Coolmore syndicate as a successful racing and breeding operation. O'Brien's ability to pick world-class

yearling colts and train them to perfection at Ballydoyle led to multiple Classic and other major triumphs – and the successful horses would then stand at the Coolmore Stud to be syndicated as stallions.

In Canada in 1968 O'Brien, acting for a wealthy American owner, spotted a yearling son of the then unproved stallion, Northern Dancer. The colt was Nijinsky. Ridden by Piggott, a principal jockey for Ballydoyle during the great years of the late 1960s and 1970s, Nijinsky made history in 1970 by winning the Triple Crown (2000 Guineas, Derby and St Leger) amidst other victories. The fabulous bloodline of Northern Dancer was a key to success for Coolmore and Nijinsky himself later became a top-class sire.

O'Brien retired in 1994, exactly 50 years after his first victory as a trainer. Ballydoyle was formally taken over by the Coolmore Stud. In the nearby village of Rosegreen, a statue of Vincent O'Brien by Jim Connolly reminds visitors of the great man with his gentle smile and firm authority.

Inside the perfectly-maintained grounds of Ballydoyle, a glorious sculpture of Nijinsky by Emma MacDermott shimmers in the sunlight.

Vincent O'Brien (above left) built Ballydoyle as world-leading stables where Nijinsky now shimmers gloriously in bronze (above).

MILL REEF and BRIGADIER GERARD

Newmarket in May 1971 hosted one of the finest-ever Classic races. The 2000 Guineas featured two of the decade's great thoroughbreds, Mill Reef and Brigadier Gerard, as well as the strongly-backed My Swallow – between the three horses, they had won 18 out of 19 of their races; My Swallow and Mill Reef were the most highly-rated but it was Brigadier Gerard, ridden by Joe Mercer, who burst clear for an emphatic three-length win.

Mill Reef (1968–1986) would never again be beaten. The little horse proceeded as a three-year-old to an unprecedented year of success in 1971. He won six successive Group One races including a magical quartet of the Derby, the Eclipse Stakes, the King George VI & Queen Elizabeth Stakes and the Prix de l'Arc de Triomphe. Ridden throughout his racing career by Geoff Lewis, Mill Reef won the affection of the British public to a degree achieved by few other horses. He later became one of the most successful stallions at the National Stud in Newmarket, including siring two Derby winners. Mill Reef is commemorated at the National Stud with a statue by leading equine sculptor John Skeaping.

Brigadier Gerard (1968–1989), named after Arthur Conan Doyle's swashbuckling hero, was owned by John Hislop and trained throughout his career by Major Dick Hern. He would prove unbeatable as a miler. Carefully raced, avoiding the soft going where he struggled to find top form, the Brigadier won a staggering 15 straight victories with an impeccable record at distances between five furlongs and a mile and a quarter, finishing with 17 wins out of 18 starts. The Brigadier was one of the best and most popular of all thoroughbreds.

The one blemish on his record came, as a four-year-old, when he was defeated in the Benson & Hedges Gold Cup at York over a mile and a quarter. Yet the Brigadier recovered to finish his career winning the Queen Elizabeth II Stakes and the Champion Stakes before retiring to stud.

Regarded as one of the great milers of the 20th century, Brigadier Gerard is celebrated – fittingly at the Rowley Course at Newmarket, the scene of that Classic victory in 1970 – through a life-size statue, appropriately also by John Skeaping, which stands in front of the pre-parade ring. The Brigadier continues to exude power and confidence.

Two great horses celebrated in bronze at Newmarket: Mill Reef (above left) and Brigadier Gerard (above).

RED RUM

The Nation's Favourite

RED RUM
1965–1995

Bronze
Philip Blacker
Aintree
Racecourse,
Liverpool
1988

Racing memories of the 1970s were not confined to the Flat. The jumps produced an equine legend – as famous as any horse ever. Red Rum (1965–1995) became, in 1977, the first horse to win the Grand National three times (and he was runner-up on the other two occasions he raced).

The story of Red Rum is full of romance. Born in Ireland, he was bred to be a sprinter on the Flat – actually dead-heating in his first race, coincidentally at Liverpool. After a change of owners, he started to race as a steeplechaser. He was spotted in the 1972 Scottish Grand National (where he finished fifth) by Ginger McCain, a taxi-driver with a small stable in Southport close to the sands, who recommended him to owner Noel Le Mare in his search for a potential horse for the Grand National. But Red Rum suffered from weak bones and appeared lame. McCain had the answer; regular gallops

in the shallow, salt-water surf of the sea at Southport transformed Red Rum.

Then came the Grand National of 1973. Red Rum, aged eight and ridden by Brian Fletcher, was 20 lengths or more behind the favourite Crisp. The sporting nation gasped, many with sadness, as the valiant Crisp slowed and was caught in a dramatic finish by Red Rum. Red Rum won again, triumphantly, in 1974 despite giving weight to dual Cheltenham Gold Cup winner L'Escargot. Could Red Rum win the National an unprecedented third time? Runner-up in both 1975 and 1976, it seemed that the story had ended. But the fairy-tale did continue. The 12-year-old, ridden now by Tommy Stack, had one further attempt and that glorious third victory was achieved in 1977.

Retired after his 1977 triumph, Red Rum continued to enjoy the public spotlight, opening the Blackpool lights and leading the parade at Aintree on many emotion-filled occasions. He died in 1995, at the age of 30, and is buried facing the winning post at Aintree. His death was front-page news.

A majestic statue at Aintree ensures that, at the home of the Grand National (whose fortunes he revived with attendances increasing dramatically), Red Rum continues to be in the public eye. It was the first full-size equine sculpture by Philip Blacker – himself a successful former jockey. It captures a sense of vitality and movement. The sculptor wanted, in his design, to reflect the great racehorse revelling on the beach at Southport.

"It's hats off and a tremendous reception. You've never heard one like it before at Liverpool. Red Rum wins the National for the third time" *Peter O'Sullevan*

Red Rum and trainer Ginger McCain together (far left) after winning the 1977 Grand National and in bronze at Aintree (above and right).

"The horse would be up on his toes ... jig-jogging, slightly sideways. His mane and tail would be blowing free, as if he were out on the sands, and his head and neck would be held in that unmistakeable pose, high and outstretched."

A portrait bust of Ginger McCain, sculpted by Nigel Boonham, was unveiled in 2012 at Aintree by the parade ring – just a short distance from the statue of the great horse he trained to glory.

Red Rum is still in the limelight at Aintree. Sport and art combined magnificently.

MARY PETERS

Irish Eyes are Smiling

MARY PETERS
1939–

Bronze
John Sherlock
Monsalto House,
Belfast
2009

Mary Peters gives
her all in the long
jump on her way to
pentathlon gold in
Munich (below left).

The biggest and warmest smile of the decade came at the 1972 Olympic Games in Munich. Mary Peters (1939–) became the pride of Northern Ireland, and indeed the whole of Britain, when she won the gold medal in the pentathlon at the 1972 Olympic Games in Munich – the only British athletics gold medal of the Games.

It was a triumph for the tenacity and courage of the 33-year-old Ulsterwoman, now an athletics 'veteran'. She fought off the challenge of the local German star Heidi Rosendahl in two days of tension. Peters had built up a good lead on the first day after the 100 metres hurdles, shot put and the high jump. On the second day, nervously, her lead was cut following the long jump. The gold medal position came down to the final event, the 200 metres, Rosendhal's best event. The German, a top-class sprinter, duly won but an arm-pumping, lung-bursting effort by Peters, stretched to the limit, produced a fourth place and a personal best time. Peters had won the gold medal by just 10 points,

4,801 points to 4,791, a world record. One-tenth of a second slower and the medal would have been silver. The smile of Mary Peters lifted a nation.

The win was overshadowed the following day when 11 Israeli athletes and officials were killed in the Olympic village by Palestinian terrorists. Yet, the memory of that victory smile lives on.

Born actually in Lancashire, Mary Peters moved with her parents to Belfast when she was 11. These became severely violent and troubled times in Northern Ireland. Peters trained in a local gym fortified to keep out the bombers. Her victory led to a popularity that has never waned. She was BBC Sports Personality of the Year in 1972 and awarded the MBE in 1973. Her later work for both sport and charity led to her becoming a Dame in 2000 and in 2009 she was appointed Lord Lieutenant of Belfast. Few athletes have been held in higher regard throughout the land.

Her triumph and smile are now recorded through a splendid sculpture by John Sherlock (on loan, at the time of photography, in the fine surroundings of Monsalto House near Belfast but awaiting a fixed home). Another statue, by the same sculptor, is planned for the athletic track in south Belfast named after Ireland's Dame.

Such was the joy on that special day in 1972 that the violence in Belfast came to a temporary halt as all shared in the celebration. Mary Peters has continued to bridge the sectarian chasm and to show that great sport, and a great sportswoman, can bring people together.

"There is no feeling on earth like standing on that Olympic rostrum, hearing the anthem, and knowing that you have achieved something beyond your wildest dreams" *Mary Peters*

ALEX HIGGINS

Another future star grew up in Belfast in a very different sport – hustling at the snooker tables of local working men's clubs: Alex Higgins (1949–2010).

The few leading professionals of the time, with their waistcoats and bow-ties, presented an urbane image and the game's popularity had dwindled. Two happenings changed everything. The BBC found that snooker presented well on colour television. A new mass audience, and not just male, was ready to be discovered. Then along came 'the Hurricane'. In 1972, one year after turning professional, Higgins defeated the pre-match favourite John Spencer to become world champion. Edgy, jiggling with adrenalin or alcohol, he played with speed, certainty and boldness. The sport exploded in popularity.

He was the 'people's champion'. He would only once more, in 1982, win the world title. His fortunes quickly declined and drunken outbursts increased. Later diagnosed with throat cancer, he died in sheltered housing.

Off the Donegall Road in Belfast, at his local pub, a painted mural (below) recalls the young, mercurial Hurricane of the 1970s with his distinctive cueing stance as if ready to play one, two, three shots ahead. Not far away is a pint of Guinness.

JOHN CURRY

Nureyev of the Ice

JOHN CURRY
1949–1994

Bronze
Stanley Taub
iceSheffield,
Sheffield
2001

A first enthusiasm for ice-skating as a competitive spectacle was, for very many in the 1970s, lit by the brilliance of John Curry (1949–1994). The first Briton to win an Olympic gold medal for men's figure-skating, he was different. His artistry helped to transform the style of the sport, bringing to the rink a combination of skating ability, ballet and modern dance beyond that previously seen.

Born in Solihull, he wanted from an early age to be a ballet dancer which his father thought "not masculine". Instead, but with parental support, he turned to ice-skating. He soon showed an unusual and special talent. Guided by coach Arnold Gerschwiler (and later in the USA by Carlo Fassi), he developed supreme skills in the jumps and spins and, with elegance of movement, in free-skating performed to music. He became British champion in 1970.

His triumphant year on the world stage was 1976 when he became the first man ever to win the European, Olympic and world titles in one season. He reached his peak at the Winter Olympic Games in Innsbruck. Leading after the compulsory figures and routines, his blend of graceful athletic strength and musical interpretation in the free dance, described by *The Times* as a performance "masterly in its cool beauty of movement", led to the gold medal. He executed three immaculate triple jumps, but it was his artistic interpretation of the music that lifted his performance to a level beyond those of his east European and north American rivals.

For Curry himself, his performance "came together technically, physically and mentally ... easily and so naturally that it was absolutely no effort". It was Britain's first medal of any kind at the Winter Olympics for more than a decade and first-ever gold for figure-skating. Later that year, at Gothenburg, he won the world championships – the first British man to do so for nearly four decades. He was awarded the OBE and voted the BBC's Sports Personality of the Year.

After his unparalleled year of competitive success, Curry turned professional and formed a new kind of ice show – a theatre of ice and dance.

His influence on British and world figure-skating was immense. Robin Cousins would succeed him as Olympic champion in 1980 and his artistic style would resonate in the great career of Jayne Torvill and Christopher Dean. In a sad ending, Curry died of an AIDS-related heart attack aged just 44.

A sculpture, commissioned by the British National Skating Association from American sculptor Stanley Taub, is a memorial to his skating genius. First unveiled at the National Ice Centre in Nottingham, it now stands, if a little awkwardly placed, in the reception area at iceSheffield.

Curry's elegant arm and leg movements are captured in perfect balance. The sculpture is a lasting reminder of a performer whose balletic style changed figure-skating. The 'Nureyev of the Ice'.

"Curry is both an ice-skater who dances and a ballet dancer who ice-skates" *Keith Money*

BILL SHANKLY

He Made the People Happy

BILL SHANKLY
1913–1981

Bronze
Tom Murphy
Anfield, Liverpool
1997

A striking feature of the 1960s and 1970s in football was the leading role played by three strong, inspirational and shrewd club managers – all by coincidence (or was it?) born into and hardened by a background in the mining communities of Scotland: Matt Busby, Jock Stein and Bill Shankly (1913–1981).

Perhaps the most significant decision in the history of Liverpool FC was to appoint Shankly as the club's new manager in 1959. A club deep in the Second Division was transformed into a major football power enjoying unprecedented success at home and abroad in the 1960s and 1970s.

At Anfield, outside the entrance to the visitors' centre, stands a larger-than-life statue of a larger-than-life character. 'Shanks' was revered by the supporters on the Kop. Commissioned by the club and crafted by Liverpool-born sculptor Tom Murphy, the statue captures Shankly with arms outstretched in post-match celebration. A Liverpool scarf is around his neck, sharing the team's triumph with the supporters, his people. "I wanted to capture the energy of his character and his tremendous presence," said the sculptor. "I wanted to make it look like a living thing."

Shankly was a good player, a wing-half with nearly 300 appearances over a war-interrupted career at Preston and five Scottish caps. He started his managerial career at Carlisle followed by stints at Grimsby, Workington and Huddersfield. (Those were days when young managers first learnt their trade with lower clubs.)

At Liverpool, Shankly's enthusiasm and drive, and humour, were infectious. A new confidence swept through the club. Liverpool won the Second Division championship in 1962 and promptly became a force in the First Division. Under Shankly's 15-year reign, Liverpool won the league title three times, the FA Cup twice and the UEFA Cup once. The people of Liverpool, and the world of football generally, were shocked by Shankly's sudden decision to resign, at the age of 60, in 1974.

An extraordinary feature of his reign was the consistency of his team selection based on a core of players in whom Shankly instilled great faith, a strong fitness regime and a clear and established team system. Not for Shankly any formula of continuous team rotation!

He died of a heart attack in 1981 at 68. The Shankly Gates at Anfield were dedicated in his memory a year later. Now, at the Kop end of the ground, this magnificent statue is a permanent reminder of Shankly's influence on the club and the city. (It is, perhaps, a sign of the times that it was funded by the club's then lead sponsor, Carlsberg.)

Fittingly, the four-sided plinth to the statue at Anfield was fashioned from Scottish granite to recall Shankly's days working at the Glenbuck pit in Ayrshire as a surface coal grader (and a memorial to its most famous sporting son is also at Glenbuck). He never forgot those roots. The inscription on the plinth simply says: 'Shankly – He Made The People Happy.'

Bill Shankly's statue by Tom Murphy (above) is ever-popular at Anfield where his successor is celebrated by the Paisley Gates (right).

"Liverpool was made for me and I was made for Liverpool"
Bill Shankly

BOB PAISLEY

If Bill Shankly laid the foundations, the 'boot room' philosophy at Liverpool was carried on with ever-greater success by Bob Paisley (1919–1996). Steeped in the club since 1939 as a player, self-taught physiotherapist and then coach with Shankly, County Durham-born Paisley stepped calmly into the manager's shoes in 1974 after Shankly's shock resignation. His players gave him total respect.

For Kenny Dalglish: "There was only one Bob Paisley and he was the greatest of them all. He went through the card in football. He played for Liverpool, he treated the players, he coached them, he managed them and then he became a director. He was never boastful but had great football knowledge. I owe Bob more than I owe anybody else in the game."

Paisley's nine years as manager yielded an extraordinary record – with six league titles, three League Cups, three European Cups and one UEFA Cup amongst the club's tally during the most successful period in its history. He would say, wryly: "Mind you, I've been here during the bad times too – one year we came second."

The Paisley Gates (left) were erected at Anfield after his death in 1996. In his birthplace of Hetton-le-Hole, a Durham mining village, a plaque unveiled in 2008 records his achievements. He is among the most successful managers in the history of British football.

DON REVIE and BILLY BREMNER

Legends at Elland Road

DON REVIE
1927–1989

Bronze
Graham Ibbeson
Elland Road, Leeds
2012

BILLY BREMNER
1942–1997

Bronze
Frances Segelman
Elland Road, Leeds
1999

Don Revie and Billy
Bremner celebrate
at Wembley (above).
Both Revie (right) and
Bremner (far right)
are now in bronze at
Elland Road.

In the late 1960s and first half of the 1970s, Liverpool's consistent rivals at the top of the game were Leeds United. Leeds were a team fashioned under the shrewd, but hard, grip of Don Revie (1927–1989). He became manager, in 1961, of a team languishing in the bottom reaches of the Second Division. After winning promotion, for nearly a decade between 1965 and 1974 Leeds would never finish outside the top four in the First Division – winning two league championships, the European Inter-Cities Cup (the first British club to do so) and the FA Cup and being runners-up in the league on no fewer than five occasions.

Revie was the architect. A skilful player with Manchester City in the 1950s (the team's strategy of a deep-lying centre-forward was even called 'the Revie plan'), Revie instilled a strong team ethic in his devoted 'family' of players at Leeds.

If Leeds came second more times than seemed unlucky given the skill of the team, the relentless nature of the fixture list took its annual toll on a side that was always in 'at the death' of each competition – never more so than in 1970 when the club was within reach of an historic treble of league championship, FA Cup and European Cup, only to fall at a late hurdle in all three competitions.

Revie left Leeds to succeed Alf Ramsey as England's manager in 1974. They would be three unhappy years, ending in calls for his sacking which he pre-empted by resigning for a lucrative job in the Middle East. He never managed in Britain again.

At the centre of it all on the field at Leeds from 1966 onwards was Revie's inspirational captain, Billy Bremner (1942–1997). He became an iconic figure at the club. A statue, by sculptor Frances Segelman, of the 'wee man' in permanent celebration greets spectators arriving at the south-east corner of Elland Road.

Scottish-born, just 5ft 5ins tall, the red-haired, hard-tackling and terrier-like midfielder made his first-team debut in early 1960 and became an automatic

"Ten stone of barbed wire"
The Sunday Times, on Billy Bremner

RAY GRAVELL

If public acclaim went first to the Welsh team's exciting world-class players, knowledgeable Welsh supporters were well aware of the foundations laid by the forwards and the hard-tackling centres.

One of those 'unsung' Welsh heroes of the 1970s and early 1980s was Ray Gravell (1951–2007). Born in rural Carmathenshire, Gravell played 23 times for Wales during the glory days of Welsh rugby. A hard-running, battling centre (by his own admission, "just a minor cog and, actually, quite an ordinary player, let's be honest"), his powerful charges from midfield, ball under his arm, auburn beard adding a touch of ferocity, were at the heart of many a Welsh attack. Gravell was a member of the Llanelli side that famously beat New Zealand during the All Blacks' tour in 1972 and was later part of two Grand Slam-winning Welsh sides.

After retirement in 1985, Gravell became an actor and well-known broadcaster. Diagnosed with diabetes in 2000, his health started to deteriorate but not his optimism. In 2006 a related infection resulted in the amputation of his right leg below the knee. He died, suddenly, just six months later. His death, aged 56, touched a Welsh nation.

A dramatic statue, sculpted by David William Ellis and unveiled in 2009, stands outside the Llanelli Scarlets ground. It is mounted on stone hewn from the mountain of Mynydd y Garreg where Gravell lived. His great compatriot, Gerald Davies, wrote of him: "For all his travelling, he never left home."

ROGER WILLIAMSON and TOM PRYCE

Motor Racing's Lost Generation

ROGER
WILLIAMSON
1948–1973

Bronze
David Annand
Donington Park
Circuit, Castle
Donington
2003

Motor racing was still a highly dangerous sport in the 1970s. Many safety measures, later to be regulated as standard, had not yet been introduced. Jackie Stewart, great world champion and campaigner for improved safety, put it simply: "Back then, racing drivers did die. It was a terrible thing, but it happened time and time again. You never really got used to it, but it was always there." Three talented British drivers in their twenties were killed on the track in the 1970s. Another was killed in an air crash. All before their careers could blossom fully.

In 1970, popular 28-year-old Etonian Piers Courage lost control during the Dutch Grand Prix at Zandvoort, hit a bridge support and burned to death in the ensuing fire. Three years later and, extraordinarily, at the same bend at Zandvoort in the Dutch Grand Prix, Roger Williamson (1948–1973) was killed at the age of just 25.

Williamson, as a young driver, came under the guidance of Tom Wheatcroft, owner of Donington Park. Success followed, including three British Formula Three Championships. He was widely regarded as a potential world champion. On the eighth lap of the Dutch Grand Prix, one of his tyres exploded. He lost control and hit a crash barrier, secured by badly-mounted posts which flipped his car back onto the track where it landed upside down. Brave attempts by fellow British driver David Purley to rescue the trapped driver failed. (Purley was later awarded the George Medal for his bravery.) Williamson's fuel tank burst into flames.

Another promising British driver was Tony Brise, a protégé of twice former world champion Graham Hill and, in 1975, driving for his Embassy Hill team. On a foggy November evening, a light aircraft piloted by Hill and carrying a number of his team, including Brise, crashed in a landing attempt in north London. All occupants were killed.

No accident on the track was more bizarre, though, than the one that caused the death of promising Welsh driver, Tom Pryce (1949–1977).

Pryce, born in Ruthin in north Wales, was moving up the formula ranks. In 1975 he won the prestigious, if non-championship counting, Race of Champions at Brands Hatch and became the first Welshman to win a Formula One race. He was fast becoming a real contender. In 1977, racing in the third grand prix of the season at the Kyalami circuit in South Africa, Pryce crested a rise in the slipstream of another driver. A teenage marshal ran across the track to attend a small fire in another driver's car. Pryce was unable to dodge the marshal

TOM PRYCE
1949–1977

Bronze plaque
Neil Dalrymple
Clwyd Street,
Ruthin
2009

"He was in a class of his own and could easily have been the Ayrton Senna of his day" *Tom Wheatcroft, on Roger Williamson*

VIRGINIA WADE

Jubilee Champion

"For she's a jolly good fellow" rang out around the Centre Court at Wimbledon in July 1977 as Britain's Virginia Wade (1945–) received the trophy on court from the Queen after clinching the ladies' singles title in an emotional three-set win over Holland's Betty Stove. It was the Queen's Silver Jubilee year, as well as the centenary of the Wimbledon Championships. Flags were everywhere. The *Daily Telegraph* described it as "rather like the last night of the Proms".

Born in Bournemouth, Wade moved, as a one-year-old, with her parents to South Africa where her father became the Archdeacon of Durban and she learned her tennis. The family moved back to England when she was a 15-year-old. A tennis career was launched that spanned the end of the amateur era and the game going 'open' to professionals, as well as amateurs, in 1968. She was, in fact, the winner of the world's very first 'open' tournament, the British hard courts championship held at Bournemouth.

Later that year, Wade showed her great promise by winning the first US Open, defeating Billie-Jean King in the final at Forest Hills – the first and so far only British woman to win that tournament. Her prize money was $6,000 – the winner's prize money in 2012 was $1,900,000. She won a further major singles title in Australia in 1972. With her many doubles titles, she is the only British woman to have won titles at all four Grand Slam tournaments.

Strong-serving, dark-haired and talented, no player of her time was more aggressive, more ready to attack and volley at the net. Wade was in the world's top 10 for over a decade. It seemed that a singles title victory at Wimbledon would elude her until, as a 31-year-old, that memorable day came in 1977 before the Queen. It was her 16th attempt to win the title.

Wade's appearance in the final was secured with a fine win over defending champion Chris Evert in a thrilling three-set semi-final. (It was nearly another all-British final; Sue Barker lost in the other three-set semi-final.)

She continued to compete in the singles at Wimbledon up to 1985 when she played her 24th consecutive year – a remarkable and all-time record. Her record of 64 wins in singles matches at Wimbledon is only exceeded by Billie-Jean King. She was awarded an OBE in 1986. She also became the first female member of the committee of the All England Club.

For Britain, Wade was the third woman to win a post-war Wimbledon singles title, joining Angela Mortimer and Ann Jones. (Sue Barker also won the French title in 1976.) These were days of women's success which have not since been enjoyed at this level.

Virginia Wade's portrait bust, sculpted by Ian Rank-Broadley, stands in front of the ivy-clad frontage of the Centre Court at Wimbledon alongside other British ladies' champions. She bears a gentle smile – no wonder, a Wimbledon singles title is the most honoured title in the game.

VIRGINIA WADE
1945–

Bronze
Ian Rank-Broadley
All England Club,
Wimbledon,
London
2004

"All the singing. It was so friendly. Just like a fairy-tale"
Virginia Wade

EMLYN HUGHES

Crazy Horse

EMLYN HUGHES
1947–2004

Bronze
Chris Kelly
Abbey Road,
Barrow-in-Furness
2008

A number of football players of renown from the 1970s have sadly met an unexpected or early death. One such player was Emlyn Hughes (1947–2004).

Hughes was a boy from Barrow who started with the local club before joining Blackpool as a teenager in 1964, then a First Division side. With the latter, he moved back to the marauding midfield position which he would occupy for most of his career. Bill Shankly, anxious to add new force in a transitional stage for Liverpool, watched and then bought him as a 19-year-old after barely two dozen league games at Blackpool. Story has it that, after signing Hughes in 1967 and driving him to Anfield for the first time, he was stopped by the police. Shankly said: "Don't you know who I've got in this car? The next captain of England."

Hughes was a central engine of the Liverpool team throughout the 1970s. His enthusiasm, and sometimes over-enthusiasm, led to the nickname of 'Crazy Horse'. He became the club's captain in 1973, winning that year his first of four league championship titles with Liverpool. The FA Cup was won in 1974 and the UEFA Cup in 1973 and 1976.

There were also many disappointments. The heights and depths of his emotions were never more clearly shown than in 1977. Chasing an unprecedented treble of league championship, FA Cup and European Cup, Liverpool lost the FA Cup final to rivals Manchester United. Hughes was a desolate figure – clear to millions of television viewers. Four days later, the smile was back and radiant as he led Liverpool to their first European Cup trophy in a 3–1 win over Borussia Mönchengladbach in Rome (a title retained the following year with a hard-fought 1–0 win over Club Brugge at Wembley).

Hughes was indeed captain 23 times out of his 62 international appearances for England. He was never, though, fully convincing for Alf Ramsey or, later, Don Revie although he was a regular during the spirited caretaker reign of Joe Mercer.

He left Liverpool in 1978 after 665 appearances for the club. A few years were left at Wolves, Rotherham and Hull. Fame and limelight were only resumed, but popularly so, with his appearances as a cheerful captain on the BBC's *A Question of Sport*. In 2003 he was diagnosed as suffering from a brain tumour. He died the next year, aged 57. His sad loss of health, coupled with the relatively recent memory of his exuberance, was deeply poignant.

It is in Emlyn Hughes' birthplace of Barrow (they like civic statues in Barrow) that a statue, funded by the regional development agency as a public sculpture and unveiled in 2008, dramatically celebrates a favourite son. "It's a big dynamic statue," said sculptor Chris Kelly. "You can see every muscle in the legs and the shorts are turned up like Emlyn used to wear them."

It is an imaginative and evocative reminder of a distinctive footballer of the 1970s.

"I knew after just seeing him once that he was a winner"
Bill Shankly

PETER OSGOOD
JEFF ASTLE
ROBBIE JAMES
and DAVIE COOPER

The 1960s and 1970s were still decades in football when a loyal bond could exist between a player, his club and his local community of a depth and longevity that is fast diminishing. Many statues proudly honour 'local heroes' from this period, several who died early.

Peter Osgood (1947–2006) became a cult hero at Chelsea. His languid style, physical strength, skill, eye for goal and air of confidence (often bordering on arrogance) were much loved by the fans at Stamford Bridge. Osgood died unexpectedly, aged 59, following a heart attack. Now, a nine-foot-high, imposing statue by Philip Jackson greets fans at

the West Stand. 'Ossie' was a player who captured the imagination and support of the fans of the Blues, a symbol of the team.

At the Hawthorns, home of West Bromwich Albion, fans pass through the Astle Gates in tribute to Jeff Astle (1942–2002), the club's iconic centre-forward of the late 1960s and early 1970s and still the club's leading goalscorer. He scored 174 goals in 361 matches and is revered at the club for his strike that won the 1968 FA Cup final. He died aged 59 in 2002. The cause of death was a degenerative brain disease over many years. The repeated act of heading, at the front of his brain, the heavy leather balls of his day had, the coroner found, contributed to his death. Thankfully, much lighter polyurethane balls have for some time been used.

Robbie James (1957–1998) was the favourite of the fans during Swansea's 'golden period' in the late 1970s and early 1980s. He played 484 times in two separate spells with the club and his goals

were a regular feature. He won 47 caps for Wales. He was just 40 when he died suddenly on the field at Llanelli where he was player/manager. A portrait statue by Peter Nicholas, full of Welsh fire in the striker's eyes, is now seen outside Swansea's Liberty Stadium.

Davie Cooper (1956–1995) suddenly collapsed with a brain haemorrhage aged 39. One of the most gifted of all Scottish players with over 500 appearances for Rangers and 22 Scottish caps, he was an exciting winger with a caressing skill in his left foot (some said his only one). His home town of Hamilton honoured his memory with a statue, by Kenny Mackay, four years after his death. He was a player who brought a little magic to the game.

Four heroes of the fans: (clockwise from left) Peter Osgood, Jeff Astle, Davie Cooper and Robbie James.

Four more 'club heroes' celebrated in bronze: (clockwise from left) Roy Sproson, Ted Bates, Hugh McIlmoyle and John Ritchie.

ROY SPROSON
TED BATES
HUGH McILMOYLE
and JOHN RITCHIE

Visitors arriving at Vale Park, the home of Port Vale FC, have since the end of 2012 been greeted by a 16-foot-high sculpture by Mike Talbot of Roy Sproson (1930–1997) leaping to head the ball. Here, Sproson is a legend – a one-club man who made 837 starting appearances (and five as a substitute) over a 20-year career with the club. It is a record in league football. By the end of his playing career, he was four years older than the manager!

Ted Bates (1918–2003) arrived at Southampton FC on his 19th birthday and became part of the club – as player, coach, manager, director and president – for the next 66 years. It was under his shrewd direction as manager, over 18 years, that the club rose from obscurity in the Third Division to the First Division in the 1960s for the first time. A first statue was unveiled at the new St Mary's Stadium in March 2007 – not to applause but to outrage. The legs were too short and, even worse, the face looked more like the then-chairman of Portsmouth! A new statue was commissioned from a different sculptor, Sean Hedges-Quinn, and unveiled a year later. Ted Bates is gently waving, his club tie in place and quiet dignity in his face.

At Carlisle United, during three separate spells at the club, Hugh McIlmoyle (1940–) became a particular favourite of the fans with his goals and forceful play. A statue of him by Chris Kelly was chosen to celebrate the club's centenary. Outside Carlisle's Brunton Park ground, McIlmoyle rises up for another strong header towards goal – or some, with less vision, would say into the main road of traffic outside the ground.

John Ritchie (1941–2007) was Stoke's swashbuckling centre-forward in the successful days under manager Tony Waddington. His exploits are now recalled by a portrait statue by Andy Edwards quietly positioned at the ground. A youthful Ritchie, hair around his ears, is fronted by a small but full-length statuette of an older and less hirsute version celebrating another goal.

In the late 1970s black footballers started to make a significant impact at the top level of British football. The town centre in West Bromwich will, from July 2014, site a distinctive sculpture celebrating three pioneer players of the Baggies. England winger Laurie Cunningham, defender Brendon Batson and striker Cyrille Regis played for the club with great success. A 10-foot-high sculpture,'Celebration' by Graham Ibbeson, is due to be unveiled on the 25th anniversary of Cunningham's death in a road accident in Spain.

BRIAN CLOUGH

Ol' Big 'Ead

BRIAN CLOUGH
1935–2004

Bronze
Les Johnson
Old Market Square,
Nottingham
2008

In his autobiography, Brian Clough (1935–2004) started one chapter: "My wife said to me in bed one night, 'God, your feet are cold'. I said, 'You can call me Brian in bed'."

This larger-than-life sporting figure is still prominent in bronze in the centre of Nottingham through a striking nine-foot-high sculpture by Les Johnson. His hands are clasped above his head as he acknowledges the fans and shares in their celebration. Clough is again among the people of Nottingham with whom he shared so many triumphs.

His unique management style was built on a shrewd understanding of his players and how to get the very best out of them – at times boosting their confidence, at others ruling dictatorially. He dealt with his club chairman in a similar manner: "We debate for around 20 minutes, and then decide that I was right."

His success over 18 years as manager of Nottingham Forest should not obscure his earlier career. He was a prolific goal-scoring centre-forward with

Middlesbrough (his home town and where a statue of Clough, by Vivien Mallock, stands in the local park and recalls his early days, Clough's training boots hanging loosely over his shoulder) and later Sunderland, winning two England caps. His playing career was cut short by a serious knee injury.

Clough turned to management aged 30, then the youngest manager in the game, learning his apprenticeship at Hartlepools United before moving to Second Division Derby County – and, with assistant Peter Taylor (1928–1990), inspiring the latter to promotion and then, extraordinarily, to the First Division title the next season in 1972. The period between Derby and Nottingham Forest, spent briefly with Brighton and a torrid 44 days at Leeds, is now best remembered in the book and film, *The Damned United*.

He put Nottingham on the world footballing stage. Becoming manager of the unfashionable Second Division side in 1975 and re-joined by Taylor in 1976, promotion to the First Division was clinched in Clough's second full season in charge. And then, to the astonishment of most, straight to the league championship title in the following season. Clough was the first manager since Herbert Chapman to achieve championship titles managing two different clubs.

Two successive European Cup victories followed – knocking out defending champions Liverpool in the first round before defeating Sweden's Malmo 1–0 in the 1979 final in Munich and then,

Brian Clough
as manager of
Nottingham Forest
in 1977.

"I wouldn't say I was the best manager in the business. But I'm certainly in the top one" *Brian Clough*

controversial, seemingly more so as his career developed, could Clough really have worked with the FA? Was he the best manager England never had?

Clough was awarded the OBE in 1991. He died in 2004. It is in the heart of Nottingham, with the statue unveiled before a crowd of 5,000 or more in the Old Market Square, that he now stands. Clough's hands are together above his head proudly sharing in the celebration and joyful support of the fans. He is wearing that sweatshirt (one can immediately visualise the familiar green top) and tracksuit bottoms. He is among his adopted people. Passers-by often use the plinth as a spot to rest. Clough would have liked that. At the unveiling before a crowd of more than 5,000 admiring fans, his wife, Barbara, said: "I think he would be surprised by the turnout – but then again, possibly not."

If Nottingham and Middlesbrough took the lead in immortalising Brian Clough in bronze, Derby has now honoured the partnership of Clough and Taylor that lifted the Rams to the peak of English football. A majestic larger-than-life statue, sculpted by Andrew Edwards, was unveiled in 2010 outside Pride Park Stadium. (Somewhat mistifyingly, perhaps due to an unusual chemical reaction from the copper content, the sculpture started to turn yellow in small patches. Clough and Taylor would not have been pleased. Repairs have now been made.)

The sculpture shows the two men, arms around each other's shoulders, holding together the 1972 league championship trophy. Clough's eldest son, Simon, declared: "They were a partnership in every sense. Together they were formidable."

They were years at Derby and Nottingham that will not be forgotten.

Brian Clough's playing days are recalled in Middlesbrough (left) and his partnership with Peter Taylor is celebrated at Derby County (right).

a year later, a victory by the same score over Hamburg in Madrid. Clough would always recall that first night in Munich: "When I sit in my garden and close my eyes I can still see that moment when Robertson makes his mark ... Trevor Francis is hurtling towards the far post ... and 'Robbo' sends over the perfect cross. One-nil. Pass me the European Cup. Thank you."

England overlooked him in 1974 and appointed Don Revie. Charismatic and

CHAPTER SEVEN

THE EIGHTIES &
NINETIES

In the 1980s and 1990s, there were seismic changes in the competitive structure of many of our major sports and in the way sport is 'consumed' by millions of fans.

A major driving force for change was the substantial investment poured into sport in order to attract subscribers to the new media of satellite television. No sport was more affected than football where the top clubs broke away in 1992, with the blessing of the Football Association, to form the Premier League and enjoy the spoils of sponsorship and sums offered by television companies as they competed for 'live' sport. Major beneficiaries of these financial rewards have been the leading players in the main spectator sports.

The Olympic Games became potentially 'open' to all at Seoul in 1988 and even rugby union embraced professionalism in 1995. Governing bodies recognised the reality; sport at the highest level is a full-time occupation.

Sport became ever more international. Overseas players began to play an increasing role in football, cricket and rugby in Britain. International competitions also acquired an ever-higher profile – not only the well-established Olympic Games and football's World Cup and European Championship but also golf's Ryder Cup and newly-formed world competitions in cricket and rugby union. The Paralympic Games became firmly established.

The Bradford and Hillsborough stadium disasters in the 1980s brought personal tragedy and fundamental changes in safety regulations. Major sports stadia could never be the same again.

As for statues and memorials, this is an unfinished period. Memorials for deceased heroes inevitably follow several years after the individual's sporting contribution. Many leading participants from this period are, fortunately, still with us, although some towns and clubs have not been shy to celebrate their achievements. Other personalities have sadly died, some too young. Already, we can experience many statues and memorials that vividly recall highs and lows of British sport in the last two decades of the 20th century.

JOHNNY OWEN

The Matchstick Man

JOHNNY OWEN
1956–1980

Bronze
James Done
St Tydfil Shopping
Centre,
Merthyr Tydfil
2002

Boxing remains a hard and potentially dangerous sport. Few sporting deaths have hit the consciousness, and conscience, of the British public more than that in 1980 of Johnny Owen (1956–1980). Thin, if wiry, the determined 'Matchstick Man' from Merthyr Tydfil was challenging for the world bantamweight title – his ultimate sporting dream. He was in Los Angeles fighting the reigning champion, Mexican Lupe Pintor. Owen never recovered after a 12th round knock-out.

Over 20 years later, in 2002, a distinctive statue, sculpted by James Done, was unveiled in his memory in a central shopping centre in Merthyr Tydfil. Owen is ready to box, doing what he loved best. The frail form, the protruding ears, determination in the face, Lonsdale belt around his waist – it is a warm but haunting statue. Taped to his sock, as always when he fought, is a Welsh leek; the original was given to him by an old lady and always worn for luck.

One of eight children in a working-class family, Owen soon joined the line of fine boxers from Merthyr Tydfil. Quiet, reserved, with a skeletal frame, Owen was a terrier in the ring – full of perpetual motion and a relentless determination. Turning professional as a 20-year-old, he gained the British bantamweight title a year later. Stirring performances followed to win the Commonwealth title and then the European championship. Owen had won 25 of his 27 professional fights. He was ready in 1980 for the ultimate challenge – a WBC world title fight.

His thin frame always looked young and frail against the experienced Pintor. Yet, Owen was a fighter. The contest was level after eight rounds. Then Owen started to tire. A final thundering right sent him to the canvas towards the end of the 12th round. He lost consciousness and slipped into a coma. Seven weeks later he was pronounced dead, aged 24. It transpired that he had an unusually delicate skull. The accident could have happened at any time.

The statue was unveiled by Owen's father – accompanied, movingly, by Pintor. The unveiling ceremony was concluded with a rousing rendition of the Welsh national anthem.

Boxing continues to occupy awkward and ambivalent territory in the minds of many sports fans. We have uneasiness at the physical dangers; it is the only sport where there is a deliberate intent to aim at the head, and hurt, an opponent. Can one look at the haunting statue of Johnny Owen without feeling that unease? Yet, still, the raw contest for physical supremacy between two men at their fittest and most committed can thrill and inspire.

A leek (left), taped to his sock, reflects the Welsh roots of Johnny Owen on his statue in Merthyr Tydfil.

"It was a sporting accident. Sport is beautiful. He was a great warrior" *Lupe Pintor*

BRADLEY STONE and JIM MURRAY

Medical supervision and support in boxing may have improved significantly but Johnny Owen's death would, sadly, not be the last in the ring.

Outside the Peacock Gym in Canning Town in east London stands the statue (above left) of Bradley Stone (1970–1994), a young boxer who died fighting for the British super bantamweight title. A fearsome left hook knocked him out in the 10th round. A few hours later, he fell into a coma and never recovered. The statue, by Ann Downey, was unveiled in 1995.

Jim Murray (1969–1995), aged 25, collapsed in the 12th round, with just 34 seconds left, of a British bantamweight title fight in Glasgow. Counted out, the severity of his injury only became apparent when he arrived in hospital. A clot had formed during the fight, causing pressure on his brain and his collapse. He never recovered. An imposing statue (above right) by Alison Bell, unveiled in 1996 and high on a plinth in a carefully-tended public space in Newmains on the outskirts of Glasgow, movingly recalls local boy Jim Murray and his fight to realise his dream.

STEVE OVETT

Brighton Racer

STEVE OVETT
1955–

Bronze
Peter Webster
Madeira Drive,
Brighton
2012

By 1980, the rivalry between Steve Ovett (1955–) and Sebastian Coe at the pinnacle of world athletics dominated headlines in Britain and around the world.

It was a golden period for British middle-distance running. Ovett had captured the world mile record and equalled Coe's 1500 metres record. They were very different personalities with different styles, Ovett's raw edge and power contrasting with the smooth, floating elegance of Coe, and they appealed to different sets of fans – of which there were legions. Ovett was BBC Sports Personality of the Year in 1978 and Coe in 1979. As the Moscow 1980 Olympics approached, 24-year-old Ovett was favourite for gold in the 1500 metres and Coe for the 800 metres – with the final of the shorter distance coming first.

Along the south coast, in Brighton, there is a lasting memory of that iconic race when Britain's two world-class middle-distance runners competed for gold in the 800 metres, head-to-head for only the second time in international competition. It was a robust, bumping and pushing contest made for a racer. That racer was Brighton-born Ovett. The triumph that day belonged to him ... but he had to concede to Coe in the 1500 metres six days later as his rival smoothly and stunningly accelerated to gold, celebrating with relief and outstretched arms, with Ovett in third place. The following year, Ovett and Coe exchanged world records in the mile three times during a 10-day

period. A sporting rivalry had taken each athlete to a new peak. It was a magical period in British athletics. Coe went on to retain his 1500 metres title in the 1984 Olympics in Los Angeles.

This was also a decade of transformation in athletics. Amateurism was on its last legs. While notionally retained until the 1988 Olympics, athletes were allowed to enjoy the growing benefits of sponsorship and advertising and to build up trust funds. Appearance money became standard for the top athletes. Important in the long term, the way was open for athletes from poor backgrounds to pursue athletic careers.

In Brighton, following a campaign led by a local schoolteacher, a life-size bronze statue of Ovett was commissioned by the council from local artist, Peter Webster. It depicted Ovett in that final, bursting stride to glory in the 1980 Olympics. Erected in 1987 in Preston Park where Ovett frequently used to train in his home town, it was sadly stolen in 2007, sawn-off from its plinth above Ovett's right ankle. Police later recovered a leg and a few small pieces, the rest feared sold for scrap. The London 2012 Olympics inspired a campaign for a replacement and, shortly before the start of the Games, a fine new sculpture of Brighton's great athlete (made an OBE in 2000) was erected by the seafront. The distance from the statue to the pier and back is 800 metres.

Permanent is the memory of Steve Ovett's triumph and those glory days of British middle-distance running.

"Ovett, those blue eyes, like chips of ice"
David Coleman

TESSA SANDERSON

Other great British athletes emerged in the 1980s to claim world records and Olympic titles. A first, stunning, record-breaking throw in the final of the javelin in Los Angeles in 1984 won the gold medal for Tessa Sanderson (1956–). Jamaican-born but brought up in Wolverhampton, she became the first British black woman to win an Olympic gold medal. Her career, spanning six Olympic Games and including gold medals at three Commonwealth Games, was one of the longest for a British athlete.

A set of intriguing, if neglected, railings (above), designed by Kate Maddison, in tribute to Tessa Sanderson now skirt a housing development in Wednesfield in outer Wolverhampton – built, perhaps a little ironically, on land that formed part of the playing fields of her former school.

BALLYREGAN BOB

Top Dog

BALLYREGAN
BOB
1983–1994

Bronze
James Osborne
Brighton & Hove
Greyhound
Stadium, Hove
1998

Next, we go to the dogs – to the greyhound racing stadium at Hove on the south coast. In 1985 and 1986 the sport was lifted by the exploits of one extraordinary dog. His name would join the 'greats' to be mentioned along with the legendary Mick the Miller of the 1930s. Ballyregan Bob (1983–1994) was as fast and dominant as any greyhound has ever been.

With an Irish pedigree (and much-loved by his Irish supporters), Ballyregan Bob was bred in the south of England. His local track was Hove. Astonishingly in retrospect, he lost his first four races before becoming, in the words of his trainer George Curtis, "the perfect racing machine". Curtis knew he had a special greyhound on his hands.

Ballyregan Bob won 41 of his next 43 races. A stirring burst of speed over the back straight to win the trainers' championship meeting at Walthamstow in 1985 demonstrated his class. An injury kept him out of the Greyhound Derby and, subsequently, he mostly competed in the longer, six-bend races – a distance at which his stamina and speed were unsurpassed.

A winning streak started in August 1985 unparalleled in the history of the sport. Greyhound racing had again discovered a superstar. Most races were won comfortably but a semi-final win, in the 1986 St Leger at Wembley, became legendary when, boxed in after the first bend and as two of the field were more or less crashing to the deck, Bob literally hurdled over one of them to avoid a fall and then, to the delirium of the crowd, made up a distance on the leader (ironically, one of Bob's litter brothers) that seemed impossible. Huge crowds attended his races and were treated to dominant displays as his trail of victories extended. He set track records all around the country where he competed.

On December 9 1986, at 9.19pm, Ballyregan Bob stood on the verge of a new world record. Could he become the winner of 32 races in succession? Appropriately, that final race was at his home track of Hove. It was broadcast live on television by the BBC. The traps flew open and Ballyregan Bob was in third place going into the first bend, then he moved up to second place and, showing his familiar ease of acceleration, by the last bend the world record was never in doubt as the crowd cheered him home more than nine lengths clear of any follower.

Ballyregan Bob alongside Mick the Miller in Tring's National History Museum (left).

"He is the fastest I have ever seen. Only bad luck can beat him. No other dog will" *George Curtis, trainer*

Joachim Reisner's sensitive sculpture stands in Bradford's city centre (above), a permanent memory of the 1985 disaster. Memorials at Hillsborough (right) and Anfield (far right) of the 1989 disaster continue to be honoured by relatives and fans.

BOBBY ROBSON

Sir Bobby

BOBBY ROBSON
1933–2009

Bronze
Sean Hedges-Quinn
Portman Road,
Ipswich
2002

England losing in a penalty shoot-out to West Germany (the eventual champions) in the semi-final of the 1990 World Cup in Italy is an enduring memory of this period. (Yes, it was Stuart Pearce and Chris Waddle who missed.) Few men have experienced the highs and lows of the game, over such a long period, as Bobby Robson (1933–2009).

Born in County Durham (his father was a coalminer), Robson's playing career spanned nearly 20 years, mainly with Fulham and then West Bromwich Albion, and included 20 caps for England. It was as a manager, though, that his greatest success came. He took over at Ipswich Town in 1969 when the club were in the Third Division. After one or two mediocre years, the momentum accelerated. By 1973 Ipswich were in fourth place in the First Division and, in the following nine seasons, finished lower than sixth only on one occasion – and in that year (1978) won the FA Cup with a 1–0 victory over Arsenal. They were league runners-up twice and won the UEFA Cup in 1981. Success was achieved with many young players but was crucially led by two astute buys from Holland, Arnold Muehren and Frans Thijssen. Robson was amongst the first to sign continental players for English football.

In 1982 he left Ipswich to manage England. He was manager for the next eight years, leading the national side to the quarter-finals in the 1986 World Cup, losing to two goals from Diego Maradona.

(Robson would comment on the travesty of the first: "That was no hand of God. That was the hand of a rascal.") Failure to qualify beyond the group stage in the 1988 UEFA European Championship led to vilification in the press. Yet, he continued and lifted the reputation of England by reaching the World Cup semi-finals in 1990 – losing in *that* shoot-out – after which he left ("with dignity and grey hair" said an FA spokesman).

There was still time, in a career of extraordinary longevity, to serve successful spells as manager at PSV Eindhoven, Porto, Barcelona (where he engaged a young assistant called Jose Mourinho) and Newcastle. Knighted in 2002, he became an icon at Newcastle – where he is celebrated (twice) in bronze. A portrait bust, sculpted by Tom Maley, graces the players' entrance at St James' Park and in 2012 a full-size statue by the same sculptor was unveiled outside the ground.

Sir Bobby is also remembered with deep affection at Ipswich. "The years in charge at Portman Road were among the happiest of my career. I still think of them as 'my baby' and I always will." A life-size statue by Sean Hedges-Quinn (who also sculpted nearby Alf Ramsey) was commissioned by the club's supporters' association in celebration of Robson's 13-year spell as manager and unveiled opposite the Cobbold Stand at Portman Road in 2002. A youthful Bobby Robson points enthusiastically to his players – or is it to direct spectators on their way to the ground?

"We don't want our players to be monks. We want them to be football players because a monk doesn't play football at this level"
Bobby Robson

TASKER WATKINS
and SID WATKINS

Tasker Watkins stands proudly outside the Millennium Stadium (right, top). A portrait bust of Sid Watkins is prepared for Silverstone (right, bottom).

Many recent sporting sculptures reflect community pride in men from this period whose sporting contributions have largely been made 'outside the field of play'.

At the magnificent Millennium Stadium in Cardiff, a nine-foot-high bronze statue stands of Tasker Watkins (1918–2007), sculpted by Roger Andrews in 2009. Awarded the Victoria Cross after extraordinary bravery during the Second World War, he later became Deputy Lord Chief Justice and was knighted in 1971. Rugby was his passion. President of the Welsh Rugby Union for 11 years (1993–2004), he oversaw turbulent years of change including the switch from the amateur era to professionalism in 1995 and the move, in Wales, from club to regional rugby. Tasker Watkins stands dressed smartly in a suit, medals worn proudly at his front.

Sid Watkins (1928–2012) was 'The Prof' of motor racing. Recruited by Bernie Ecclestone in 1978, he was the medical adviser to the FIA for more than two decades (and made an OBE in 2002). As trackside safety consultant, he helped transform the medical back-up necessary to maximise care and recovery. Many drivers owe their lives to him. Ron Dennis, head of McLaren, declared: "It is probably fair to say that he did more than anyone, over many years, to make Formula One as safe as it is today." A fine portrait bust, by Amy Goodman, was commissioned after Sid Watkins' death for the British Racing Drivers Club at Silverstone. It radiates warmth and sensitivity.

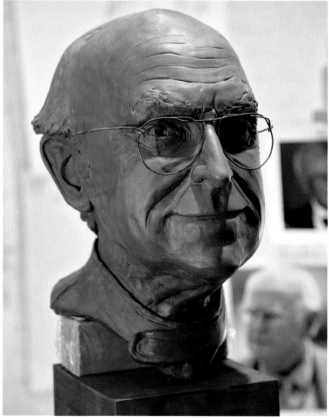

JACK WALKER
TOMMY BURNS
and DEREK DOOLEY

Owners of football clubs are not usually
candidates for recognition in bronze. But
Jack Walker (1929–2000) was different.
Brought up on the terraces at Blackburn,
he was 'one of them'. ("If they don't
win then I am bloody miserable on a
Sunday.") After the sale of the family's
steel business, he pursued his dream of
putting Blackburn back on the footballing
map. In 1995 the dream became reality.
Rovers won the championship title on a
dramatic last day. Tears of joy ran down
Jack Walker's face. A memorial statue
by James Butler of Blackburn's greatest
supporter, in celebration, now stands at the
back of Ewood Park.

More than 400 appearances by Tommy
Burns (1958–2008) as a fine midfield
player for Celtic were followed by roles
as manager and subsequently as youth
development officer and first-team coach.
Diagnosed with melanoma skin cancer,
he died two years later at age 51. He is
commemorated by a relief sculpture
outside Celtic Park close by other major
figures in the club's history.

In February 1953 Sheffield Wednesday's

highly promising 23-year-old centre-
forward, Derek Dooley (1929–2008),
suffered a double fracture of the leg.
Worse, a cut became infected. His leg had
to be amputated. (He declared: "I'll stay
in football. I don't mind if they stand me
up and use me as a corner flag.") Dooley
was appointed Wednesday's team manager
in 1971 with modest success. After a
boardroom takeover in 1973, Dooley was
sacked without warning on Christmas Eve.
He vowed never to return.

Unexpectedly offered a job by the 'old
enemy', he worked for Sheffield United in
a variety of roles. When he finally attended
a local derby match at Hillsborough in
1992, he was given a standing ovation
by both sets of supporters. A subsequent
spell as chief executive followed. After
ownership changes, Dooley (awarded the
MBE in 2003) was surprisingly asked
back in 2006 as club chairman, a role he
performed with dignity and pleasure. A
fine statue by Paul Vanstone now stands at
Bramall Lane. No man has united the fans
of Sheffield more than Derek Dooley.

Three men of football:
(clockwise from
top) Jack Walker at
Blackburn, Derek
Dooley at Sheffield
United and Tommy
Burns at Celtic.

TONY ALLCOCK

Master Bowler

TONY ALLCOCK
1955–

Bronze
Martin Williams
Thurmaston
Shopping Centre,
Leicester
2006

In a corner of a shopping centre in Thurmaston, on the outskirts of Leicester, we turn to the apparently genteel world of bowls. Unexpected in this setting, a sculpture of Tony Allcock (1955–) shows the locally-born, curly-haired, master bowler, knees bent and eyes focused, carefully releasing a bowl along its curved path towards the jack.

Bowls, with a history dated back to the Middle Ages and beyond, developed into an internationally competitive sport strongly in the 1960s and 1970s. The World Bowls Championships were first held, in Australia, in 1966. The creation of quality indoor surfaces, and the potential of television and sponsorship, led to the World Indoor Bowls Championships in 1979 (first held in Scotland). The sport was, nevertheless, still perceived to be for 'older men'. The first prominent world champion, and bowls' most publicly-recognised figure for many years, was the genial-looking, pipe-smoking David Bryant. Then along came Tony Allcock.

Brought up in Leicestershire into a keen bowling family, he started, as an 11-year-old, playing bowls on the lawn behind his parents' house and then on the corner of cricket fields. He soon became a formidable player. Young, slim-hipped, blond curly hair, a playful look in his eye and with a certain swagger, Allcock enlivened the sport's public image. He was just 31 when, in 1986, he won the first of his three world indoor titles and six years later he won the World Bowls Championships outdoors, a title retained

four years later. (It was rare for a bowler to be such a master of both the indoor and outdoor game.) He won numerous other titles including many pairs victories with the irrepressible Bryant. Allcock was the game's leading figure for over a decade.

He retired early, aged 47, still at the top of the game, declaring: "In reality, at the top level, bowls is a young man's game." He turned to a successful dog boarding and breeding operation, regularly winning prizes at Crufts. He was not lost to the sport. He became chief executive of the English Bowls Association, determined to take the game forward in the modern era but without losing its traditions.

In Leicester, proud of its sporting figures, the local authority commissioned this delightful full-size sculpture of the master bowler by Martin Williams in 2006. Bowling through a shopping centre, rather than along lush green lawns, Tony Allcock is still a distinctive figure.

"The greatest all-round bowler in the history of the sport"
David Gourley

GRAHAM GOOCH

Essex's Heavy Hitter

GRAHAM
GOOCH
1953–

Bronze
John Doubleday
New London Road,
Chelmsford
1992

Graham Gooch (1953–) may himself have been surprised by Chelmsford borough council's decision to include him in their public art in 1992 – but they are not shy in Essex. Gooch is from Leytonstone ... and Essex is proud of him. He now wields his bat in a striking larger-than-life statue in a precinct of Chelmsford barely a six-hit from the county cricket ground.

Gooch received his first call-up for England as a 21-year-old against Australia at Lord's. He was out for a 'pair', no score in either innings. Gooch was a strong hitter, literally bearing one of the heaviest bats in the game, and the selectors remained confident the runs would come.

This was a tumultuous and changing time for world cricket. The 'Kerry Packer revolution' at the end of the 1970s led to major changes as cricket strived to adapt to a new age: not least more sponsorship and money for the high-profile international players, new experimental formats and competitions and increased focus on the one-day game.

Test series for the Ashes (now with a commercial sponsor) continued to be major events. In 1981 came the sensational victory by England over Australia at Headingley in the third Test. With England 227 runs behind after the first innings and forced to follow on, hotel rooms vacated and with wickets falling, a comeback led by a swashbuckling 149 not out from Ian Botham changed the game. With eight wickets from Bob Willis ripping apart Australia's second innings, a most

unlikely victory was won – and then the series. Gooch's batting contribution at Headingley was, however, minimal.

His Test career was recovering when, amidst controversy, he led the rebel tour to South Africa in 1982 against the wishes of the game's authorities (and the UK government). He was dropped from the national side for three years.

When recalled, Gooch blossomed. He was re-appointed captain in 1989 and became a run-machine for England. Never more so than when a mammoth first innings of 333 runs at Lord's against India in 1990 was followed by a second innings of 123 – an individual total in one match of 456 runs never surpassed in Test history.

When he retired from first-class cricket in 1997, he had become the all-time highest run-scorer in top-class cricket (if Test and first-class matches are combined with one-day cricket at List A level). Gooch, who was awarded the OBE in 1991, is still England's highest Test scorer with 8,900 runs including 20 centuries. His work ethic was legendary. If his upright stance and high bat-lift were not as elegant as some, his record stands comparison with any.

For Essex, six county championship titles in the period from 1979 to 1992 and multiple other domestic honours secured Gooch's hero status in his home county. This striking statue is by John Doubleday, himself an Essex man. It shows Graham Gooch, moustachioed and wearing his Essex sweater, well back in the middle of a firm stroke. A true heavy hitter from Essex.

"He became the best player of blinding speed in the world"
Christopher Martin-Jenkins

DICKIE BIRD

Cricket's Umpire

DICKIE BIRD
1933–

Bronze
Graham Ibbeson
St Mary's Garden,
Barnsley
2009

No more individualistic or popular umpire than Dickie Bird (1933–) has raised a finger to give a batsman out. It was an emotional moment when a distinctive life-size sculpture by Barnsley-born sculptor Graham Ibbeson was unveiled in St Mary's Garden, close to Bird's childhood home near the town centre, in 2009.

Calm, consistent and unarguably impartial, Harold Bird ('Dickie' from his schooldays) was respected throughout the cricket world. His commonsense and humour calmed many a tense, and potentially explosive, incident on the field. Cautious with LBW decisions ("I have to be certain"), he umpired in 66 Test matches – then a world record – and 69 one-day internationals including three World Cup finals.

He wasn't a bad player himself. A right-handed batsman, he represented his beloved Yorkshire and, later, Leicestershire but failed to become a regular first-team player – correctly Bird would agree, but adding, "If you had compared me to Boycott in the nets, you would have picked me as the Test player." He retired aged 32 before, a few years later, turning to umpiring. His first Test appointment was appropriately at Headingley in 1973. His white cap and infectious humour made him a popular figure – not only with the public but also the players.

In 1994 the International Panel of ICC Umpires was established from which a 'neutral' umpire would be chosen for all Test matches. Dickie Bird was the first.

"A Barnsley icon, a Yorkshire icon and a cricketing icon"
Michael Parkinson

He grew into a national and beloved institution. A standing ovation greeted him as he came out at Lord's, through a guard of honour formed by players from both England and India, for his last Test match in 1996. Awarded the MBE in 1986 and the OBE in 2012, Bird may well regard his Freedom of Barnsley as an equal honour.

The life-size, and lifelike, statue shows Bird in a familiar pose. Ibbeson was keen that the statue should have humour and affection. His white cap, shoulders ready to twitch in that idiosyncratic fashion and forearm stretching as the finger is raised – all became a compelling feature of international cricket and are now a permanent feature in Barnsley. The sculpture received a royal visit in 2012 when Prince Charles met the famous resident. Enjoying the statue, Prince Charles enquired whether the sculptor had put the finger the wrong way round. Dickie Bird gave a chuckle.

Dickie Bird, jumpers around his waist and cap in place, gives another batsman out in Barnsley.

NICK FALDO

Master Golfer

NICK FALDO
1957–

Bronze
Paul Ferriter
Lough Erne Resort,
County Fermanagh
2009

S tanding tall, golf club held by his side, his stance is assured but relaxed. The statue is of a golfer who knows that he is at the top of the world's game. Nick Faldo (1957–) was, in the late 1980s and early 1990s, simply the best golfer in the world.

Britain has enjoyed periods of great success in golf during the last 30 years or so. (Before that, Henry Cotton had stood alone with his Open victories in 1934, 1937 and 1948.) The breakthrough, internationally, came with Tony Jacklin winning both the Open (at Royal Lytham in 1969) and the US Open (at Hazeltine National in 1970). A golden period then followed with major wins for Nick Faldo, Sandy Lyle and Ian Woosnam. Faldo became Britain's most successful-ever golfer. The game itself has flourished with vastly increased numbers of courses and participants.

Brought up in a small council house in Welwyn Garden City in Hertfordshire, Nick Faldo was inspired as a 13-year-old when he watched on television as Jack Nicklaus competed in the 1971 US Masters. Within five years Faldo had become a leading tour professional.

Yet, to the astonishment of many, he spent nearly two years in the mid-1980s remodelling his swing under coach David Leadbetter to withstand better the pressures of major championship golf.

"Nick Faldo should be remembered among the greats of this or any era" *Jack Nicklaus*

Faldo's search for improvement, if not perfection, was seemingly insatiable. His qualities of concentration and commitment were supreme if not always endearing to all.

In 1987 all came to fruition. Faldo won the Open Championship at Muirfield with an all-par final round that demonstrated his class and soundness under pressure. In 1989 he became the first Englishman to win the US Masters – and then won again in 1990. Faldo gained further major triumphs by winning the Open twice more in 1990 and 1992. He was officially ranked the world's number 1 for a period of 98 weeks in the early 1990s. In 1996 Faldo enjoyed one more glorious victory in the US Masters.

His record of six major championships and 40 titles on the professional tour around the world is unsurpassed for a British golfer. Faldo also has a leading record for Europe in the Ryder Cup, making more appearances and winning more matches than any other player in that event's history.

Faldo's achievements have already been celebrated in bronze. It is perhaps a sign of our commercial sporting times that life-size statues of Faldo (by Irish sculptor Paul Ferriter) stand at and promote prestigious

golf courses bearing the Nick Faldo design – one at Lough Erne Resort in County Fermanagh in Ireland and another, in identical form, at the Oceanic Faldo course in Portugal.

Faldo welcomed Ferriter at his course at Lough Erne. Renowned for his attention to detail, Faldo gave his full focus to the sculptor when they met as the latter moved around his subject with a camcorder. Then, tape measurements were made. As if planning an approach shot to the green with his caddy and with only a hint of levity, Faldo warned, "It's got to be accurate, this one."

Knighted in 2009, Nick Faldo ranks as one of the great post-war British performers in the world of sport.

Nick Faldo on his way to victory at Augusta in the US Masters in 1996.

BERNARD GALLACHER
SEVE BALLESTEROS
JACK NICKLAUS
and PAYNE STEWART

The Ryder Cup (in which British and, since 1979, other European golfers combine to take on theUSA) became, from the mid-1980s, one of sport's leading international events.

Bernard Gallacher (1949–), an eight-time player in the Ryder Cup, was non-playing captain in three dramatic contests in the 1990s. A professional at Wentworth for 25 years until 1996, his time at the club is celebrated by a life-size statue by David Wynne, striking a drive by the first tee.

Synonymous with the Ryder Cup is Seve Ballesteros (1957–2011). No player led the European charge in the 1980s and 1990s more than the charismatic Spaniard. Winner of five majors including three Opens, he was as popular in Britain as any home-grown player. His free-flowing swing is celebrated by a bronze statue by Paul Ferriter outside the Heritage Club in Ireland which the Spaniard promoted.

Two other golfers have statues in Ireland, both American. Jack Nicklaus (1940–), winner of 18 major titles including three Open wins, is one of the game's all-time great players. A statue by Paul Ferriter now stands at the Nicklaus-designed Killeen Castle golf course in County Meath. Waterville on Ireland's west coast is the scene of a moving, happy statue of Payne Stewart (1957–1999) by Jim Connolly. The colourful American, winner of three major titles and a tough competitor in five Ryder Cup matches, was due to be captain at Waterville before his premature death in an airplane accident.

Four Ryder Cup golfers in bronze: (clockwise from top) Bernard Gallacher at Wentworth and Jack Nicklaus, Payne Stewart and Seve Ballesteros in Ireland.

JONATHAN EDWARDS

Triple Jumper Supreme

JONATHAN
EDWARDS
1966–

Mosaic
*Shannon Ridd and
Jonathan Rodney-
Jones*
Ilfracombe
2002

Rings of stones in mosaic, spaced apart and embedded in a lawned area, stretch out like large footprints towards the sea at Ilfracombe in Devon. From a start line to the farthest stone ring measures over 60 feet in length. It is, astonishingly, the length of a triple jump – still a world record – made in 1995 by locally-born Jonathan Edwards (1966–).

The son of a local vicar, Edwards went to school nearby where his athletic talents were soon noted. With a sprinter's speed and an easy technique on the hop, skip and jump, he developed into Britain's best triple jumper. Given the chance in 1991 of competing in the world championships, he declined. His strong religious belief prevented him, in his mind, from competing on a Sunday – a conflict reminiscent of Eric Liddell in 1924. By 1993, though, after long deliberations with his father, he changed his mind and competed in Stuttgart, winning a bronze medal. A world-class future beckoned.

His breakthrough year was 1995. His speed and skill reached their sensational peak at the world championships in Gothenburg. An early jump smashed the world record with a leap over 18 metres. The record lasted barely 20 minutes as Edwards broke it again with his next attempt – that soaring hop, skip and jump of 18.29 metres, over 60 feet, the first in the world to pass that mark. "I hadn't got a great step in my first jump. This time my step was near perfect and I had a sensation of flying." Edwards won all 14 competitions he entered in that glorious year. He had extended the boundaries of his event. From a relatively unknown athlete at the beginning of the year, he was now a world sporting star.

Despite never again reaching that record distance, his career continued at the highest level. Although favourite, he was pipped into second place in the 1996 Olympics. Determined, Edwards recovered his top position and achieved the Olympic gold medal in 2000 in Atlanta. At one point in 2002, he was reigning gold medal winner at the Olympics, world championships, Commonwealth Games and European championships. Awarded the CBE in 2001, he retired in 2003, one of Britain's most successful medal-winning athletes. His public career has continued as a television presenter and an active member of Britain's organising team for the London 2012 Olympics.

Now, in Ilfracombe, this imaginative and attractive memorial stretches out on the seafront, commissioned by the proud local authority of Jonathan Edwards' birth town. It celebrates an extraordinary athletic moment. It is a world record which, more than a generation of athletes later, still shows no sign of being beaten.

"It's been a remarkable time for an ordinary, skinny little guy who jumps into a sandpit for a living" *Jonathan Edwards*

The memorial at Ilfracombe measures out the world-record triple jump of Jonathan Edwards (above) with detail of his footprint also recalling his Olympic triumph (left).

FRANKIE DETTORI

The Magnificent Seven

To horse-racing – and to recall an extraordinary day in 1996.

As racegoers enter the main gates at Ascot, many make an instinctive bow towards a sculpture of Frankie Dettori (1970–), albeit a little squeezed against a side wall, in tribute to his achievement on Saturday, September 28 1996. Dettori had urged his mount, Fujiyama Crest, into the lead in the seventh and final race of the day during the Royal Ascot festival. Chased by Pat Eddery on the fancied Northern Fleet, Dettori held on to win by a neck. Dettori, exhausted, still managed his trademark flying dismount. It was a sporting landmark. Seven races on the card, seven winners! Extraordinary scenes of jubilation ensued and the champagne flowed.

Dettori, Italian-born, came to England as a stable jockey for Luca Cumani in 1985. In 1990 he became the first teenager since Lester Piggott to ride 100 winners in a season. He won the Derby on Authorized in 2007 – but it is that day in September 1996 for which Dettori will forever be remembered.

It was a high-class programme at Ascot. Romantic punters might have backed a set of three or four victories for Dettori but surely not seven at cumulative odds of 25,095–1? Early wins on Wall Street and Diffident (a 12–1 outsider) set Dettori up for the Queen Elizabeth II Stakes, the highlight of the day. He sparked Mark Of Esteem alight at just the right time to win by a length and a quarter. In the fourth, Dettori guided Decorated Hero through

a packed field. The fifth, on Fatefully, was won by a neck. Six consecutive winners would be a record – and the BBC postponed its other programmes to see Dettori make history on Lochangel. Unprecedented ... but more was to follow. Yes, Dettori achieved that extraordinary clean sweep of seven wins on Fujiyama Crest (a 12–1 outsider at the start of the day) in the last race of the day.

In September 2001, five years and a day after that astounding feat, a sculpture of Dettori in flying dismount, by David Roper-Curzon, was unveiled by the entrance to the Members Enclosure at Ascot. Since then, its position has been moved – and its head remodelled for a closer likeness to Dettori.

As for Fujiyama Crest? When he came up for sale at the end of his racing career, he was bought by ... Frankie Dettori. "This horse made me famous. So, giving him a home for the rest of his life is the least I can do."

FRANKIE DETTORI
1970–

Bronze
David Roper-Curzon
Ascot Racecourse, Ascot
2001

"I just punched the air. I was so exhausted I nearly fell off"
Frankie Dettori

Frankie Dettori performs a flying dismount off Mark Of Esteem during his extraordinary day at Ascot.

PETER O'SULLEVAN

The Voice of Racing

PETER
O'SULLEVAN
1918–

Bronze
Angela Connor
Aintree
Racecourse,
Liverpool
1997

Sports commentators can play a significant and lasting role in our enthusiasm, knowledge and enjoyment. Some have become closely identified with a particular sport and its public persona – including the well-known voices of Dan Maskell (tennis), Murray Walker (motor racing), John Arlott and Brian Johnston (cricket), Bill McLaren (rugby), Harry Carpenter (boxing), David Coleman (athletics) and John Motson (football) and even the individualistic Eddie Waring (rugby league) and Sid Waddell (darts). None, though, has had a longer career, possessed a greater authority or conveyed a more warming enthusiasm than Peter O'Sullevan (1918–).

Born in County Kerry but brought up in Surrey amidst horses and paddocks, his rapport with animals and care for their welfare started at an early age. There is a lovely story of his childhood. His grandparents, by whom he was being brought up at that time, invited over friends who brought their horses with them. Peter's pony was turned out of its own box and loosed in a far-off paddock. It was pouring with rain. Peter went missing. The police were called. Eventually, two hours later, a report came back that a child had been seen in a paddock holding an umbrella over a pony.

O'Sullevan admits that his love of horse-racing also increased when, as a 10-year-old, he had a sixpenny bet on the winner of the 1928 Grand National. It is a love that has enriched the sport.

The 'Voice of Racing' called home the horses, on radio and television, for more than 14,000 races (yes, 14,000). It was the voice of a man who cared passionately about his sport. He started on radio and then, in the late 1940s, gave some of the earliest commentaries on television in any sport.

For countless fans, O'Sullevan's distinctive tones were an essential part of the Derby and the Grand National. He himself became a national institution. His 50th consecutive year of commentating on the Grand National was reached in 1997. He was knighted by the Queen in that same year – the first sports broadcaster to have been given that honour.

It is at Aintree that a portrait statue, by Angela Connor, of Peter O'Sullevan stands in his honour. It was unveiled beside the parade ring in 1997 by the Princess Royal to celebrate O'Sullevan's 50th and final Grand National. Although many of us miss the familiar trilby, it is warming and right that, at the home of the Grand National, this great sports commentator should be honoured.

Racing commentator
Peter O'Sullevan
at work (left); both
O'Sullevan (right) and
'the Noble Lord', John
Oaksey (far right),
are commemorated
in bronze.

"The sound of Sir Peter calling the horses should be one of our exports into outer space to signify the depth of our civilisation"
Sue Mott

JOHN OAKSEY

In 2009, the Princess Royal unveiled another statue to a great figure of horse-racing – John Oaksey (1929–2012). Aristocratic by birth (4th Baron Trevethin and 2nd Baron Oaksey), Oaksey was a leading amateur jockey for many years, good enough to ride the winner of the Hennessy Gold Cup and the Whitbread Gold Cup and once (in 1963) second in the Grand National. He became a well-known racing journalist for the *Daily Telegraph* and the *Sunday Telegraph* for three decades as well as an authoritative television commentator (lastingly called 'the Noble Lord' by John McCririck).

No contribution, though, has been greater than his work as driving force behind the Injured Jockeys Fund founded in 1964. The new residential centre for the Injured Jockeys Fund in Lambourn, fittingly called Oaksey House, was formally opened in September 2009. A life-size bronze statue (above) by Willie Newton stands in the grounds of the new centre. John Oaksey has a racecard in hand and wears his distinctive trilby. The Princess Royal certainly gave an approving smile.

JOEY DUNLOP

King of the Roads

JOEY DUNLOP
1952–2000

Bronze
Amanda Barton
Seymour Street,
Ballymoney,
County Antrim
2002

Britain continued over these two decades to enjoy success at the highest level in motor racing. Nigel Mansell and Damon Hill won the Formula One World Championship in the 1990s. Both, fortunately, still alive and no statues (yet). On two wheels, though, leading British racers of this period died prematurely and are remembered in bronze.

Joey Dunlop (1952–2000), pride of Northern Ireland and perhaps the greatest-ever road motorcycle racer, died in a minor 125cc race in Tallinn in Estonia – losing control in the wet conditions and, fatally, hitting a tree. The shy, part-time publican from a small town in Northern Ireland was one of the province's most famous sportsmen. Fifty thousand mourners or more, including bikers from all parts of Britain and Ireland and people from all backgrounds, lined the streets at his funeral. He was akin to royalty.

Dunlop's career spanned more than 30 years. He won countless victories around the road circuits of Ireland including the

Ulster Grand Prix 24 times and the North West 200 13 times. In 1986 he secured his fifth consecutive Formula One World Championship title. He won 26 Isle of Man TT races including three 'hat-tricks' (wins in three different engine classes in the same year) with victories spanning an extraordinary period from the first in 1977 to a final three wins, before a grandstand of spectators roaring in exultation, in 2000. (He was always happiest on the 'roads' rather than the purpose-built circuits.) The most versatile rider of his generation, he simply loved to race.

A hero in his land, Dunlop and his Honda motorcycle – a 20-year association that began in 1980 – were an inseparable image along with his distinctive canary yellow helmet.

Quietly, his charity work was a source of great pride and satisfaction, collecting clothing and materials locally and taking them himself to countries such as Bosnia and Romania. He was awarded the OBE in 1996 for his charity work, to add to his existing MBE for motorcycling.

A fascinating sculpture by Manx sculptor, Amanda Barton, brings Joey Dunlop and his Honda motorcycle back together. There are two versions of the sculpture. One is in the Isle of Man overlooking the Bungalow section of the TT course on Snaefell Mountain that he graced for a quarter of a century. Another stands in a memorial garden in Dunlop's home town of Ballymoney in Northern Ireland. Joey's hair flops youthfully, as ever, over his smiling face.

Joey Dunlop in action in his famous yellow helmet (left) and in bronze at Ballymoney (above); fellow racers in bronze are Steve Hislop (far right, top) and brother Robbie Dunlop (far right, bottom).

"I never really wanted to be a superstar. I just wanted to be myself"
Joey Dunlop

STEVE HISLOP
and ROBBIE DUNLOP

Three years after the death of Northern Ireland's Joey Dunlop, Scotland lost its own great motorcycle racer of modern times, Steve Hislop (1962–2003). 'Hizzy' died aged 41 after a career in which he won the British 250cc championship, 11 TT titles and the British superbike championship – which he won in 1995 and regained in 2002 (after a serious crash in 2000 which resulted in a broken neck). Planning to qualify as a commercial pilot, Hislop was killed in a helicopter accident. His funeral was headed by a massive

motorbike cavalcade – one repeated when a life-size statue, by David Annand, was unveiled in 2009 in Hawick. The statue is but a short distance from that of Jimmie Guthrie, Hizzy's childhood hero.

Just eight years after the death of his elder brother, Robert Dunlop (1960–2008) also died in a motorcycle road racing crash. A four-time TT winner and highly popular in Northern Ireland, his career was halted by a major accident in the 1994 Formula One TT. He recovered to be a formidable 125cc rider ('the Mighty Micro'). A life-size sculpture, also by David Annand, of 'Robbie' in celebration stands in a memorial garden in Ballymoney close by that of his brother, Joey.

CHAPTER EIGHT

INTO A NEW CENTURY

As sport moved into the 21st century, the major trends of the previous two decades continued. The nexus between commerce and sport has become ever-stronger – top-class sport being central in the battle for television viewers and broadcasting and sponsorship income being vital for leading sports and clubs. Football's Premier League, perhaps with Formula One, has become the most commercially successful sporting competition in the world.

Professional sport has become ever more global. Riches in football have attracted foreign owners to Britain. Barriers to international movement of players have long gone. Foreign sportsmen and women, of the highest quality, feature regularly in our major sporting events and on our screens. Many have been adopted 'as if our own'. International competitions, from the Rugby World Cup to the Olympics, have been central to our attention and memories.

Leading sportsmen and women earn salaries, and sponsorship income, beyond any level previously contemplated. Many

have become global 'celebrities'. (There is apparently a golden statue by a Thai sculptor of David Beckham, in his floppy hair days, in a temple in Bangkok.) Some older fans may express nostalgia for past times when their heroes, they will claim, reflected values of fair play and loyalty now less evident. Yet, sport has a wonderful and continuing ability of producing men and women (and animals) who inspire and bring lasting pride.

Sporting sculptures continue to be created around the country – but generally reflect heroes of earlier decades. These are inevitably early days for statues or memorials of figures from the current century. Many of the 'immortalised' stars of this era are sporting heroes whose longevity of achievement straddles decades. We start with an Olympian legend who triumphed in three different decades and end with a sculptural exhibition celebrating the London 2012 Olympics.

Our sporting heritage is a continuing history. There will be many more immortals of British sport.

STEVE REDGRAVE and MATTHEW PINSENT

Golden Olympians

STEVE
REDGRAVE
1962–

Bronze
Neale Andrew
Higginson Park,
Marlow
2002

Our first hero celebrated in the new century is a figure who, astonishingly, was also an Olympic champion in the 1980s. Steve Redgrave (1962–), winner of gold medals at five consecutive Olympic Games stretching from 1984 to 2000, is one of Britain's very greatest Olympians. Matthew Pinsent (1970–), with gold medals in four consecutive Games, is barely a stroke behind.

Their 100th race together came at the 1996 Olympics where, by less than a second, they retained their men's coxless pairs title – Britain's only gold medal at those Games. Immediately afterwards, an exhausted Redgrave gave people "permission to shoot me if they see me in a boat again". Four years later they were together again striving for Olympic gold.

If sport is remembered for its greatest moments, two rank in the highest echelon. The first came at Sydney in the coxless fours at those 2000 Olympic Games. The British four – Redgrave, Pinsent, James Cracknell and Tim Foster – were seeking to overcome the Italian crew, the world champions. Was it one Olympics too many for 38-year-old Redgrave? The British led ... but the Italians relentlessly made up ground. In a finish of unbearable tension, Redgrave and his crew summoned the strength to hold on to win by the fine margin of 0.38 seconds. Redgrave's

seemingly impossible record of a fifth gold had been achieved.

At 6ft 5ins, Redgrave exuded power. His first win, as part of the coxed four in 1984, was the first British gold medal in rowing since 1948. (His record would supersede even that of the earlier great British rower, Jack Beresford, gold medallist in three Olympics in the 1920s and 1930s.) In addition to his Olympic haul, Redgrave has nine world gold medals and numerous other achievements to his record. Sixteen years as an Olympian required dedication and physical and mental strength beyond compare. He became Sir Steven Redgrave in 2001.

Matthew Pinsent was also 6ft 5ins of power, with a lung capacity and strength beyond normal belief. Norfolk-born, he was educated at Eton and Oxford (where he rowed in three university boat races against Cambridge, twice on the winning crew). It was in 1990 that Redgrave

Matthew Pinsent (left) and Steve Redgrave (middle) celebrate winning the coxless fours in the Sydney 2000 Olympics.

"It is no shame to lose to a boat which contains Redgrave. He is not only beyond praise, he is beyond imagination"
Carlo Mornati, the Italian stroke

STEVE REDGRAVE
and MATTHEW PINSENT

continued

STEVE
REDGRAVE
1962–
and
MATTHEW
PINSENT
1970–

Bronze
Sean Henry
River and Rowing
Museum,
Henley-on-Thames
2002

formed his partnership with Pinsent, then aged 19. World and Olympic titles in the coxless pairs followed. Pinsent would win 10 world gold medals, one more than his great friend. He too was knighted, in 2005.

That supreme effort in Sydney could not be matched, or could it? Four years later in Athens, Pinsent made his own bid for gold in four consecutive Games as the British coxless four (Pinsent with Cracknell, Ed Coode and Steve Williams) fought against the Canadian world champions for the Olympic title. With 200 metres to go, the Canadian crew took the lead and headed for victory. But Pinsent had one last gasp. He increased the stroke-rate and, with supreme physical and mental effort, forced the boat over the line with final strokes of superhuman strength. Victory had been achieved by inches. Journalist Simon Barnes graphically described it as "perhaps the most remarkable outpouring of one man's spiritual powers I have ever seen".

There are two sculptures near the Thames. An eight-foot-tall statue of

Redgrave and Pinsent display their gold medals at Atlanta 1996 (right), reward for countless hours of training reflected in Sean Henry's sculpture at Henley-on-Thames (far right).

Redgrave was unveiled in Marlow by the Queen in 2002. Around Redgrave's neck are five medals, loosely forming the Olympic rings and representing his record five gold medals. His face has an intensity and will-to-win that drove Britain's great Olympian. The pose, with his weight resting on his right leg and his left arm raised, was used (according to sculptor, Neale Andrew) by classical Greek sculptors in their depiction of athletes – thus creating a direct link between Redgrave and the early Olympic theme. Redgrave, at the unveiling, simply commented: "The statue seems to be a good likeness ... but I would have liked to see it with a few less pounds around the middle."

The second sculpture has a different feel. It is at the River and Rowing Museum in Henley-on-Thames – but, sadly, in the car park rather than more prominently by the river. It is a life-size statue showing Redgrave and Pinsent together in training. The sculpture has been strongly patinated, the colouring of the rowers' kit and faces giving it a distinctive look and drawing the viewer in for a closer study. It was the intention of sculptor Sean Henry to reflect the years of dedication that lie behind all world-class athletes. "I was struck by the thousands of hours both men have spent training over the years when compared with the few hours of competition."

The dedication, determination and sacrifice behind achievement in world-class sport, and the dream of glory, are reflected in this distinctive sporting sculpture of two great British Olympians.

MARTIN JOHNSON

World Cup Captain

MARTIN
JOHNSON
1970–

'LINE-OUT'
Bronze
Gerald Laing
Twickenham
Stadium,
Twickenham
2010

The structure of rugby union had changed fundamentally in the last decade of the 20th century. International rugby in the 21st century was now a full-time professional sport. At senior club level, the old format of friendly games arranged by amateur clubs survived no longer. Leagues with promotion and relegation were introduced in 1987 under commercial sponsorship. Pressure for more international events led to the first Rugby World Cup in the same year. The competition's commercial success culminated in an era-changing deal between Rupert Murdoch's television empire and the governing bodies of the three big southern hemisphere nations of Australia, New Zealand and South Africa.

A professional game in the southern hemisphere and an amateur in the northern was unthinkable – the loss of players from the north would be too great. The inevitable followed. In 1995, the Rugby Football Union (RFU) finally accepted professionalism. (It was, ironically, one century after the RFU's refusal to permit 'broken-time' payments had led in 1895 to rugby's split and the creation of the professional Northern Union.) The Heineken Cup was established as a competition for European clubs accompanied by a Champions League. Players became ever fitter and stronger. The century-old Five Nations tournament became the Six Nations Championship with the addition of Italy. Rugby at the highest level was now a potentially highly rewarding, if gruelling, full-time sport.

The Rugby World Cup of 2003 provided lasting memories – none more so than Jonny Wilkinson's drop-goal in the final minute of extra time to clinch the World Cup for England against Australia in Sydney by 20–17. England were led on the pitch by the calm judgment and indomitable strength of their captain Martin Johnson (1970–). Johnson, a towering 6ft 7ins lock forward, played for England for 11 years winning 84 caps, toured three times with the British Lions and was a stalwart of an outstanding Leicester club side. The World Cup victory was the culmination of his playing career and, under Clive Woodward as coach,

Martin Johnson climbs highest in the 2003 Rugby World Cup final against Australia (left). A 27-foot-tall sculpture of a generic line-out greets visitors to Twickenham (right).

"It was just something about him, the way he spoke.
It had an effect on his people – to make them feel bigger"
Jonny Wilkinson

MARTIN JOHNSON
continued

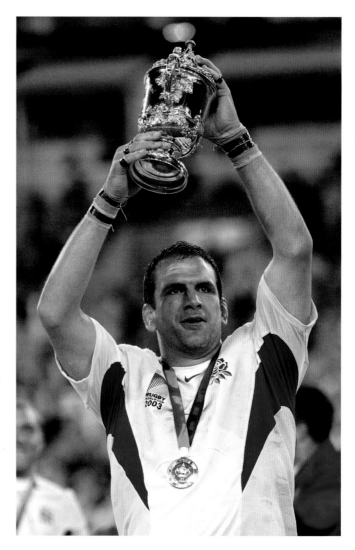

The England captain raises the most sought-after trophy in rugby – the Webb Ellis Cup (above). Johnson was the obvious choice to open the Wall of Fame at Twickenham in 2005 (left).

a successful period for English rugby. Johnson captained his country in 39 matches, of which 34 were victories.

At the home of English rugby, around the iconic Twickenham Stadium, a number of sculptures by Gerald Laing illustrate the action, strength and excitement of the sport in a generic way – but not as sculptures of individual players. Twickenham opened, though, a new Wall of Fame in 2005 as part of its World Rugby Museum. It is a celebration of 100 great players from all over the world who have played at Twickenham. Memories are recalled, through photographs, as buttons are pressed. A button away and blond-haired David Duckham is in full stride or Richard Sharp is making a piercing run. Who was chosen to open the Wall of Fame? The undisputed choice was Martin Johnson.

Since 2010 a massive, 27-foot-tall, dramatic sculpture by Gerald Laing,

depicting a rugby line-out, has greeted spectators arriving at the plaza outside the South Stand at Twickenham. It is a distinctive landmark. The sculpture was originally created in clay, scanned onto a computer and, in giant form, set in bronze by the foundry. Engraved around the plinth are statements of five core values of the game – teamwork, respect, enjoyment, discipline and sportsmanship.

Martin Johnson (now a CBE) was at the unveiling. He barely reached the waist of the standing players as he looked up. The ball is close to the fingers of the line-out catcher. Does he take it cleanly or not? In 2003, Martin Johnson certainly won the ball for England.

NICK DUNCOMBE
and JASON LEONARD

Scrum-half Nick Duncombe is recalled fondly in a statue at Harlequins (far left). Jason Leonard, England's most-capped player, stands tall in metal above the A13 (left).

In the dominant England pack for much of that period of international success was England's most-capped player, prop forward Jason Leonard (1968–). He won 114 caps before his retirement in 2004. Although no longer a first-choice selection, he appeared in all seven matches of the 2003 World Cup campaign, coming on as a key extra-time substitute in the final. Barking-born Jason Leonard (OBE) now stands high above the traffic passing on the A13 in a group of metal sculptures including other locally-born sporting heroes Alf Ramsey, Bobby Moore, Geoff Hurst and Beverley Gull.

If players like Martin Johnson and Jason Leonard enjoyed lengthy international careers, one promising player who did not was Nick Duncombe (1982–2003). He made his England debut aged just 20 at scrum-half and, showing skill and courage, a long international future lay ahead. Head coach Clive Woodward said: "Nick was one of the brightest and most talented players." Yet, after two international caps and aged just 21, Duncombe died in 2003 of meningitis contracted during a short holiday abroad.

A statue by sculptor Nathan David at the ground of Nick Duncombe's club, Harlequins, in Twickenham, recalls a young player full of vigour and vision – and the sadness of a life and career tragically cut short.

BEST MATE and KAUTO STAR

Jump Legends

BEST MATE
1995–2005

Bronze
Philip Blacker
The Green,
East Lockinge
2008

Great racehorses continue to provide vivid memories. Two of the finest from this period are now celebrated in bronze, both legends of National Hunt racing.

With a third successive victory in the Cheltenham Gold Cup in 2004, ridden as usual by jockey Jim Culloty, Best Mate (1995–2005) joined Golden Miller, Cottage Rake and Arkle in an elite group of three-time winners. Supremely consistent, Best Mate won 14 times from 22 starts and never fell. He became one of the nation's best-loved horses. Withdrawn from the 2005 Cheltenham Gold Cup with a burst blood vessel just days before the race, Best Mate's return was at Exeter in November. There, in front of the packed stands, the 10-year-old pulled up in clear distress, stumbled to his knees and died of a heart attack. First on the scene was his trainer, Henrietta Knight, who knew immediately what had happened. It was dramatic, poignant and headline news.

In 2008 a life-size statue was commissioned from leading equine sculptor Philip Blacker. It shows Best Mate peacefully and happily grazing. It stands, as intended, on the village green at East Lockinge, not far from Knight's

KAUTO STAR
2000–

Bronze
William Newton
Haydock
Racecourse,
Newton-le-Willows
2012

BEST MATE and KAUTO STAR
continued

Oxfordshire stables. Another version of the same statue was unveiled at Cheltenham where Best Mate's record, as well as statue, stands alongside those of Golden Miller and Arkle. It is, though, in this peaceful country setting of East Lockinge that this warm, beautiful sculpture seems at home.

By the end of the decade another steeplechaser was about to join racing's immortals. French-bred Kauto Star (2000–) moved to England in 2004 to be trained by Paul Nicholls for new owner Clive Smith. He won the Cheltenham Gold Cup twice and the King George VI Chase no fewer than five times. In all, he recorded 23 victories (including 16 Grade 1 races) over eight seasons and 41 starts. The margin and authority of many victories added to his claim to stand high in the all-time ranking lists. Strong, with

a distinctive white blaze on the head, Kauto Star became a nation's favourite, an affection enhanced by his recovery from setbacks and perhaps no more so than in 2009 with his second Gold Cup victory, avenging the previous year's defeat behind stablemate Denman.

The public's affection was warmly demonstrated in the 2012 Gold Cup when he was pulled up on the first circuit. Kauto Star, with jockey Ruby Walsh, was applauded to the unsaddling area as if a winner. Retirement beckoned and it would be his last race. A future in dressage may, though, still await this legendary horse.

A statue of Kauto Star (perhaps the first of several) was unveiled in 2012 at Haydock Park, the scene of many of his wins including a record fourth victory in 2011 in the Betfair Chase. Sculptor William Newton aimed to "capture the supreme confidence of the great horse". Kauto Star was in attendance at the unveiling, still fresh, vibrant and the centre of attention. A supreme equine athlete.

"The horse of my lifetime"
Ruby Walsh,
on Kauto Star

YEATS
PERSIAN PUNCH
and MOTIVATOR

Memorable racehorses of the Flat from this period are also celebrated in bronze.

Perhaps the finest racehorse was Yeats. This Irish thoroughbred, a bay stallion trained by Aiden O'Brien, won his place in racing folklore by being the first horse to win four consecutive victories in the Ascot Gold Cup at Royal Ascot. Injured when favourite for the 2004 Derby, Yeats won seven Group I races and was for four years European Champion Stayer. His fourth victory in the Ascot Gold Cup came in 2009 when, ridden by Johnny Murtagh, he accelerated to victory. The legend of Yeats is now permanently celebrated in the parade ring at Ascot through a magnificent larger-than-life sculpture by Charlie Langton unveiled by the Queen in 2011. Yeats is truly regal.

At Newmarket, the scene of his victory in the Jockey Club Cup on Champions Day in 2003 (his last before his sudden death at Ascot the following year), Persian Punch (1993–2004) is recalled through a statue by Philip Blacker. The 'people's horse' was one of the most popular and courageous horses of the Flat over many years.

In 2005 Motivator (2002–), ridden by Johnny Murtagh and owned by an Ascot-based consortium, won the Derby at Epsom with ease in one of the fastest-ever times in that legendary race. A sculpture by Gill Parker now stands in glorious view at Ascot conveying a real sense of shimmering speed and flight.

As the years pass, we look forward to more equine legends from this period being immortalised in bronze.

Three champions of the Flat celebrated in bronze: Yeats (top), Persian Punch (middle), and Motivator (bottom).

ALEX FERGUSON

The Boss

ALEX FERGUSON
1941–

Bronze
Philip Jackson
Old Trafford,
Manchester
2012

It was November 1986. The glory days at Manchester United were gone; the club was struggling and looking for a new manager after the sacking of Ron Atkinson. Bobby Charlton recalled watching Alex Ferguson (1941–) as manager of Scotland; one impression was overwhelming: "It was of a man who had an extraordinary force of personality. When he spoke, or when he danced up and down the touchline, his players took notice. It was a ferocity I knew we needed at Old Trafford." Ferguson was appointed and a reign of more than 25 years and the longest in the club's history began.

Ferguson, Glasgow-born, was himself a talented striker with a good scoring record at several clubs including Rangers. He has always appreciated the goalscorer's art. His full-time management career began at St Mirren followed by a highly-successful period in charge of Aberdeen, leading the club to victory over Real Madrid in the 1983 UEFA Cup Winners' Cup, before managing Scotland (after the death of his hero Jock Stein) for a brief spell before United called.

His early days at Manchester United were by no means successful. Results were mediocre and with the club still lowly in the First Division, rumours of a sacking continued ... and then were put aside as United won the FA Cup in 1990. (Would Ferguson have survived those early years today?) The record since has been one of unparalleled success as United became the dominant force in British football and one of the richest clubs worldwide.

By Ferguson's retirement in 2013, United had won the Premier League 13 times, the FA Cup five times, the League Cup four times and the UEFA Champions League twice. Few sporting moments have been more dramatic that the two late goals in 1999 at the Nou Camp in Barcelona which enabled Ferguson's United to beat Bayern Munich to win the Champions League and clinch the unprecedented golden treble alongside Premier League and FA Cup success. He was knighted in 1999.

Many great players have been integral to United's success under Ferguson's management. In addition to those legends immortalised in bronze outside Old Trafford, fascinating welded-steel sculptures by Amy Goodman of other Red Devil 'greats' now appear in one of United's hospitality suites. Three sculptures are of players, bought during Ferguson's reign, who rank among United's greatest: Eric Cantona, imperious, with his hands on his hips and head to the side; Peter Schmeichel at full stretch; and Wayne Rooney having just unleashed one of his trademark thundering drives.

In 2012, Alex Ferguson joined the other greats of United's history immortalised in bronze outside Old Trafford. A fine larger-than-life statue by Philip Jackson was unveiled to recognise Ferguson's contribution to the club over a quarter of a century. It captures the character and authority of this driven Scot. Watching his players, arms crossed, fierce determination in his eyes, Ferguson is 'the Boss'.

"Football is like a drug which is difficult to give up"
Alex Ferguson

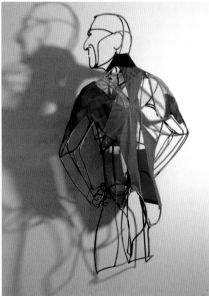

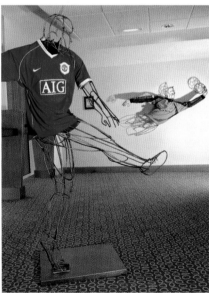

Alex Ferguson at Old
Trafford (left); Eric
Cantona (top), Wayne
Rooney and Peter
Schmeichel (above) in
action inside.

SIR ALEX FERGUSON

TONY ADAMS
and THIERRY HENRY

Premier Gunners

TONY ADAMS
1966–
and
THIERRY HENRY
1977–

Bronze
MDM/2020
Emirates Stadium,
Arsenal,
London
2011

The 1990s and early 2000s were dramatic years for football at the highest level. Attracted by the huge increase in television revenues, the top clubs in the First Division of the Football League broke away and, with the support of the Football Association, formed the Premier League in 1992. The bargaining strength, and salaries, of leading players escalated. Players from around the globe were drawn to the riches of the Premier League and clubs could, or thought they could, afford to pay for them.

In this new age, was the British-born player with lifelong commitment to a single club a dying breed? Would non-British players, attracted to the spoils of the Premier League, ever capture the long-standing passion of a club's community in the way of 'footballers of old'? Arsenal would say 'yes' to both.

Tony Adams (1966–), born in Essex, was with the club for the whole of his playing career, nearly 20 years in the top flight. He was the lynchpin at the core of the disciplined Arsenal defence.

A strong leader, Adams was appointed skipper at 21 and remained club captain for the next 14 years. Champions of the First Division of the Football League in 1989 and 1991, he also led Arsenal to success in the new Premier League, twice completing the League and FA Cup double

(in 1998 and 2002) and becoming the only player to captain a title-winning team in three different decades. He won 66 international caps for England, captaining his country at Euro 96 on home soil. He has remained a symbol of commitment, discipline, leadership and character for the faithful of Arsenal.

The Premier League quickly became a magnet for great players around the world. Many such players have sparkled at British clubs but not stayed at them for more than a few seasons as freedom of movement (and the careful calculation by players, and their clubs, of a player's commercial value) has resulted in constant transfer activity. Could a non-British player attract such passion and admiration within a club and

Statues of Tony Adams (above) and Thierry Henry (right) celebrate iconic goals against Everton and Tottenham respectively.

"I never thought in my wildest dreams that I would have a statue like this in front of the stadium of the team I love"
Thierry Henry

its supporters in the 21st century as to lead to permanent recognition in bronze?

Born in a suburb of Paris, Thierry Henry (1977–) joined Arsenal in 1999 and became Arsenal's outstanding striker during his eight seasons with the club – a world-class player with exceptional pace, skill, balance and the coolness of a finisher. He was central to Arsenal's success in the Premier League (twice) and the FA Cup (three times), including the double-winning side of 2002. His goals helped Arsenal reach the final of the UEFA Champions League and he became the club's all-time top scorer. (He is also the French national team's leading goalscorer.)

When Arsenal celebrated their 125th anniversary in 2011, three statues were unveiled outside the Emirates Stadium, the new, sponsored ground itself a symbol of the commercial success of the Premier League. Herbert Chapman, the club's legendary manager of the 1930s, was again honoured.

Two players were also chosen to symbolise the spirit of Arsenal. Tony Adams is immortalised in celebration of a goal in the match against Everton that clinched the Premier League title in 1998. Thierry Henry is on his knees acknowledging a glorious goal against local rivals Tottenham Hotspur in 2002 – the first non-British player in the Premier League to be immortalised in bronze.

KEIRON CUNNINGHAM

King of St Helens

KEIRON
CUNNINGHAM
1976–

Bronze
Vanessa Marston
Chalon Way, St
Helens (now at
Langtree Park)
2010

Rugby league has continued, as ever since the formation of the Northern Union, to be central to the pride of many industrial towns of the north – and none more so than the glass-making town of St Helens near Liverpool. No figure of recent times has symbolised the community's pride in its famous rugby league club more than Keiron Cunningham (1976–).

One of the original founding clubs of the game, St Helens have enjoyed enormous success over much of the league's history. In 2007, after another victory at Wembley in the Challenge Cup, the local council publicly acknowledged the club's contribution: "The club have been marvellous ambassadors for our borough and we [wish] to honour the club for their sporting and community achievements over their long and prestigious history." The permanent symbol would be a statue of the player voted by the people of St Helens. The player chosen, with over 10,000 votes, was Keiron Cunningham.

Born in St Helens, Cunningham became the coveted number 9, a world-class hooker renowned for his bursting runs and his ability to poach tries from a short distance. He retired in 2010 after a 17-year career with the club and over 400 appearances. During that time, St Helens won five Super League championships, seven Challenge Cup victories and two World Club Challenge titles. His final appearance was also the last match at the club's famous Knowsley Road ground. And the final try? A typical, bursting plunge over the line by Cunningham.

His career coincided with major changes in the structure of the sport. The Super League was created in 1996, fuelled by the funds of Rupert Murdoch's News Corporation in a ruthless battle to dominate broadcasting of the sport both here and, importantly, in Australia. Rugby league in Britain switched from a winter to a summer season – and now runs concurrently with the Australian season. If more money came into the sport from television, many (wrongly) predicted its demise after sporting history was turned on its head with the decision of rugby union to go 'professional' in 1995. Several leading league players switched codes, ironically, to the now more lucrative union game. Cunningham, himself, was tempted by offers but chose to remain loyal to his home-town club and rugby league.

His familiar rugged, bursting style, ball tightly under his right arm, is recalled in a fine nine-foot-high statue by Vanessa Marston, first unveiled in 2010 in the centre of St Helens and since moved to a position outside the club's new ground. The statue is a glorious reminder that sport can still act as a strong binding force within a community.

"It's a strange feeling to be immortalised in bronze but it's nice to be erected while I am still breathing"
Keiron Cunningham

ALEX MURPHY and MARTIN OFFIAH

Two other heroes from modern decades of rugby league will also shortly be represented in bronze in the five-figure statue being prepared for Wembley Stadium to celebrate rugby league's traditional association with Wembley through the holding there of the Challenge Cup final.

Amongst the greats of the game, Alex Murphy (1939–) has a unique record in being the only player to captain three different sides to victory in the Challenge Cup (St Helens in 1961, Leigh in 1971 and Warrington in 1974). Murphy, an OBE, won 27 caps for Great Britain.

More recently, the exploits of Martin Offiah (1996–), more popularly known as 'Chariots', are legendary. One of the fastest players in the game and one of its most prolific try-scorers, he will forever be remembered for the try he scored for Wigan in the 1994 Challenge Cup final against Leeds when he brought the stadium to its feet with a 90-metre solo run. Offiah won 33 caps for Great Britain.

With sculptor Stephen Winterburn working on the figures in his studio at the time of writing, the monumental sculpture will become a national focal point for rugby league fans.

Alex Murphy (left) and Martin Offiah (right) being prepared for Wembley by sculptor Stephen Winterburn.

TOM DALEY and AMY WILLIAMS

Sculpture and the Olympics

TOM DALEY
1994–

Wire-mesh
Nikki Taylor
Cross Bath, Bath
2012

The spotlight of the world's sporting attention in 2012 was on the London Olympics. Sculpture and sport came together in the lead-up through a fascinating exhibition presented by a public art organisation based in Bath, *Art at the Edge*. Thirty British sculptors were commissioned to create sculptures representing a range of different Olympic sporting events. The result was a unique series of works, initially all in maquette-size but later added to by a number of large-scale sculptures in Bath itself, reflecting not only sporting excitement but also the breadth and diversity of modern sculpture.

The works ranged from conceptual impressionist pieces to more traditional figurative sculptures. Most represented different sports in a generic way – from basketball to fencing, cycling to taekwondo – but a number were based on specific sporting individuals. These now contribute to our collection of sporting heroes in sculpture.

One fascinating life-size wire-mesh sculpture by Nikki Taylor stood for a period in the delightful setting of the Cross Bath at Thermae Bath Spa. It represented Tom Daley (1994–) in action. Daley, leading diver from the 10-metre platform, was Britain's youngest competitor at the 2008 Olympics in Beijing. European champion

"Faster, Higher, Stronger"
Olympic motto
(English translation)

Amongst the Art at the Edge exhibition in Bath were wire-mesh sculptures by Nikki Taylor of Olympic sprinter Jason Gardener (left) and diver Tom Daley (right) and a classical part-headless sculpture in marble by Ben Dearnley of swimmer Mark Foster (below).

TOM DALEY and AMY WILLIAMS
continued

in 2008 and 2012, he also won the world championships in Rome in 2009. He joyously won a bronze medal at the London 2012 Olympics. The same sculptor also produced a distinctive vision of Jason Gardener (1975–), Bath-born sprinter and a member of the British 4 x 100 metres relay team which won the gold medal at the 2004 Olympic Games, to symbolise the speed and beauty of the sprint athlete.

Elsewhere, a larger-than-life torso of swimmer Mark Foster (1970–), carved out of Bath stone by Ben Dearnley and classical in its representation, stood in a central square in Bath. Foster carried the flag for Great Britain in the opening ceremony at the 2008 Olympic Games in Beijing. A specialist over the 50-metre course, by medal count he is among Britain's most successful swimmers – winner of five world championship titles

(at freestyle and butterfly).

The sculpture with perhaps the strongest visual impact, and one representing a great Olympic moment for Britain, is that of Amy Williams (1982–). Her stunning triumph in Vancouver in 2010, winning the gold medal in the women's skeleton event, was the first British gold medal in an individual event at the Winter Olympics for three decades and the first British individual gold medal for a female participant for 58 years. Her success, and accompanying joy, excited the sporting nation. Graceful and powerful, the three-quarter life-size bronze sculpture by Alan Dun is a delightful combination of sport and art.

The 2012 Olympics also became an occasion to recall, around Britain, many of our nation's past Olympic figures. Events included: the installation of a new memorial to 'founding' father William Penny Brookes in Much Wenlock; a fresh headstone in Dorset for Charles Bennett ('the Shapwick Express') who in 1900 was the first British athlete to win an

AMY WILLIAMS
1982–

Bronze
Alan Dun
Victoria Art
Gallery, Bath
2012

Olympic skeleton gold medallist Amy Williams on her way to victory in Vancouver (top) and celebrated in bronze by sculptor Alan Dun (left).

Olympic gold medal; a plaque to recall the birthplace of 1924 sprint champion Harold Abrahams (with fellow-athlete Eric Liddell well-established in bronze); a replacement sculpture in Brighton of runner Steve Ovett; an unusual sculpture of triple jumper Jonathan Edwards crafted from old train parts for a tour of key stations along the East Coast Main Line; a rather bizarre commercially-produced statue of Kelly Holmes (since stored); and a return of Mary Rand to her home town and the Freedom of Wells. Birmingham Council, recognising the global nature of sport, welcomed the Jamaican athletics team (who trained in the city) with a six-foot-high wicker sculpture of the great Usain Bolt in his famous pose pointing to the sky in victory – but, unfortunately, presented him extending his right arm whereas the golden sprinter uses his left!

We end with a delightful statue celebrating both the Olympics and a community's pride in its Olympians. The area of Badenoch and Strathspey, centred around Aviemore and the Cairngorm National Park in Scotland, has apparently produced a higher percentage of Olympians per head of its 13,500 population than any other area of Britain.

In a community-led sculpture, 14 home-grown winter Olympians (from skiers Alain and Noel Baxter to curling's Douglas and James Dryburgh) are now celebrated in an elegant three-figure work by the Aviemore-based artist, Dudley Evans. The sculpture, unveiled in 2007 by Lord Coe, stands prominently on the village green at Aviemore. Based on local granite, it is topped by a torch bearing the Olympic flame. The three figures represent the Olympic ideals 'Faster, Higher, Stronger'.

Memorials remind us of past Olympics, including records from the first London Olympics in 1908. How many stars of 2012 will later be celebrated in bronze? The Games established, thrillingly, the reputation of many British sporting sportsmen and women.

Sculpture will continue to be a powerful medium for celebrating legendary figures and memories comprised in our sporting heritage. Many more heroes of British sport will, in years to come, be immortalised in bronze.

A sculpture in Aviemore (right) celebrates the many Olympians who have come from the region. With the Olympic flame above, the three figures represent the Olympic motto 'Citius, Altius, Fortius' ('Faster, Higher, Stronger').

The first London Olympics, in 1908, are still recalled (along with the golden performance of the British team) by a memorial near the site of the old White City Stadium.

POSTSCRIPT

The flow of new sporting sculptures around Britain continues. Our enthusiasm for commemorating heroes of the past in bronze or permanent memorial shows no sign of diminishing.

Football statues reflecting legendary players associated with particular clubs continue to appear, endorsing, for that club or stadium, a sense of tradition and history: Nat Lofthouse will stride out in bronze at Bolton later in 2013 through a sculpture by Sean Hedges-Quinn; Fred Keenor, Cardiff's captain in the club's 1927 FA Cup final win over Arsenal, is now commemorated through a sparkling statue by Roger Andrews; Arsenal, in turn, joyfully add to their memory of fine European players with Dennis Bergkamp (in flying action) joining Thierry Henry in bronze at the Emirates Stadium.

Amongst other sports, much-loved rugby commentator, Bill McLaren, is now warmly recalled by a portrait bust in his Scottish border town of Hawick. One of golf's founding course architects, Alister McKenzie is recorded by an unusual life-size wood carving at Hazel Grove GC in Manchester. Taking a different form, cricket's Bedser twins, Alec and Eric, are celebrated by a new bridge over the Basingstoke canal bearing their name at Woking near where they were brought up, the bridge will in due course bear not only their name but also statues of the bowling twins at either end.

Sculptors and designers are at work. Subjects of planned statues include: Samuel Ryder, founder of golf's Ryder Cup, in St Albans town centre; Dorothy Round, Wimbledon ladies' champion, in Edgbaston; Henry Cooper in London's East End courtesy of the London Ex-Boxers Association; Basil D'Oliveira at the New

Fred Keenor (right) again enjoys Cardiff's 1927 FA Cup win through a sculpture by Roger Andrews. Graham Ibbeson's sculpture of Laurie Cunningham, Brendon Batson and Cyrille Regis in 'Celebration' takes shape in clay for West Bromwich (far right).

The rugby league statue for Wembley by Stephen Winterburn takes shape. Martin Offiah kneels with Alex Murphy behind in a maquette (left). Bill McLaren is commemorated in Hawick (below).

Ground in Worcestershire; Jimmy Sirrel and Jack Wheeler at Notts County; and Jimmy Dickinson at Portsmouth. In the centre of West Bromwich a sculpture, 'Celebration' by Graham Ibbeson, will reflect the club's pioneering black footballers Laurie Cunningham, Brendon Batson and Cyrille Regis.

Perhaps most notably, Wembley Stadium will be the site of a 20-foot-high sculpture to match that of soccer's Bobby Moore. Rugby league will be celebrating the game's long and close association with Wembley, old and new, as a place of pilgrimage for the Challenge Cup final through a sculpture by Stephen Winterburn of five of the game's legends. Sporting sculpture continues to thrive.

If readers wish to follow these developments, please visit **www.sportingimmortals.com** *where it is intended to capture, through photographs, the continuing story of the immortals of British sport.*

CREATING A
SPORTING SCULPTURE

How is a sporting sculpture created? The story is a fascinating blend of research and design, inspiration and perspiration, craftsmanship and technical skill. The overall project frequently takes six to 12 months, and sometimes more, to complete. This is a layman's attempt at a summary of a typical process.

DESIGN

A basic challenge for the sculptor is, of course, to ensure that his or her work reflects a strong likeness of the particular sporting individual; not always easy if based solely on photographs or video and,

A small maquette of Brian Clough and Peter Taylor reveals the pose and detail of the proposed sculpture (right). Leading equine sculptor Philip Blacker carefully works final detail into the clay sculpture (far right).

almost certainly, the first critical judgment that will be made by any viewer. Perhaps the most important design challenge, though, is to capture a pose, feature or look that enhances the spirit and memory of the individual: Brian Clough and Peter Taylor with arms around each other's shoulders in friendship and triumph; Dickie Bird with umpiring finger raised; Red Rum trotting gently in the surf; or Fred Trueman's individualistic, full, thrusting bowling action.

This leads to the first significant three-dimensional working task: the production of a small-scale model, a 'maquette', no more than one-third of the eventual size and often much smaller. Sculpted generally in clay, or sometimes plasticine, this is used to develop and test the proposed shape, proportions and feel of the sculpture – and to obtain the approval of the commissioning (and paying) client. Sometimes, different design options will be offered. The maquette will be worked, and re-worked, to produce virtually all the features and precise dimensions (but reduced) of the final sculpture.

SCULPTING IN CLAY

The next major step is 'scaling up' to full size. A large-scale sculpture (and, frequently, the earlier maquette) will require an 'armature' or framework around which the sculpture can be built. Generally made of aluminium wire or other metal, it will be bent, twisted and welded into the required shape and measurement. Where further 'body' is

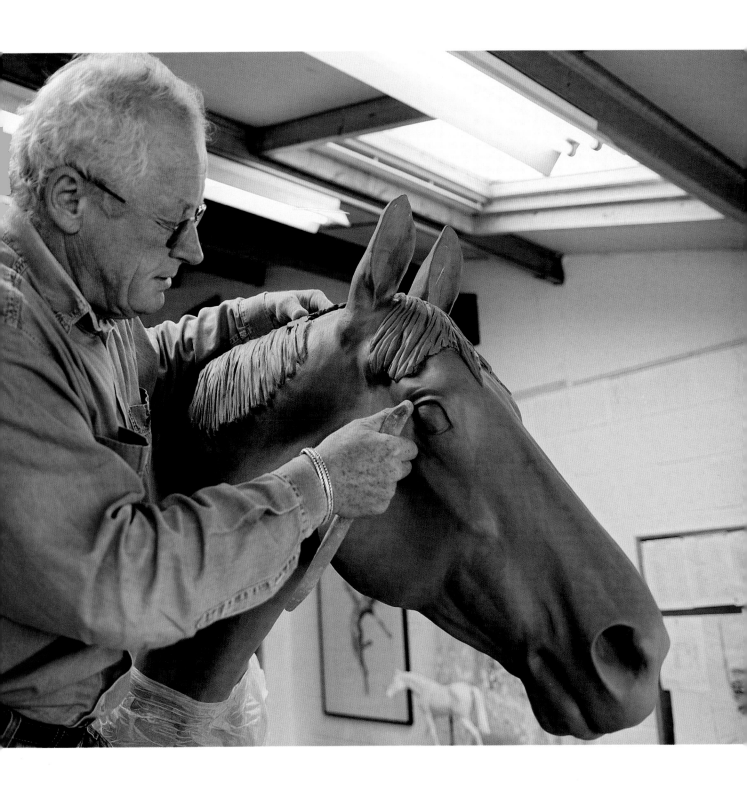

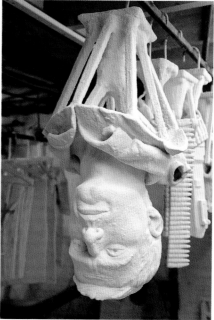

CREATING A SPORTING SCULPTURE
continued

required, chicken wire or similar may be used to surround the armature to support the clay.

The sculptor then turns to the clay modelling, the heart of the craft, adding and shaping the clay around the armature and building up the sculpture to its final detail and dimensions. Hours of skill, craftsmanship and discipline are required until the final work, finished in clay, is ready. The essential creative phase of the sculptor is completed.

MOVING TO THE FOUNDRY
Yet, in terms of the final sculpture, this is only halfway. The sculptor, of course, does not sculpt in bronze; it is the team at the foundry who cast the work into metal. The partnership between the sculptor and the foundry is vital. Astonishingly, the bronze casting process most commonly used – the 'lost wax' method – is, in basic principle, thousands of years old.

The large-scale clay sculpture is cut carefully into sections. It will be weeks and often months before it comes together again. A series of skilled and painstaking processes follow at the foundry:

~ Specialised rubber coatings are applied to create a mould of each section which captures, in 'negative' form, the shape and fine detail of the original sculpture. Outer coatings of plaster encase a solid 'jacket' around the flexible rubber.

~ The casing and mould are cut open. The sculptor's original work is removed and no longer used in the casting process.

~ A 'positive' wax replica of each section is created by applying a series of hot wax coatings to the inside of the rubber mould and working the wax into the minute recesses of the mould to ensure a faithful reproduction of the detailed surface of the original. After cooling and 'slushing out' of the mould, a skin of wax – around 3mm or 4mm thick – is left on the interior.

~ The rubber mould is removed. The remaining wax halves of each section are joined together and the seams carefully blended. A wax replica has been created. The sculptor may make final touches finessing the finest details of his work.

The wax model is now prepared by the foundry for the bronze casting – an ancient craft carried out with modern-day skills and techniques:

~ A tree-like system of wax tubes or 'sprues' is attached to each wax piece rising to a funnel-shaped wax cup. This creates channels through which the molten bronze will eventually flow and the gases created by the intense process escape.

Andrew Edwards applies touches of detail to the wax model before the casting process begins (above left). The upside-down head of Brian Clough, in a ceramic shell and with 'sprues' attached, is ready for the bronze pouring (above).

The pouring of molten bronze, heated at more than 1100 degrees centigrade, is a dramatic stage in the process (right).

CREATING A SPORTING SCULPTURE
continued

~ The 'investment' process follows and creates a ceramic shell around the work. Layers of slurry and silica are applied, repeatedly, to the exterior of the wax model and dried until the required thickness is achieved. The interior core of the wax model is similarly compacted.

~ Heated in a kiln, each piece is hardened into a ceramic shell. The wax itself melts out at the bottom. The wax is 'lost' – leaving cavities into which the molten bronze will flow and fulfil the ancient principle: "Wherever there was wax, there will be bronze."

~ After checking that no cracks have appeared and another firing in the kiln, each ceramic shell piece is placed firmly in sand ready to support the pouring of molten liquid bronze.

CASTING IN BRONZE
Bronze is still the medium of choice for most large-scale sculptures. Why bronze? It is an alloy made up in largest part of copper but with, importantly, a small percentage of tin, zinc or other metal which enables the copper alloy to flow in liquid form and so create, in lasting form, all the subtle detail of the sculpture.

Bronze ingots are melted down in a furnace at around 1100 to 1200 degrees centigrade. A glowing pre-heated pot or crucible is lifted and used, colourfully, to pour the molten bronze into each ceramic shell piece – and the bronze is left to cool.

The ceramic shell, including any inner core material, is broken up and removed. The spruing system is cut from the cast. What is left is the final solid bronze.

WELDING, CHASING AND PATINATION
Still in pieces, the skilful and lengthy task begins of welding and 'chasing' the various sections of the bronze sculpture together to form a cohesive whole, carefully removing any evidence of join and repairing any other imperfections. Steel rods may be inserted through the legs or body and affixed to the final plinth to support the weight of the work. The sculpture has come together once again.

The work is ready for 'patination' or colouring, usually achieved by applying a blend of chemicals to the sculpture which react with the copper and create different surface colours. A good patina enhances the sculpture and the feel of the piece.

The sculpture is finally waxed in order to seal the surface and given a final polish. It is ready to be mounted for installation. The sculpture complete, Fred Trueman returns to Yorkshire. Brian Clough and Peter Taylor are reunited in Derby.

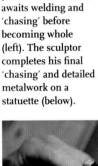

Fred Trueman, cast in bronze but still in pieces at the foundry, awaits welding and 'chasing' before becoming whole (left). The sculptor completes his final 'chasing' and detailed metalwork on a statuette (below).

A bronze statuette of Muhammad Ali undergoes chemical 'patination' or colouring (below).

DIRECTORY OF SCULPTORS

*Set out below are brief details of most of the sculptors whose works (specified in italics after the sculptor's name) are featured in this book.
'FRBS' indicates a Fellow of the Royal British Society of Sculptors and 'ARBS' an Associate member.*

ANDREW, NEALE ARBS
Harold Larwood, Steve Redgrave
Neale Andrew (1958–) is a renowned sculptor whose first public commission, The Defence of Newark, commemorated the English Civil War. A portrait bust of former Prime Minister, John Major, stands in the House of Commons. Other public works include an over life-size Robin Hood for Doncaster/Sheffield Airport.

ANDREWS, ROGER
Tasker Watkins
A Welsh sculptor, Roger Andrews (1949–) has a particular reputation in the field of military sculpture. He has also developed a popular series of figurines and architectural miniatures.

ANNAND, DAVID ARBS
John Rattray, Stirling Moss, Mike Hawthorn, Colin Chapman, Jim Clark, John Surtees, Roger Clark, Roger Williamson, Mike Hailwood, Steve Hislop, Robert Dunlop
A Scottish-based sculptor, David Annand (1948–) has a leading reputation for motor racing figures. Renowned non-sporting works include Nae Day Sae Dark, a tribute to Scottish poet William Soutar, in Perth. (*Pictured below*)

ATTWOOD, CARLTON
Harold Fleming
Carlton Attwood was a Wiltshire-based artist and sculptor. Other public works include the replacement Golden Lion statue in Canal Walk, Swindon.

BARTON, AMANDA
Joey Dunlop
Based in the Isle of Man, Amanda Barton is

known for her life-size sculpture of George Formby in Douglas. Another is planned for Wigan. She also sculpted the figures in the Ramsey Library of Godred Crovan (the founder of the last dynasty to rule Mann and the Isles) and his son Olafi.

BELL, ALISON ARBS
Jim Murray
Alison Bell works primarily in portraiture. Subjects in bronze in private collections have included Henry Moore, Ayrton Senna and John Smith. Her works also include a popular series of Wee Souls bronzes.

BEWS, PHILIP
Brian Bevan
Philip Bews (1951–) has worked on a wide range of public art projects, often civic in collaboration with architects and structural engineers. Examples include works in Wythenshawe Park in Manchester and Newby Hall in Yorkshire.

BLACKER, PHILIP ARBS
Jim Driscoll, Red Rum, Desert Orchid, Generous, Best Mate, Persian Punch
One of the world's leading equine sculptors, Philip Blacker (1949–) was a former jumps jockey with over 300 winners and a fourth place in the Grand National. He has since applied his equine knowledge to a sculpting career which began with a new trophy for Aintree and his life-size sculpture of Red Rum. Commissions have continued for leading venues and owners around the world.

BOONHAM, NIGEL FRBS
Ginger McCain, West Auckland FC
Nigel Boonham (1953–) is a Past President of the Society of Portrait Sculptors. Amongst his works are many distinguished portrait bronzes including Dame Cicely Saunders, pioneer of the hospice movement, for the Royal College of Physicians, Diana, Princess of Wales, at the National Hospital of Neurology, and Cardinal Basil Hume in Newcastle.

BOYT, JUDY FRBS
Diomed, Golden Miller
Judy Boyt (1954–) started work in the ceramics

industry. Her 15-foot-high award-winning sculpture, Rebellion, for Standard Life is sited in the City of London. Many of her works, including her study of Diomed and Galileo in Epsom, have been recognised by the annual British Sporting Art Trust Sculpture Awards. She has, since 1992, designed the Mitsubishi silver trophy awarded annually at the Badminton Horse Trials.

BURN, GEORGE
Harry Clasper, Robert Chambers, James Renforth
George Burn lived in Newcastle and his skills as a sculptor seem to have been in great demand on Tyneside in the late 18th century. As well as those for the great Tyneside rowers, he sculpted the monument to Colonel Edward Perkins at Birtley in Gateshead and the statue of Garibaldi in the Blaydon Library.

BUTLER, JAMES RA FRBS
Reg Harris, Stan Cullis, Billy Wright, Duncan Edwards, Jack Walker
James Butler (1931–) is a Royal Academician. Major works include a twice life-size portrait statue of President Kenyetta in Nairobi, a portrait statue of Field Marshal Earl Alexander of Tunis in Wellington Barracks, London, a memorial to the Fleet Air Arm on London's Embankment, a memorial statue of Richard III in Leicester, and a portrait bust of the Queen Mother. He also designed the 50 pence piece commemorating Roger Bannister's four-minute mile for the Royal Mint.

CLAPPERTON, THOMAS
Jimmie Guthrie
Scottish-born Thomas Clapperton (1879–1962) served in India in the First World War and subsequently produced many significant war memorials. Other works include the statue of Robert the Bruce at Edinburgh Castle and the Sir Walter Scott memorial in Galashiels.

CONNOLLY, JIM
Vincent O'Brien, Payne Stewart
An Irish sculptor and social campaigner, Jim Connolly was the founder of Rural Resettlement Ireland which helps disadvantaged families in the cities move to the country. His sculptures

include actor Richard Harris as King Arthur from his film, *Camelot*, in Limerick, and Eamon Da Valera in Ennis, County Clare.

CONNOR, ANGELA FRBS
Peter O'Sullevan
Angela Connor is well known for her large-scale sculptures, including distinctive water mobiles, as well as her figurative sculpture and portrait busts which include the Queen and other members of the Royal Family. Public figurative works include a large-scale statue of General Charles de Gaulle in Carlton Gardens, London, and the bust of Sir Laurence Olivier at the National Theatre, London.

DALRYMPLE, NEIL
Tom Pryce
Based in Ruthin in the Vale of Clwyd, Neil Dalrymple works in ceramic and stoneware, specialising in sculptures of game fish and wildlife.

DAVID, NATHAN FRBS
Nick Duncombe
Nathan David is probably best known for his sculptures of dancers. His works include a portrait head of Dame Margot Fonteyn at the Royal Opera House, Juliet at the Royal Ballet School, and Mother and Child at Queen Mary's Hospital, London.

DEARNLEY, BEN
Mark Foster
Wiltshire-born, Ben Dearnley (1964–) has been strongly influenced by classical sculpture. His works include a series of fragmented sculptures, based on Olympic and Paralympic champions, exhibited as The Avenue of Champions in Salisbury Cathedral in 2012.

DIMBLEBY, NICHOLAS ARBS
Jimmy Hill
Nicholas Dimbleby studied at Edinburgh College of Art. His public figurative sculptures include Captain Cook in Great Ayton, Yorkshire, James McNeil Whistler by the Thames Embankment, and Christie Hennessy, Irish singer/songwriter, in Tralee town square.

DIZENGREMEL, LAURY
Ken Jones
Born in Paris, Laury Dizengremel (1954–) has worked on many community art projects around the world including for the United Nations. She led the Tennis Terracotta Warrior project for the ATP/Tennis Masters Cup in Shanghai.

DONE, JAMES
Johnny Owen
A Cardiff-based sculptor, James Done (1940–) has worked for major porcelain manufacturers including Wedgwood. One of his best-known public works is his statue of comedian Tommy Cooper in Caerphilly.

DOUBLEDAY, JOHN
Graham Gooch
Major works of Essex-based John Doubleday (1947–) include Sherlock Holmes outside Baker Street station in London, Charlie Chaplin in Leicester Square, the Beatles in Liverpool, Admiral Nelson in Gibraltar, the Royal Marines Commando Memorial in Lympstone, Devon, and the Battle of Maldon Monument in Blackwater Estuary, Essex.

DUN, ALAN
Amy Williams
Alan Dun (1950–) works from his studio near Bath. Portraits include studies of computer scientist Alan Turing and war veteran Harry Patch. A recent commission is a bicentenary sculpture for the Kennet and Avon Canal. A keen cyclist, he was the curator of the Sculpture and Sport: A Celebration for 2012 exhibition organised by Art at the Edge.

DUNLOP, BONAR
Gareth Edwards
Born in New Zealand, Bonar Dunlop (1916–1992) joined the International Brigade in Finland and later the RAF before moving to Australia, working on public war memorials and as a commercial artist. A rugby enthusiast, he started work on sculptures of sporting figures. A retrospective exhibition of his work was held at the Museum of Rugby in Twickenham in 2004.

EDWARDS, ANDREW
Steve Bloomer, Stanley Matthews, Gordon Banks, John Ritchie, Brian Clough/Peter Taylor
Born in the Potteries, Andrew Edwards was one of the trio of sculptors responsible for the three-figure memorial to Stanley Matthews at Stoke and later The Fine Lady on a White Horse at Banbury Cross. Individually he has become a leading sculptor of sporting figures and other projects in the Midlands. (*Pictured below*)

EINO
Roger Bannister
Eino (1940–) is an internationally-acclaimed Finnish-American sculptor based in Nevada, USA. A runner all his life, including training with such athletes as Finland's Lasse Viren, Eino believes that art, science and sport are the three pillars of life. He wishes his sculpture of Roger Bannister to find a permanent home in the UK as a symbol of the athlete's inspirational achievement.

EPSTEIN, JACOB
Herbert Chapman
American-born, Jacob Epstein (1880–1959) became a British citizen in 1907. He was a world-famous leader of modern sculpture producing many bold and controversial works with his highly original style. More conventional bronze works include such well-known sculptures as Jan Smuts in Parliament Square, London. He was knighted in 1954.

FERRITER, PAUL
Old Tom Morris (Rosapenna Golf Resort), Nick Faldo, Seve Ballesteros, Jack Nicklaus
Paul Ferriter (1967–) (son of Gaelic footballer,

DIRECTORY OF SCULPTORS
continued

Sean Ferriter, former captain of Donegal and Ulster) is well known for his golfing figures. As well as works featured here, sculptures include Christy O'Connor Jnr in Portugal.

GOODMAN, AMY
Graham Hill, Sid Watkins, Eric Cantona, Peter Schmeichel, Wayne Rooney
Working from her studio near Andover after a period in France, Amy Goodman (1974–) is a portrait artist and sculptor specialising in welded steel and bronze works and is renowned for her equestrian and other animal works. (*Pictured below*)

GRAY, HARRY
Alexander Obolensky
Harry Gray (1963–) is a Cambridge-based sculptor who has undertaken many leading and innovative public sculptures including the original Battle of Britain Monument at Dover, the Reformers Tree in Hyde Park, London, and a series of sculptures outside the University Library in Cambridge.

HAWKEN, ANTHONY
Sam Bartram
Based in Blackheath, Anthony Hawken (1948–) is widely represented around the country including in the British Museum and the Victoria and Albert Museum. His bronze portrait busts of celebrities include Melvyn Bragg and, in progress, Sir Patrick Stewart.

HEDGES-QUINN, SEAN
Alf Ramsey, Bob Stokoe, Bobby Robson, Ted Bates
Sean Hedges-Quinn (1968–), based in Suffolk, initially worked in the film industry as a model-maker and sculptor. His 'sporting' career began with a sculpture of Sir Alf Ramsey at his local club, Ipswich Town. This has been followed by several other works of sporting figures. A recent sculpture is Captain Mainwaring, from *Dad's Army*, erected in Thetford.

HENRY, SEAN FRBS
Steve Redgrave/Matthew Pinsent
Sean Henry's (1965–) prolific and wide-ranging work has gained international acclaim. A major public work is Couple, a 13-metre-high/18-metre-wide bronze and steel sculpture completed in 2007 and sited 250 metres out to sea at Newbiggin-by-the-Sea in Northumberland.

HODGKINSON, PETER
Tom Finney, Stan Mortensen
Peter Hodgkinson was born in Preston. His sculpture of Tom Finney was his first major public work.

HOLLAND, SAMANTHA ARBS
William McGregor
Samantha Holland's public art, among significant works reflecting our maritime heritage, includes the national memorial at the Royal National Lifeboat Institute at Poole, the Dic Evans memorial for the Welsh boat coxswain in Anglesey, unveiled by the Prince of Wales, and The Mariners, a 35-foot-high sculpture at St Mary's Island, Chatham.

IBBESON, GRAHAM
William Webb Ellis, Don Revie, Fred Trueman, Dickie Bird, Laurie Cunningham/Brendon Batson/ Cyrille Regis
A well-known sculptor based in Barnsley, Graham Ibbeson (1951–) has created bronze sculptures in many towns and cities across Britain. Other public works include the statue of Eric Morecambe in Morecambe, Laurel and Hardy in Ulverston, and Les Dawson in Lytham St Annes. He sculpted a piece to commemorate the London 2012 Olympic Mountain Bike competition.

JACKSON, MARK
Ludwig Guttmann
Mark Jackson (1984–) ('Jacko', the son of former General Sir Mike Jackson) left the Army in 2003 after an injury in a parachuting accident while on holiday in Spain. Retrained as a sculptor, his life-size work in Windsor of a soldier wearing modern combat gear uses bronze and stone brought back from Afghanistan.

JACKSON, PHILIP CVO FRBS
Bobby Moore, Bobby Moore/Geoff Hurst/Martin Peters/Ray Wilson, Matt Busby, Bobby Charlton/ Denis Law/George Best, Peter Osgood, Alex Ferguson
A Fellow of the Royal Society of Arts and a sculptor of renown, Philip Jackson (1944–) has his studio in West Sussex. He was appointed a

Commander of the Royal Victorian Order (CVO) in the Queen's 2009 birthday honours list. Significant public sculptures include the Queen in Windsor Great Park, King George VI for the Dartmouth Royal Navy College, the memorial to the Queen Mother in The Mall, London, and the recent Bomber Command Memorial in Green Park, London. (*Pictured below*)

JEFFERY, JULIAN
Stanley Matthews
Julian Jeffery (1973–) is a Midlands-based sculptor who worked with Carl Payne and Andrew Edwards on the memorial of Stanley Matthews in Stoke and, later, The Fine Lady on a White Horse at Banbury Cross.

JENNINGS, DOUGLAS ARBS
Johnny Haynes
Douglas Jennings (1966–), formerly with Madame Tussauds, is a prominent sculptor whose portraits and statues can be seen worldwide including in the Royal Collection at Buckingham Palace. High-profile public commissions include an acclaimed portrait of US President Barack Obama.

JOHNSON, LES FRBS
Brian Clough (Nottingham)
Born in Australia where he studied before coming to Britain, Les Johnson's major public commissions include Landed, erected outside the Excel Exhibition Centre in the Docklands to pay tribute to the dock workers of the Port of London, the statue of Air Chief Marshal Sir Keith Park in Waterloo Place, London, and a 14-foot-high memorial, commemorating enslaved Africans and their descendants, to be sited in Hyde Park, London.

KELLY, CHRIS
Willie Horne, Emlyn Hughes, Hugh McIlmoyle
Chris Kelly is an experienced figurative sculptor based in Yorkshire. Other public works include The Shepherd which celebrated the centenary of the Royal Welsh Agricultural Show staged in Builth Wells in Wales.

MAP OF SPORTING SCULPTURES

Listed below are the locations (generally by town, city or London borough) of each sculpture or memorial photographed in this book.
This list and the map on the page opposite are based on the counties, including metropolitan counties, of Great Britain and Ireland.

ENGLAND

BEDFORDSHIRE
Harold Abrahams (Bedford)

BERKSHIRE
Frankie Dettori (Ascot)
Bernard Laurence Hieatt (Reading)
Motivator (Ascot)
John Oaksey (Lambourn)
Yeats (Ascot)

BUCKINGHAMSHIRE
Ludwig Guttmann (Aylesbury)
Matthew Pinsent/Steve Redgrave (Henley-on-Thames)
Steve Redgrave (Marlow)

CHESHIRE
Brian Bevan (Warrington)

COUNTY DURHAM
West Auckland FC (West Auckland)
Arthur Wharton (Darlington*)

CUMBRIA
Donald Campbell (Coniston)
Willie Horne (Barrow)
Emlyn Hughes (Barrow)
Hugh McIlmoyle (Carlisle)

DERBYSHIRE
Steve Bloomer (Derby)
Brian Clough/Peter Taylor (Derby)

DEVON
Francis Chichester (Plymouth)
Jonathan Edwards (Ilfracombe)

DORSET
Charles Bennett (Kinson)

ESSEX
Graham Gooch (Chelmsford)

GLOUCESTERSHIRE
Fred Archer (Cheltenham)
Arkle (Cheltenham)
Dawn Run (Cheltenham)
Golden Miller (Cheltenham)

HAMPSHIRE
Ted Bates (Southampton)
Hambledon Club (Hambledon)

HERTFORDSHIRE
Ballyregan Bob (Tring)
Eclipse (Hatfield)
Mick the Miller (Tring)

KENT
Matthew Webb (Dover)

LANCASHIRE
Tom Finney (Preston)
Stan Mortensen (Blackpool)
Jack Walker (Blackburn)

LEICESTERSHIRE
Tony Allcock (Thurmaston)
Colin Chapman (Kirkby Mallory)
Jim Clark (Kirkby Mallory)
Roger Clark (Kirkby Mallory)
Mike Hailwood (Kirkby Mallory)
Stirling Moss (Kirkby Mallory)
John Surtees (Kirkby Mallory)
Roger Williamson (Castle Donington)

LONDON (GREATER)
Tony Adams (Islington, N5)
Charles Alcock (West Norwood, SE27)
Fred Archer (Fitzrovia, W1)
Eric Ashton/Billy Boston/Alex Murphy/
  Martin Offiah/Gus Risman
  (Wembley, HA9*)
Roger Bannister (Croydon, CR9)
Sam Bartram (Charlton, SE7)
Jack Beresford (Chiswick, W4)
Herbert Chapman (Islington and Highbury,
  N5)
Henry Cooper (Southwark, SE1)
Nick Duncombe (Twickenham, TW2)
Steve Fairbairn (Barnes, SW13)
Bob Fitzsimmons (Fitzrovia, W1)
C B Fry (Croydon, CR0)
Kitty Godfree (Wimbledon, SW19)

W G Grace (St John's Wood, NW8 and
  Fitzrovia, W1)
Beverley Gull (Dagenham, RM9)
Johnny Haynes (Fulham, SW6)
Thierry Henry (Islington, N5)
Jack Hobbs (Kennington, SE11)
Geoff Hurst/Bobby Moore/Martin Peters/
  Ray Wilson (East Ham, E13)
Ann Jones (Wimbledon, SW19)
Jason Leonard (Dagenham, RM9)
Line-Out Statue (Twickenham, TW2)
Thomas Lord (Marylebone, NW1)
Daniel Mendoza (Bethnal Green, E2)
Bobby Moore (Wembley, HA9)
Young Tom Morris (Fitzrovia, W1)
Angela Mortimer (Wimbledon, SW19)
Bill Nicholson (Tottenham, N17)
Peter Osgood (Chelsea, SW6)
Fred Perry (Wimbledon, SW19)
William Renshaw (Fitzrovia, W1)
Dorothy Round (Wimbledon, SW19)
Tom Sayers (Highgate, N6)
Bradley Stone (Canning Town, E16)
Virginia Wade (Wimbledon, SW19)
Matthew Webb (Fitzrovia, W1)
Walter Wingfield (Wimbledon, SW19)

MANCHESTER (GREATER)
Jimmy Armfield/Geoff Hurst/Simone
  Perrotta (Ashton-under-Lyne)
Dick Barlow/Albert Hornby (Manchester)
Colin Bell (Manchester)
George Best/Bobby Charlton/Denis Law
  (Manchester)
Matt Busby (Manchester)
Eric Cantona (Manchester)
Keiron Cunningham (St Helens)
Basil D'Oliveira (Middleton)
Eric Evans (Audenshaw)
Alex Ferguson (Manchester)
Football League (Manchester)
Reg Harris (Manchester)
Joe Mercer (Manchester)
Munich Clock (Manchester)
Wayne Rooney (Manchester)
Peter Schmeichel (Manchester)
Henry Taylor (Chadderton)
Bert Trautmann (Manchester)

MERSEYSIDE
Dixie Dean (Liverpool)
Hillsborough Memorial (Liverpool)
Kauto Star (Newton-le-Willows)
Ginger McCain (Aintree)
Peter O'Sullevan (Aintree)
Bob Paisley (Liverpool)
Lester Piggott (Newton-le-Willows)
Red Rum (Aintree)
Bill Shankly (Liverpool)

NORFOLK
Jem Mace (Beeston)

NORTHAMPTONSHIRE
Graham Hill (Silverstone)
Sid Watkins (Silverstone)

NORTHUMBERLAND
Harry Clasper (Whickham)
Jackie Milburn (Ashington)
James Renforth (Gateshead)

NOTTINGHAMSHIRE
Brian Clough (Nottingham)
Harold Larwood (Kirkby-in-Ashfield)
Tommy Simpson (Harworth)
Bendigo Thompson (Nottingham)

OXFORDSHIRE
Roger Bannister (Oxford)
Best Mate (East Lockinge)

SHROPSHIRE
William Penny Brookes (Much Wenlock)

SOMERSET
Tom Daley (Bath)
Mark Foster (Bath)
Jason Gardener (Bath)
Mary Rand (Wells)
Amy Williams (Bath)

STAFFORDSHIRE
Gordon Banks (Stoke-on-Trent)

Stanley Matthews (Stoke-on-Trent)
John Ritchie (Stoke-on-Trent)
Roy Sproson (Stoke-on-Trent)

SUFFOLK
Brigadier Gerard (Newmarket)
Hyperion (Newmarket)
Lord Gyllene (Newmarket)
Mill Reef (Newmarket)
Alexander Obolensky (Ipswich)
Persian Punch (Newmarket)
Alf Ramsey (Ipswich)
Bobby Robson (Ipswich)

SURREY
Desert Orchid (Sunbury-on-Thames)
Diomed/Galileo (Epsom)
Bernard Gallacher (Virginia Water)
Generous (Epsom Downs)
Lester Piggott (Epsom Downs)
Special Cargo (Esher)

EAST SUSSEX
Mike Hawthorn/Lofty England (Goodwood)

WEST SUSSEX
Ballyregan Bob (Hove)
Steve Ovett (Brighton)
Tom Sayers (Brighton)

TYNE AND WEAR
Robert Chambers (Newcastle)
Jackie Milburn (Newcastle)
Bob Stokoe (Sunderland)

WARWICKSHIRE
Randolph Turpin (Warwick)
William Webb Ellis (Rugby)

WEST MIDLANDS
Jeff Astle (West Bromwich)
Sydney Barnes (Birmingham, since removed)
Brendon Batson/Laurie Cunningham/Cyrille
  Regis (West Bromwich*)
Stan Cullis (Wolverhampton)
Duncan Edwards (Dudley)
Jimmy Hill (Coventry)
William McGregor (Birmingham)
William Perry (Tipton)
Tessa Sanderson (Wolverhampton)
Billy Wright (Wolverhampton)

WILTSHIRE
Harold Fleming (Swindon)
Walter George (Calne)

YORKSHIRE (EAST)
Jack Harrison (Kingston upon Hull)

YORKSHIRE (NORTH)
Brian Clough (Middlesbrough)
George Hardwick (Middlesbrough)
Wilf Mannion (Middlesbrough)
Barry Sheene (Scarborough)
Fred Trueman (Skipton)

YORKSHIRE (SOUTH)
Dickie Bird (Barnsley)
John Curry (Sheffield)
Derek Dooley (Sheffield)
Double Trigger (Doncaster)
Jimmy Hagan (Sheffield)
Hillsborough Memorial (Sheffield)
Joe Shaw (Sheffield)

YORKSHIRE (WEST)
Bradford Fire Memorial (Bradford)
Billy Bremner (Leeds)
Beryl Burton (Morley)
John Charles (Leeds)
Douglas Clark (Huddersfield)
Len Hutton (Leeds)
Northern Rugby Football Union
  (Huddersfield)
Don Revie (Leeds)

SCOTLAND

EDINBURGH (CITY)
Eric Liddell (Edinburgh)
John Rattray (Leith)

FIFE
Jim Baxter (Hill O'Beath)
Jim Clark (Kilmany)

Old Tom Morris (St Andrews)
Young Tom Morris (St Andrews)
Allan Robertson (St Andrews)

GLASGOW (CITY)
Tommy Burns
John Greig/Ibrox Memorial
Jimmy Johnstone
Jim Murray
Jock Stein
Brother Walfrid

HIGHLAND
Strathspey/Badenoch Olympians (Aviemore)

SCOTTISH BORDERS
Jimmie Guthrie (Hawick)
Steve Hislop (Hawick)
Bill McLaren (Hawick)

SOUTH LANARKSHIRE
Davie Cooper (Hamilton)

WALES

CARDIFF
Jim Driscoll
Gareth Edwards
Fred Keenor
Gwyn Nicholls
Tasker Watkins

CARMARTHENSHIRE
Ray Gravell (Llanelli)

DENBIGHSHIRE
Tom Pryce (Ruthin)

MERTHYR TYDFIL
Jimmy Owen
Eddie Thomas
Howard Winstone

NEWPORT
Ken Jones (Blaenavon)

RHONDDA CYNON TAF
Arthur Linton (Aberdare)

SWANSEA
Ivor Allchurch
Robbie James

WREXHAM
Billy Meredith (Chirk)

NORTHERN IRELAND

ANTRIM
Joey Dunlop (Ballymoney)
Robert Dunlop (Ballymoney)
Alex Higgins (Belfast)
Mary Peters (Belfast)

ARMAGH
William McCrum (Milford)

FERMANAGH
Nick Faldo (Enniskillen)

LONDONDERRY
Bertie Peacock (Coleraine)

REPUBLIC OF IRELAND

DONEGAL
Old Tom Morris (Downings)

KERRY
Steve Casey (Sneem)
Payne Stewart (Waterville)

LAOIS
Seve Ballesteros (Laois)

MEATH
Jack Nicklaus (Dunsany)

OFFALY
Mick the Miller (Killeigh)

TIPPERARY
Nijinsky (Rosegreen)
Vincent O'Brien (Rosegreen)

JERSEY

Harry Vardon (Grouville)

* Sculpture planned for this location.

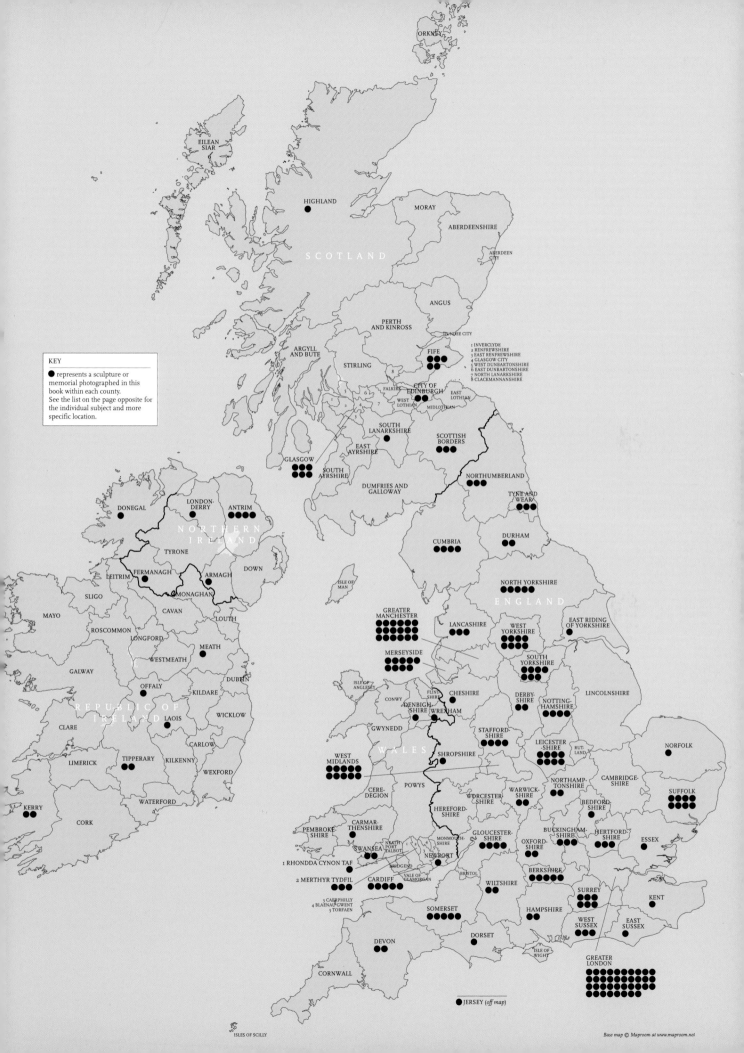

KEY

● represents a sculpture or
memorial photographed in this
book within each county.
See the list on the page opposite for
the individual subject and more
specific location.

ORKNEY

HIGHLAND

MORAY

ABERDEENSHIRE

ABERDEEN
CITY

SCOTLAND

ANGUS

PERTH
AND KINROSS

DUNDEE CITY

EILEAN
SIAR

1 INVERCLYDE
2 RENFREWSHIRE
3 EAST RENFREWSHIRE
4 GLASGOW CITY
5 WEST DUNBARTONSHIRE
6 EAST DUNBARTONSHIRE
7 NORTH LANARKSHIRE
8 CLACKMANNANSHIRE

ARGYLL
AND BUTE

STIRLING

FIFE

CITY OF
EDINBURGH

FALKIRK
WEST
LOTHIAN

EAST
LOTHIAN

MIDLOTHIAN

GLASGOW

SOUTH
LANARKSHIRE

EAST
AYRSHIRE

SCOTTISH
BORDERS

SOUTH
AYRSHIRE

NORTHUMBERLAND

TYNE AND
WEAR

DUMFRIES AND
GALLOWAY

DONEGAL

LONDON-
DERRY

ANTRIM

NORTHERN
IRELAND

TYRONE

DOWN

CUMBRIA

DURHAM

ISLE OF
MAN

NORTH YORKSHIRE

ENGLAND

EAST RIDING
OF YORKSHIRE

LEITRIM

FERMANAGH

ARMAGH

MONAGHAN

SLIGO

CAVAN

LOUTH

GREATER
MANCHESTER

LANCASHIRE

WEST
YORKSHIRE

MAYO

ROSCOMMON

LONGFORD

WESTMEATH

MEATH

MERSEYSIDE

SOUTH
YORKSHIRE

LINCOLNSHIRE

GALWAY

DUBLIN

ISLE OF
ANGLESEY

CONWY

FLINT-
SHIRE

CHESHIRE

DERBY-
SHIRE

NOTTING-
HAMSHIRE

OFFALY

KILDARE

DENBIGH-
SHIRE

WREXHAM

REPUBLIC OF
IRELAND

LAOIS

WICKLOW

GWYNEDD

STAFFORD-
SHIRE

LEICESTER
-SHIRE

RUT-
LAND

NORFOLK

CLARE

CARLOW

WALES

SHROPSHIRE

CAMBRIDGE-
SHIRE

LIMERICK

TIPPERARY

KILKENNY

WEST
MIDLANDS

WARWICK-
SHIRE

NORTHAMP-
TONSHIRE

SUFFOLK

WEXFORD

CERE-
DIGION

POWYS

WORCESTER-
SHIRE

BEDFORD-
SHIRE

HEREFORD-
SHIRE

BUCKINGHAM-
SHIRE

HERTFORD-
SHIRE

ESSEX

KERRY

WATERFORD

PEMBROKE-
SHIRE

CARMAR-
THENSHIRE

NEATH
PORT
TALBOT

MONMOUTH-
SHIRE

GLOUCESTER-
SHIRE

OXFORD-
SHIRE

CORK

SWANSEA

NEWPORT

BRISTOL

1 RHONDDA CYNON TAF

BRIDGEND

2 MERTHYR TYDFIL

CARDIFF

VALE OF
GLAMORGAN

BERKSHIRE

WILTSHIRE

HAMPSHIRE

SURREY

KENT

3 CAERPHILLY
4 BLAENAU GWENT
5 TORFAEN

SOMERSET

DORSET

ISLE OF WIGHT

WEST
SUSSEX

EAST
SUSSEX

DEVON

GREATER
LONDON

CORNWALL

● JERSEY (off map)

ISLES OF SCILLY

Base map © Maproom at www.maproom.net

ACKNOWLEDGEMENTS

Sam Lloyd and I called this adventure 'Project Dessie' after our first visit to photograph a sporting statue, Desert Orchid, the great steeplechaser at Kempton Park. Numerous trips have followed around sporting Britain. Our thanks go to all the clubs and venues visited; each has been welcoming and supportive.

The co-operation received from so many sculptors, and the insight learned into their skill, has been a delight. I am particularly grateful to David Annand, Philip Blacker, Andy Edwards, Eino, Amy Goodman, Philip Jackson and Stephen Winterburn for the time spent with us. A & B Fine Art Foundry, Castle Fine Arts Foundry and Talos Art Foundry also kindly provided an introduction to the fascinating world of bronze casting.

In researching the broader historical background, I owe a considerable debt to three fine books: Richard Holt's outstanding *Sport and the British: A Modern History*; its companion *Sport in Britain 1945 – 2000* by Richard Holt and Tony Mason; and Julian Norridge's imaginative *Can We Have Our Balls Back, Please? How the British Invented Sport*. My journey discovering Britain's sporting statuary was aided, in its final furlong, by the helpful database of full-length statues in *The Sporting Statues Project*, initiated in 2012 by Chris Stride, Ffion Thomas and John Wilson from Sheffield University.

Many friends provided suggestions, mostly constructive, and Bill Maclagan kindly read and contributed to an early draft. The book was given shape and direction by the publishers, Vision Sports Publishing, and I am particularly grateful to Jim Drewett, Doug Cheeseman and John Murray for their helpful input, guidance and creativity. Any errors are, of course, my responsibility.

A key challenge has been to take and present photographs of Britain's sporting statues in a way that reflects the skill of the sculptor and excites the imagination of the sports fan. I am so grateful to my friend and colleague on this project, Sam Lloyd, for producing such a stunning collection of images on which this book is fundamentally based.

Ultimate thanks go to my wife, Jenifer, for her advice and encouragement. Without her support, this book would not have been completed. Admittedly, she once declared that "it will never sell". On this occasion, I hope she is wrong. She was right, though, that a book combining sport and art would provide a rewarding challenge. 'Project Dessie' has been a fascinating and fun project.

IAN HEWITT
July 1 2013

PICTURE CREDITS

All photographs are by Sampson Lloyd except:

Baxter, Walter: 303 (right)
Bridgeman Art Library: 12 (bottom), 14, 16 (top left, top right), 70 (bottom)
British Museum: 21
Colorsport: 220
Getty Images: 82 (left), 167 (top right), 192, 194 (left), 204 (top), 224 (right), 229, 242, 250 (bottom right), 254, 259, 260, 264 (left), 268, 271 (top, bottom), 272 (top, bottom), 274 (bottom), 278 (top, bottom), 282 (top), 290, 292 (top left, bottom left), 294, 299 (top right)
Getty Images/AFP: 41 (bottom), 200 (top), 266 (bottom), 267 (middle right), 280, 282 (bottom), 296 (left), 299 (top)
Getty Images/Archive Photos: 71 (right)
Getty Images/Bob Thomas Sports Photography: 175, 194 (middle, right), 208, 214, 216, 230, 234 (top), 274 (top), 284 (top)
Getty Images/Hulton Archive: 26 (left), 38 (bottom), 44, 46 (left), 50 (left), 62 (top), 67 (top), 71 (bottom), 74, 84, 86 (top, bottom), 89, 90 (top), 94, 96, 98, 102 (top), 104 (left), 108, 114 (top), 119, 124, 130, 133, 134, 140, 146, 151, 156, 159, 161, 164, 168 (top left, bottom left), 170 (top), 172, 181, 182, 184, 186 (top), 188 (top), 190, 196 (middle left), 200 (bottom), 202 (top), 210 (top), 212, 240 (top)
Getty Images/Picture Post: 137, 152, 246
Getty Images/Popperfoto: 19, 30, 33, 38 (top), 43, 54 (left), 56, 58, 68 (top, bottom), 70 (top), 72, 91 (bottom), 92 (left), 120 (left), 137, 144 (left), 144 (bottom right), 149 (left), 162, 167 (top left), 176, 196 (top left, bottom), 202 (bottom), 204 (bottom), 210 (bottom), 226, 234 (bottom), 262 (top)
Hewitt, Ian: 51 (top), 143 (bottom), 185 (right)
Ibbeson, Graham: 302 (right)
Kelly, Ken: 71 (top left)
Newton, William: 313
Royal Veterinary College: 12 (top)
Topham Picturepoint/Press Association Images: 224 (left)
Tyne & Wear Archives & Museums: 22
Warrington Wolves: 126
Wenlock Olympian Society: 34

All Sampson Lloyd's photographs in this book were taken with Nikon equipment.
Camera bodies used were Nikon D3, D3S, D4 and D800. Lenses used were primarily
Nikon 200-400 f4, 70-200 f2.8 and 24-70 f2.8.